VIEW OF

CW00833054

HEBREWS

OR THE TRIBES OF ISRAEL IN AMERICA

SECOND EDITION, IMPROVED AND ENLARGED

BY ETHAN SMITH

PASTOR OF A CHURCH IN POULTNEY, (VT.)

ৎ ৎ

"THESE BE THE DAYS OF VENGEANCE."
"YET A REMNANT SHALL RETURN"
"HE SHALL ASSEMBLE THE OUTCASTS OF ISRAEL; AND GATHER
TOGETHER THE DISPERSED OF JUDAH"

ৎ ৎ

PUBLISHED AND PRINTED BY
SMITH & SHUTE
POULTNEY, (VT.)
1825

Be it remembered, that on the sixteenth of April, in the fortyninth year of the Independence of the United States of America, SMITH & SHUTE, of the said District, have deposited in this office the title of a book, the right they claim as proprietors, in the words following, to wit: *"View of the Hebrews or the Tribes of Israel in America"*, Exhibiting Chap. I. The Destruction of Jerusalem. Chap II. The certain Restoration of Judah and Israel. Chap. III. The Present State of Judah and Israel. Chap. IV. An Address of the Prophet Isaiah to the United States relative to their Restoration. Second edition, Improved and enlarged. By ETHAN SMITH, pastor of a church in Poultney (Vt.) 'These be the days of vengeance.' 'Yet a remnant shall return.' 'He shall assemble the outcasts of Israel; and gather together the dispersed of Judah.' In the conformity to the act of the Congress of the United States, entitled "An act for the encouragement of learning, by securing the copies of maps, charts, and books, to the authors and proprietors of such copies, during the limes therein mentioned." JESSE GOVE, Clerk of the District of Vermont. A true copy of record, examined and sealed by J. Gove, Clerk.

Published by
Ancient American Archaeology Foundation
P.O. Box 370, Colfax, Wisconsin 54730

ISBN 1-930679-61-0
Printed by
Hayriver Press
Colfax, Wisconsin
2002

FOR THE SECOND EDITION.
The importance of the question, *Where are the Ten Tribes of Israel?* the speedy sale of the first edition of this work; and the obtaining considerable additional evidence relative to the origin of the American Indians; have led the way to the publishing of a second edition of this View. Additional evidences are adduced from various sources; especially from *Hunter's Narrative* -*Baron Humboldt on the Kingdom of New Spain*- and the *American Archaeology*. These authors, without particular design, have furnished what is deemed material evidence upon this subject.

Some objections are noted, and replies made to them. The writer has had his ears open to objections; and he is of opinion that none have been made, but what are capable of a fair solution.

Poultney, April 1, 1825.

RECOMMENDATIONS.

Testimonials in favour of this work have not been wanting. The following will be here inserted.

The Pawlet Association certify, that they have heard the Rev. E. Smith read a considerable part of his "View of the Hebrews;" that they do highly approve of the *plan* and *execution* of the work; do wish its publication; and cordially recommend it to the perusal of all classes of people.

Voted, unanimously, Attest, Rufus Cushman, *Scribe.*

Extracts from Reviews of the First Edition.
"We have been exceedingly gratified in taking a 'View of the Hebrews,' through the glass that Mr. S. has put to our eye; and it is presumed that none will turn away dissatisfied with such a medium of vision, unless they are dissatisfied that they may not look *longer*. -The subject is large enough to engage a more extended discussion; but perhaps Mr. S. has said all that need be said at present. Undoubtedly further inquiries will be made, and more satisfactory results obtained ere long."

[*Boston Recorder.*]

"Of this we feel convinced, that the religious community are indebted to Mr. S. for the pains he has taken in this his sketch of the Hebrews; and we hope that his labour will be amply remunerated, not only in seeing the salutary tendency of his book in exciting Christians to their duty in reference to the Jews, but also in its rapid sale. The sentiments interspersed are calculated to be profitable to the pious; as well as informing to the reader, who is merely in pursuit of interesting historical knowledge." "We consider the moral tendency of the publication to be truly valuable. No person can read it without some benefit, unless his heart be strangely perverted." "One of the impressions which this work is calculated to make is, the awful guilt and danger contracted by a rejection of Jesus Christ as our atoning Saviour. This we see in the terrible destruction of Jerusalem and the temple, and in the dreadful slaughter and dispersion of the Jews. Another is, the weight of obligation which now rests on Gentile Christians, and eminently on American Christians to extend the gospel to the Jews. When this people was rejected from spiritual privileges, we were graciously received; and our duty now is, by every practicable method, to persuade them to renounce their unbelief, and participate with us in the rich blessings of grace."

[*Christian Watchman,* published in Boston.]

"Certainly, if we may judge from our own feelings, such a collection of facts and details, as is presented by our author, must secure for his book an unusual degree of popularity."

[*Christian Advocate*, published at Saratoga, N.Y.]

Extracts of a letter from the Rev. Jabez B. Hyde of Eden, Erie county, N.Y. dated Feb. 4, 1825, after having read the first edition of this work.

"I have been in the sentiment of your book, that the natives of our country are the outcasts of Israel. It cannot well be doubted by any one, who has become acquainted with the religious ceremonies of the Indians, but that they have a manifest shadow of the Mosaic rituals. Most of the particulars you have mentioned in your book, I know to be facts; and were observed by the Seneca Indians. When I first came among them, the chiefs invited me to all their celebrations. For some time (when I could make it convenient) I attended, in hopes of obtaining information concerning their ceremonies. All the information I could obtain from their interpreter was, that all related to things their fathers taught them many years ago. "So our fathers worshiped the Great Spirit!" This was all the account they could give. I neglected their meetings. After I read Dr. Boudinot's 'Star in the West,' I again attended their religious ceremonies, to see if I could discern what he had represented. In 1818, a general religious excitement commenced among the Senecas. They attempted to understand and reform their old religious rites, rather than receive Christianity. This brought together their wise men, who were best acquainted with their mysteries. They spent much time to investigate their religion, its origin and what it taught, and to what it would avail. They found themselves involved in darkness. Of the meaning of the words they used in their dances, and divine songs, they were wholly ignorant. They used the words, Y-O-He-Wah, and Hal-le-lu-yah, as Dr. Boudinot has represented of other Indians. They became dissatisfied with their old rites, and consented that they would take the book which the white people call the word of God, to throw light on their path. This was the commencement of Christianity among the Senecas. This in its progress brought in two who had officiated as high priests in their religious ceremonies. With these I have had frequent opportunities. They have given me, I believe, an unreserved account of all they know of their ancient religion. Their wish has been to obtain information whether any thing is found in our scriptures similar to their religion. They have been firmly persuaded that they are the people of God; but that they have lost their way, and are bewildered in darkness. They call themselves, Hung-gwa-o-way; i.e. the real people.

In all their rites which I have learned from them, there is certainly a most striking similitude to the Mosaic rituals. Their feasts of first fruits; feasts of ingathering; day of atonement; peace offerings; sacrifices. They build an altar of stone before a tent covered with blankets; within the tent they burn tobacco for incense, with fire taken from the altar of burnt offering. All who have seen a dead human body are considered unclean eight days; which time they are excluded from the congregation. These Senecas observe their separations of females, as you notice of other Indians in your book. These Indians are well acquainted, that formerly places like cities of refuge existed among them. An old chief showed me the boundaries of one of them. I could fill sheets with details; but it would be unnecessary.

I remain yours in the bonds of the Gospel,

Jabez B. Hyde.

From the Rev. Dr. Proudfit, of Salem, NY, Salem, February 18, 1825.

"Reverend and esteemed Brother: I have examined with no inconsiderable interest your 'View of the Hebrews,' and have been highly entertained, and instructed. From the view given of their Language, and from the similarity of their customs and religious rites, with those of ancient Israel; from their belief in the existence of the one Great Spirit, as the Creator and Judge of the world; from their existing in tribes, during the lapse of so many ages; from the coincidence of their traditions with the events recorded in the inspired volume; we have in my opinion satisfactory evidence that the aborigines of our country are the remnant of the ten tribes of Israel.

I am much gratified to hear that you are preparing a second edition, with additional facts and evidences. If my name may have any influence to introduce this work to the patronage of the religious public, you have liberty to use it for the purpose. That the blessing of Israel's God may accompany this, and every production designed to excite greater exertions for the missionary cause, and extending the kingdom of the Redeemer, in the gathering of the Jews, and the fulness of the Gentiles, and hastening the progress of the millennial glory, is the prayer of your brother in the faith of Jesus, and fellow labourer in the gospel.

Alexander Proudfit.

Rev. Ethan Smith.

CONTENTS

Chapter I
The Destruction Of Jerusalem; Description of Jerusalem; Description of the Temple; Christ foretels its destruction; Various signs of the event; Seven striking portents of it; Causes of the war; Factions of the Jews; The Roman army approaching; Some prophecies have a primary, and an ultimate fulfillment;

Chapter II
The Certain Restoration Of Judah And Israel; The expulsion of the ten tribes; Arguments in favour of a literal restoration.
1. The distinct existence of the Jews; 2. Their past partial, and short possession of Canaan; 3. Express predictions of the event; 4. A mystical import given to these predictions inadmissible; 5. Their expulsion was literal; hence their restoration may be expected to be literal;

Chapter III
The Present State Of The Jews, And Of Israel; State of the Jews; State of Israel

Preliminary Remarks: 1. Israel as well as Judah are to be recovered; 2. Hence they are now in existence, but in an outcast state; 3. The last account of them; 4. Suppositions concerning them; 5. These suppositions true; 6. A prophecy in Amos viii. 11, 12, relative to a famine of the word in Israel;

Character and writings of James Adair, Esq.; Commencement of arguments in favour of the natives of America being the descendants of Israel: 1. These natives all appear to have had one origin; 2. Their language appears to have been Hebrew; Table of words; 3. The Indians have had their ark of the covenant; 4. They have had circumcision; 5. They generally have acknowledged one and only one God; 6. Testimonies of William Penn; 7. Their superior tribe; 8. Several prophetic traits of character; 9. Their being in tribes with heads of tribes; 10. Their having an imitation of cities of refuge; 11.

Various other traditions and arguments; Where they came to this country; Promiscuous testimonies, a few only of which shall be here noted; Notice of some objections, also in the Appendix.
Good original character of the natives; Natives of New Spain; Indian Pyramids; American High Places like those of ancient Israel; Pyramid of Cholula; Traditions of an ancient celebrated character, probably Moses; Traditions of a Trinity in Unity in God; Phylacteries, or ancient Hebrew writings, found on Indian Hill, in Pittsfield

Chapter IV
An Address Of The Prophet Isaiah, Relative To The Restoration Of His People; Preliminary Remarks; Exposition of Isaiah xviii

Conclusion

Appendix, (Objections answered,)

AUTHORS AND AUTHORITIES ADDUCED.
Archaelogia Americana, page 188; Adair, 80, 84, 88, 89, 92, 95, 98, 112, 116, 121, 123. Some of his arguments, 147-154.Don Alonzo de Ericilla, 158. Boudinot, 87, 91, 93, 96, 98, 100, 116, 120, 123-125, 133, 134, 138. Bartram, 113, 123-125. Buttrick, 130. Beatty, 96, 98, 116, 119. Charlevoix, 85, 174. Colden, 94, 109. Cushman, 105, 174. Clavigero, 116. Chapman, 123, 157. Carver, 123, 154. Columbus, 132. Commissioners, 137. Casas, 176. Dodge & Blight, 104. Edwards, 86, 89, 162. Esdras, 74. Frey, 118. Giddings, 88, 102. Gookin, 107. Hunter, 162. Humboldt, 177. Herman, 140. Heckewelder, 107. Hebard, 101. Hutchinson, 93, 174. Immanuel de Moraez, 97. Jarvis, 79. M'Kenzie, 97, 114,115. Long, 141, 160. Lewis & Clark, 106, 124. Morse, 91, 126, 142. Mather, 127. Melverda & Acasta, 162. Occum, 106. Pratz, 87, 175. Pedro de Cicca, 88. Penn, 107, 174. Pixley, 111, 113, 130. Robertson, 153. Sauard, 92. Smith, (Col.) 117, 126, 134, 136, 174, 175. Schoolcraft, 145. Ulloa, 88. Williams, 88, 101, 110, 114. Williams, (Roger) 107.

THE DESTRUCTION OF JERUSALEM

The land of promise was long a land of wonders. The Hebrew nation there was for many centuries the cradle of the true and only church of God on earth. There glorious things were wrought for her salvation. Patriarchs had there prayed, sacrificed and praised. There Prophets had prophesied; and the Almighty had often made bare his holy arm. There his people had too often apostatized; had been expelled from their Canaan; and again mercifully restored. There the ten tribes of Israel had renounced the house of David, and their God; and were hence banished to some unknown region of the world, to the present day; while the Jews were still retained in the covenant of their God. There God, manifest in the flesh, made his appearance on earth; performed his publick ministry;atoned for the sins of the world; and ascended to glory. There the first heralds of the gospel dispensation commenced their ministry; and thence the wonderful scheme of grace was propagated through the nations.

Jerusalem was the capital of this earthly Canaan. Glorious things were spoken of this city of our God. "Beautiful for situation, the joy of the whole earth, was this Mount Zion on the sides of the north, the city of the Great King." This, for many centuries, might be called God's Capital on earth. God said, alluding primarily to this city; "For the Lord hath chosen Zion to be an habitation for himself. Here will I dwell, for I have desired it." Here great things were done in divine faithfulness; which led the psalmist to say; "God is known in her palaces for a refuge. For lo, the Kings were assembled; they passed by together. They saw it, and so they marvelled; they were troubled, and so they hasted away." "The Lord of hosts is with us; the God of Jacob is our refuge." "In Salem stood his tabernacle; and his dwelling place in Zion. There brake he the arrows of the bow, the shield and the sword of the battle." This city of God long answered well to its name. Jeru, they shall see; Salem, peace. Long did the church, while they walked with God, there see and enjoy peace.

But alas, we find recorded of this city, temple, and nation of the Jews, a fatal reverse. They found the sentiment in their sacred oracles fulfilled; "The Lord is with you while ye be with him; but if ye forsake him, he will cast you off."

The Jews became carnal; crucified the Lord of glory; and they fell under the denunciations and the full execution of his wrath. Their lawgiver Moses and their prophets had long thundered against them solemn denunciations, that if ever they should become of the character which they did impiously assume, the most signal judgements of God should cut them off. And the Messiah uttered against them, in consequence of their rejecting him, a new edition of these fatal denunciations, which we find in Matt. xxiv. Mark xiii. Luke xix. 41-44. chap. xxi. and xxiii. 27-30; to which the reader is referred. These were to have a primary fulfilment in the desolation of Jerusalem, and of the Jewish commonwealth. This primary fulfilment Christ assured should take place on that generation. And the denunciation was fulfilled.

This fulfilment, inasmuch as it demonstrated the truth and divinity of our Saviour, exhibited a type of the destruction of Antichrist, and of the wicked at the end of the world; and shows the danger of rejecting the Son of God -ought to be duly noted in the church, and frequently contemplated. It is a subject too much neglected and forgotten in the present Christian world. I design then, to give a concise description of the event, in which Jesus Christ came in awful judgement upon the infidel Jews, and vindicated his cause against his persecutors and murderers. But some preliminary remarks will first be made.

This noted city was built on two mountains; and contained two parts, called the Upper and Lower City. The former was built on Mount Sion; the latter on Mount Acra. The city is supposed to have been founded by Melchisedec, and then called Salem, or Solyma. The warlike Jebusites possessed it when Israel entered Canaan.

In the higher city they long defended themselves against the Hebrews. Here they remained, till David subdued them; and called their city The City of David.

Herod the Great, when he repaired (or rather rebuilded) the temple, added vast strength and embelishments to this city; which accounts for its superb state and strength when it was destroyed.

Most of this city was surrounded with three walls. In some places, where it was deemed inaccessible, it had only one. The wall first built was adorned and strengthened with sixty towers. Fourteen towers rested on the middle wall. The outside one, (most remarkable for its workmanship) was secured with ninety towers.

The tower Psephinos was most celebrated. It was seventy cubits high; had eight angles; and commanded a most beautiful prospect. Here the visitor might (in a clear atmosphere) delight himself with a view of the Mediterranean, forty miles to the west; and of most of the Jewish dominions. Some of these towers were nearly ninety cubits in height; and famous for their beauty, elegance and curiosities. They were built of white marble; and had the appearance of vast marble blocks. These huge piles gave to the city, in the view of the adjacent country, a most majestick appearance.

Near the highest of these towers stood the royal palace, of the most commanding elegance. Incredible cost had furnished its pillars, porticoes, galleries, and apartments. Its gardens, groves, fountains, aqueducts, and walks, presented the richest and most delightful scenery. This was the beauty and elegance of the north side of Jerusalem.

On the east side stood the temple, and the fort of Antonio, over against Mount Olivet. This fort was built on a rock of fifty feet in height, and of inaccessible steepness, overlaid with slabs of marble. The castle of Antonio stood in the centre of this fortress. The workmanship of this castle made it more resemble a palace than a castle. A tower adorned each square of this fortress; one of which was seventy cubits high, and commanded a full view of the temple.

The temple was, in many respects, the most astonishing fabrick ever beheld. Its site was partly on a solid rock, originally steep on every side. The lower temple had a foundation of vast dimensions, said to be three hundred cubits from its lowest base. This foundation was composed of stones sixty feet in length; and the lower part of the superstructure was composed of stones of solid white marble, more than sixty feet long; and seven by nine feet in bigness. Four furlongs compassed the whole pile of building; which was one hundred cubits high; with one hundred and sixty pillars, to afford both support and ornament.

In the front were spacious and lofty galleries, with cedar wainscot, resting on uniform rows of white marble columns. Josephus asserts that nothing could exceed the exterior part of this house of God, for exquisite workmanship and elegance. Its solid plates of gold seemed to strive to out-dazzle the rising sun. The parts of the building not covered with gold, had, at a distance, the appearance of pillars of snow, or white marble mountains. And the grandeur of the internal workmanship of this magnificent dome did not fail of being fully equal to its external maginifience. Nothing superb, costly, or elegant, was spared. The different parts of the world had seemed to vie with each other, to pour their most costly treasures into this wonderful treasury of Heaven. The lower story was decorated with the sacred furniture, the table of shew bread, altar of incense, and the candlestick of pure beaten gold. The altar and table were overlaid with pure gold. Several doors of the sanctuary were fifty-five cubits in height, and sixteen in breadth, overlaid also with gold. The richest Babylonian tapestry, of purple, blue and scarlet, and of exquisite workmanship, waved within these doors. Golden vines, with leaves and clusters of grapes of gold, were suspended from the ceiling five or six feet, of curious workmanship. The temple had a huge eastern gate of pure Corinthian brass, a metal in the highest esteem. It would be a task to enumerate all the foldings of golden doors in the chambers; carved works, paintings and gildings; vessels of gold; scarlet, violet, and purple sacerdotal vestments; and all the incalculable piles of riches in this temple of Jehovah. The most precious stones, spices, and perfumes; every thing that nature, art, or riches could furnish, were stored within these stupendous and hallowed walls.

Here were the city and temple to be destroyed, for the infidelity, malice, hypocrisy, and persecution of the Lord of glory, (in himself, and his followers,) which characterized its rulers and people. Here a measure of unprecedented atrociousness was just filled up, which should bring down wrath upon them to the uttermost. This tremendous ruin our Lord foretold and fulfilled.

The last noted entrance into Jerusalem of Him, who was God manifest in the flesh, took place on the Monday before the scene of his sufferings. Amidst the acclamention of multitudes he was hailed King of Zion, with every token of joy and praise. The air rang again with their praises, uttered for all the mighty works they had seen. They sang, Hosanna! Blessed be the King that cometh in the name of the Lord! Peace in heaven; and glory in the highest. Our Lord (superior to all their adulation, and knowing how soon the hosannas of some of them would turn to, "Crucify him;"-and being touched with sympathy and pity for a devoted city, now going to fill up their guilty measure of iniquity) "beheld the city, and wept over it." He said; "If thou hadst known, even thou, in this thy day, the things which belong to thy peace! but now they are hid from thine eyes! For the days shall come when thine enemies shall cast a trench about thee, and compass thee round; and keep thee in on every side; and shall lay thee even with the ground, and thy children within thee. And they shall not leave thee one stone upon another; because thou knewest not the time of thy visitation."

The day but one after, Christ went into the temple for the last time, to instruct the people. While he was thus employed, the high priest, elders, Herodians, Sadducees, and Pharisees, gathered in turn around him, with a malicious view to entangle him in his talk. Christ returned such answers, spake such parables, and set home such reproof and conviction to their souls, as not only to astonish and silence them; but to give them some awful prelibation of the final judgement, which awaited them at his bar. He thus, in a free and pungent address to the disciples, administered the most dignified and keen reproofs for the cruelty, hypocrisy, and pride, of the Scribes and Pharisees. He foretold the malicious treatment the disciples would meet with at their hands; and then denounced the vengeance on that falling city, which for ages their crimes had been accumulating. He forewarned that this cup of divine indignation should be poured on that generation. His tender feelings of soul then melted in a most moving apostrophe: "O Jerusalem, Jerusalem! thou that killest the prophets, and stoned them that are sent unto thee! How often would I have gathered thy children together, even as a hen gathereth her chickens under her wings; and ye would not! Behold, your house is left unto you desolate. For I say unto you, ye shall not see me henceforth, till ye shall say, "Blessed is he that cometh in the name of the Lord." Upon this our Saviour left the temple. The disciples took an occasion to speak to Christ of the magnificence of the sacred edifice; how it was adorned with goodly stones and gifts. "Master, (said they,) see what manner of stones and buildings are here." "Jesus said unto them; See ye not all these things? Verily, I say unto you, there shall not be left here one stone upon another, that shall not be thrown down." How very unlikely must such an event have seemed! But it was indeed fulfilled upon that generation.

Jesus and his disciples retired to the mount of Olives. Here the temple rose before them in all its majestick elegance. The surrounding scenery naturally suggested the conversation which followed. The disciples petitioned; "Tell us, when shall these things be? and what shall be the sign when all these things shall be fulfilled?" Their minds seem to have been impressed with the preceeding discourse; and they fell most readily upon the same subject, and wished to know when such awful events should come; and what warnings should announce their approach. Our Lord replied; "Take heed that no man deceive you; for many shall come in my name, saying, I am Christ; and shall deceive many." As though he had said; This shall be one signal token of the event, both as my denunciations relate to a primary accomplishment in the destruction of Jerusalem; and to a more general and dreadful fulfilment in the destruction of Antichrist in the last days. Imposters shall abound. False religionsts shall deceive and ruin many. Let us trace the fulfilment of this and several succeeding predictions.

This was fulfilled in relation to Jerusalem. Not long after Christ's ascension, the Samaritan Dositheus appeared and declared himself the Messiah predicted by Moses. Simon Magus also declared himself "The Great power of God." Soon after, another imposter appeared from the mongrel Samaritans. The church has ever been annoyed by such kind of Samaritans, who have ever been fruitful in vile imposters, crying "Lo, here; and lo there." This imposter promised to exhibit to the people sacred utensils said to be deposited by Moses in Mount Gerazim. Here a new decision must be given from heaven, to the question between the Jews and Samaritans, as to the place of worship; a thing of which schismaticks have ever been exceedingly fond; to derive some new light upon their party question directly from above; as though decisions already given were insufficient.

Armed multitudes sallied forth to follow this Messiah, confident their Great Deliverer had at last made his appearance. But Pilate, the Roman governor, checked their fanaticism with the sword, and put their fancied Messiah to death.

Another imposter, Theudas, arose. He had the address to persuade multitudes to follow him into the wilderness, under his promise that he would cause the river Jordan to divide. The Roman procurator, Fadus, with a troop of horse, pursued them; slew the imposter, and many others; and dispersed the faction. Deceivers, under the government of Felix, were multiplied, leading off people into the wilderness under the promise and fanatical expectation that they should there see signs and wonders. The old Serpent often leads fanatical people into wildernesses of error and delusion, under similar expectations. The viligant eye of the Romas governor rested on these imposters, and was sure to frustate their designs, as oft as they appeared.

In the year 55, arose a notable Egyptian impostor, named Felix. Thirty thousand followed him, under the persuasion that from mount Olivet they should see the walls of Jerusalem fall to the ground at his command, for their easy capture of the Roman garrison there; and their taking possession of Jerusalem. They were attacked by the Roman governor; four hundred were slain; and the rest dispersed. The Egyptian imposter escaped for his life. In the year 60, another pretended Messiah appeared, engaging to break the Roman yoke, if they would follow him into the wilderness; but the deceiver and his followers soon fell a sacrifice to the vigilance of Festus, the governor. It would be too unwieldy to mention all the vile imposters of this period. They were a just retribution of righteous Heaven upon the Jews, for having rejected and put to death the true Messiah; and they fulfilled the warning given by our Lord, of a host of deceivers at that period. How prone are men to court deception. Christ had said to the Jews, 'I am come in my Father's name, and ye receive me not. If another should come in his own name, him will ye receive.' This was fulfilled; and not only then, but in every age to this day. Those who give the best evangelical evidence of their being ambassadors of Christ, many will reject; while the confident and noisy claims of egotists are by them fully allowed. "As in water face answers to face; so the heart of man to man."

Our Lord proceeds; "And ye shall hear of wars, and rumours of wars: see that ye be not troubled: for all these things shall come to pass; but the end is not yet. For nation shall rise against nation; and kingdom against kingdom; and great earthquakes shall be in divers places, and famines, and pestilences; all these are the beginning of sorrows."

The portentous thunders of wars and rumours of wars may be said to have occupied most of the time from the death of our Saviour, to the destruction of Jerusalem. The historick pages, which treat of these times, are stained with blood. A war between Herod and Aretas, king of Arabia, opened the bloody scene, after a short season of peace. In Selucia, the Greeks and Syrians rose against the Jews, who fled thither from the pestilence in Babylon, and slew fifty thousand of them. Five years after, the Jews in Perea and people of Philadelphia contended about the limits of a city, when many of the Jews were slain. Four years after this, an insult being offered to the Jews within the precincts of the temple, by a Roman soldier; and being violently resented; a Roman force rushed upon them, which so terrified the Jews, that they fled in vast disorder, and ten thousand of them lost their lives in the streets. After another four years, the Jews ravaged the country of the Samaritans, in consequence of their having murdered a Galilean, who was going to keep the passover. Many were slain. Soon after, a contention arose between the Jews in Caesarea and the Syrians, relative to the government of Caesarea. In the first encounter more than twenty thousand Jews were slain. This contention raged in many cities where the Jews and Syrians dwelt; and mutual slaughter prevailed. And in five other cities the carnage among the Jews was dreadful. At Damascus ten thousand Jews were slain in one hour. And at Scythopolis thirteen thousand were slain in one night. In Alexandria the Jews rose upon the Romans; and had fifty thousand of their people slain, without any regard to infancy or age. Soon after, in a contention at Totapata, forty thousand Jews perished. These contentions rose and increased till the whole Jewish nation took up arms against the Romans, and brought on themselves their final destruction. Thus the prediction of our Saviour quoted, received in those days a striking primary fulfilment.

Our Saviour added; "And great earthquakes shall be in divers places." These significant warnings too were accomplished in those days. Two are recorded by Tacitus; one at Rome in the reign of Claudius; another at Apamea, in Syria, where were many Jews. So destructive was the one at the latter place, that the tribute due to the Romans was for five years remitted. One also was terrifick at Crete; one at Smyrna; one at Miletus; one at Chios, and one at Samos; in all which places Jews dwelt. These are noted by Philástratus. Soon after, in the reign of Nero, both Tacitus and Eusebius inform, that Hierapolis and Colosse, as well as Laodicea, were overthrown by earthquakes. Another is noted at Rome; one at Campania; and others tremendous are mentioned as taking place at Jerusalem in the night; just before the commencement of the last siege of that city. Of these, Josephus gives the following account: "A heavy storm burst on them, during the night, violent winds arose, with most excessive rains, with constant lightning, most tremendous thunders, and dreadful roarings of earthquakes. It seemed as if the system of the world had been confounded for the destruction of mankind. And one might well conjecture that these were signs of no common event."

The famines predicted by Christ were likewise fulfilled. The one foretold by Agabus, noted in the Acts of the Apostles, was dreadful, and of long continuance. It extended through Greece and Italy; but was most severely felt at Judea, and especially at Jerusalem. The contributions noted as brought by Paul from abroad, to relieve the poor brethren there, were sent during this sore famine. Authors of that time mention two other famines in the empire, previous to the one occasioned by the siege of Jerusalem.

"Pestilences" too, the Saviour adds. Two instances of this signal judgement took place before the last Jewish war. The one took place at Babylon, where many Jews resided; the other at Rome, which swept off vast multitudes. Other lighter instances of this calamity occurred, in various parts of the empire; as both Tacitus and Suetonius record.

Our Lord also adds, "And fearful sights and great signs shall there be from heaven," Josephus (who can never be suspected of wishing to favour any prediction of Christ; and who probably knew not of any such prediction, when he wrote,) gives accounts of events, which strikingly answer to this premonition. Speaking of the infatuation of his countrymen, in running after imposters, while they neglected the plainest admonitions from heaven, he gives account of the seven following events;

1. He says; "On the 8th of the month Zanthicus, (before the feast of unleavened bread.) at the ninth hour of the night, there shone round about the altar and the circumjacent buildings of the temple, a light equal to the brightness of the day; which continued for the space of half an hour."

2. "About the sixth hour of the night, (says Josephus,) the eastern gate of the temple was found to open without human assistance." This gate was of solid brass; and so large and heavy, as to require twenty men to close it. And Josephus says, "it was secured by iron bolts, and bars, that were let down into a large threshold consisting of one entire stone." The Jews themselves concluded, from the miraculous nature of this event, that the security of their temple had fled. When the procurator was informed of it, he sent a band of men to close the door; who with great difficulty executed their orders.

3. Again, the same celebrated Jewish author says: "At a subsequent feast of pentecost, while the priests were going by night into the inner temple, to perform their customary ministrations, they first felt (as they said,) a shaking accompanied by an indistinct murmuring; and afterwards voices as of a multitude saying in a distinct and earnest manner: "Let us depart hence." How striking was this miraculus premonition. It commenced with a shaking, to call and fix the attention of these Jewish priests. Then was heard an indistinct murmur. This would make them listen with all possible heed. Then they heard the distinct voices, as of a multitude in great earnestness and haste;-

"Let us depart hence!" And their last fatal war with the Romans commenced before the next season for celebrating this feast.

4. Another sign was the following. The same author says; "A meteor, resembling a sword, hung over Jerusalem, during one whole year." This could not have been a comet, for it was stationary a whole year, and seems, from the words of Josephus, to have been much nearer than a comet, and appeared to be appropriated to that city. This reminds one of the sword of the destroying angel, stretched out over Jerusalem, I Chro. xxi. 16. This stationary position of the sword for a year, was a lively indication that the impending ruin was fatal.

5. Josephus says again: "As the high priests were leading a heifer to the altar to be sacrificed, she brought forth a lamb in the midst of the temple." Most striking rebuke to those infidel priests, who had rejected the Lamb of God who had shed his blood once for all, and abrogated the Levitical sacrifices; which yet they were impiously continuing. This wonder was exhibited in the temple, the type of the body of Christ, and at the passover, when at a preceeding passover Jesus was arrested and sacrificed; and it took place before the high priests and their attendants; so that they could never complain for want of evidence of the fact.

6. This author says: "Soon after the feast of the passover, in various parts of the country, before the setting of the sun, chariots and armed men were seen in the air passing round about Jerusalem." This strange sight occurring before sunset, and being seen in various parts of the country, must have been a miraculous portent; a sign from heaven. The Jews had said, "What sign showest thou, that we may see and believe." Now they had their signs in abundance; yet they would not believe.

7. The last and most fearful sign Josephus relates; that one Jesus, son of Ananus, a rustic of the lower class, appeared in the temple at the feast of tabernacles, and suddenly exclaimed, "A voice from the east -a voice from the west- a voice from the four winds -a voice against Jerusalem and the temple- a voice against the bridegrooms and the brides -a voice against the whole people!" These words he continued to exclaim through the streets of Jerusalem by day and by night, with no cessation (unless what was needed for the support of nature) for seven years! He commenced in the year 63, while the city was in peace and prosperity, and terminated his exclamations only in his death, amidst the horrors of the seige, in the year 70. This strange thing, when it commenced, soon excited great attention;

and this Jesus was brought before Albinus, the Roman governor, who interrogated him, but could obtain no answer except the continuation of his woes. He commanded him to be scourged, but to no effect. During times of festivals, this cry of his was peculiarly loud and urgent. After the commencement of the siege, he ascended the walls, and in a voice still more tremendous than ever, he exclaimed, "Wo, wo to this city, this temple, and this people!" And he then added, (for the first time for the seven years,) "Wo, wo to myself!" The words were no sooner uttered, than a stone from a Roman machine without the walls, struck him dead on the spot!

Such were the signs in the heavens and in the earth, which just preceded the destruction of Jerusalem. Several of them are recorded by Tacitus as well as by Josephus. The veracity of Josephus as a historian is probably allowed by all. Scaliger affirms that he deserves more credit as a writer than all the Greek and Roman historians put together.

From the conquest of Jerusalem by Pompey, sixty years before Christ, the Jews repeatedly had exhibited a most rebellious spirit against the Romans. The Jews had basely said to Pilate concerning Christ, "If thou let this man go, thou art not a friend of Caesar." But the fact was, they persecuted Christ because he would not erect a temporal throne in opposition to Caesar. Any imposter who seemed prepared to do this, they were ready to follow; and were ready to improve every apparent occasion to evince their decided hostility to the Romans. And they barely needed a prophet's eye to discern that this spirit and conduct (manifested on all occasions) would soon draw against them the Roman sword.

Judas, a Gaulonite, and Saddue, a Pharisee, had rallied the Jews with the idea that their paying tribute to the Romans would not fail to confirm them in the most abject slavery; in consequence of which, their enmity often burst forth with malignant violence, Tumults and riots increased; and Florus, the Roman governor of Judea, by his cruel exactions, increased this spirit among the Jews. Eleazer, son of the high priest, persuaded the officers of the temple to reject the offerings of foreigners, and to withhold publick prayers for them. The Roman government felt the insult; and a basis was soon found to be laid for a Roman war! Feuds and contentions increased in Judea, till Cestius Gallus marched an army thither from Syria to restore order. His march was marked with blood and desolation. The city of Zebulon, Joppa, and other villages in his way, he plundered and burned. Eight thousand four hundred of the inhabitants of the former place he slew. The district of Narbatene he laid waste, and slew two thousand of the Jews in Galilee; reduced the city of Lydda to ashes, and drove the Jews, (who made desperate sallies upon him) till he encamped within a hundred miles of the capital. Soon after, he entered Jerusalem, and burned some part of the city. But through the treachery of his own officers, he made an unexpected flight. The enraged Jews pursued him, and slew about sixty thousand of his men. Many of the rich Jews, alarmed at the Roman invasion, fled from Jerusalem, as from a foundering ship. Some suppose many of the Christians now fled to a place called Pella in the mountains of Judea. Matt. xxiv. 15-17.

Nero being informed of the defeat of Cestius, gave the command to Vespasian to press the war against the rebellious Jews. He and his son Titus soon collected an army of sixty thousand men. In A.D. 67, he marched from Ptolémais to Judea, marking his steps with ravages and desolation. Infancy and age fell before the furious soldiery. All the strong towns of Galilee and many of those of Judea fell before the victorious arms of Vespasian, who slew not less than one hundred and fifty thousand inhabitants. Signal vengeance was taken on Joppa, which had in part been rebuilt, after it had been by Cestius reduced to ashes. Vespasian was enraged at the frequent piracies of this people. The Jews of this place fleeing before him, betook themselves to their shipping. But a furious tempest overtook those who stood out to sea, and they were lost. The others were dashed vessel against vessel, or against the rocks. Some in their distress laid violent hands on themselves. Such as reached the shore were slain by the enraged Romans. The sea for some distance was stained with their blood. Forty thousand are said to have been swallowed up in the waves; and not one escaped to relate their catastrophe. Truly this was "distress of their nation, with the sea and waves thereof roaring!"

Vespasian returned from Jericho to Caesarea, to prepare for a grand siege of Jerusalem. Here he received intelligence of the death of the emperor Nero. This led him to suspend for the present the execution of his plan against the Jews. This respite to that devoted people continued about two years, and but encouraged them to deeds of greater enormity.

A spirit of faction now appeared in Jerusalem. Two parties first, and afterwards three, raged there; each contending with deadly animosity for the precedence. A part of one of these factions

the Lord, the temple of the Lord, the temple of the Lord are these."

The famine in the city became (as might be expected) still more deadly. For want of food the Jews ate their belts, sandals, skins of their shields, dried grass, and even ordure of cattle. *Now it was that a noble Jewess, urged by the insufferable pangs of hunger, slew and prepared for food her own infant child!* She had eaten half the horrible preparation, when the smell of food brought in a hoard of soldiery, who threatened her with instant death, if she did not produce to them the food she had in possession. She being thus compelled to obey, produced the remaining half of her child! The soldiers stood aghast; and the recital petrified the hearers with horror; and congratulations were poured on those whose eyes death had closed upon such horrid scenes. Humanity seems ready to sink at the recital of the woful events of that day. No words can reach the horrors of the situation of the female part of the community at that period. Such scenes force upon our recollection the tender pathetic address of our Saviour to the pious females who followed him, going to the cross: "Daughters of Jerusalem, weep not for me; but weep for yourselves and for your children; for behold the days are coming, in which they shall say, Blessed are the barren, and the wombs that never bare, and the breasts that never gave suck." Moses had long predicted this very scene. "The tender and delicate woman among you, (said he.) who would not venture to set the sole of her foot on the ground for delicateness; her eye shall be evil towards her young one, and toward her children, which she shall bear; for she shall eat them, for want of all things, secretly in the siege and straitness wherewith thine enemy shall distress thee in thy gates." Probably the history of the world will not afford a parallel to this. God prepared peculiar judgments for peculiarly horrid crimes! "These be the days of vengeance; that all things that are written may be fulfilled." Josephus declares, that if there had not been many credible witnesses of that awful fact, he never would have recorded it; for, said he, "such a shocking violation of nature never has been perpetrated by any Greek or barbarian."

While famine thus spread desolation, the Romans finally succeeded in removing part of the inner wall, and in possessing themselves of the high and commanding tower of Antonio, which seemed to overlook the temple. Titus with his council of war had formed a determination to save the temple, to grace his conquest, and remain an ornament to his empire. But God had not so determined. And "though there be many devices in a man's heart; nevertheless the counsel of the Lord that shall stand." A Roman soldier, violating the general order of Titus, succeeded in hurling a brand of fire into the golden window of the temple; and soon (as righteous Heaven would have it!) the sacred edifice was in flames. The Jews perceiving this, rushed with horrid outcries to extinguish the fire. Titus too flew to the spot in his chariot, with his chief officers and legions. With loud command, and every token of anxiety, he enforced the extinguishing of the fire; but in vain. So great was the confusion, that no attention was paid to him. His soldiers, deaf to all cries, assiduously spread the flames far and wide; rushing at the same time on the Jews, sword in hand, slaying and trampling down, or crushing them to death against the walls. Many were plunged into the flames, and perished in the burning of the out buildings of the temple. The fury of the Roman soldiers slaughtered the poor, the unarmed, and the rich, as well as men in arms. Multitudes of dead bodies were piled round about the altar, to which they had fled for protection. The way leading to the inner court was deluged with blood.

Titus finding the fire had not yet reached the inner temple, entered it with his superior officers, and surveying its magnificence with silent admiration. He found it to exceed all he had heard. This view led him to renew his efforts to save this stupendous pile of building, though so many of the out-buildings were gone. He even entreated his soldiers to extinguish the flames, and appointed an officer to punish any who should disobey. But all his renewed efforts were still in vain. The feelings of his soldiery were utterly unmanageable. Plunder, revenge, and slaughter had combined to render them deaf and most furious. A soldier succeeded in firing the door posts of the inner temple, and the conflagration soon became general.

One needs a heart of steel to contemplate the scenes which followed. The triumphant Roman soldiers were in a most ungovernable rage and fury. They were indeed instruments prepared for their work, to execute the most signal vengeance of Heaven; the flame of which was now reaching its height! The Romans slew of the Jews all before them; sparing neither age, sex or rank. They seemed determined to annihilate the Jewish race on the spot. Priests and common people; those who surrendered, and those who still fought; all were alike subjects of an indiscriminate slaughter. The fire of the temple at length completely enveloped the stupendous pile of building. The fury of the flames exceeded description. It impressed on distant spectators an idea that the whole city was in flames. The ensuing disorder and tumult, Josephus pronounces to have been such as to baffle all description. The outcry of the Roman legions was as great as they could make. And the Jews finding themselves a prey to the fury of both fire and sword, exerted themselves in the wildest accents of screaming. The people in the city, and those on the hill, mutually responded to each other in groans and screeches. People who had seemed just expiring through famine derived new strength from unprecedented scenes of horror and death, to deplore their wretchedness. From mountain to mountain, and from places distant, lamentations echoed to each other.

As the temple was sinking under the fury of the raging element, the mount on which it stood seemed in that part of it, (says the historian) to "impress the idea of a lake of liquid fire!" The blood of the slain ran in rivulets. The earth around became covered with the slain; and the victorious Romans trampled over those piles of the dead, in pursuit of the thousands who were fleeing from the points of their swords. In a word, the roar and crackling of fire; the shrieks of thousands in despair; the dying groans of thousands, and the sights which met the eye whereever it was turned, were such as never before had any parallel on earth. They probably as much exceeded all antecedent scenes of horror, as the guilt which occasioned them, in their treatment of the Lord of Glory, exceeded all guilt ever before known among men.

A tragical event had transpired worthy of particular detail. Before the temple was wrapped in flames, an imposter appeared among the Jews, asserting a divine commission; and that if the people would follow him to the temple, they would see signs, wonders and deliverance. About six thousand (mostly women and children) followed him, and were in the galleries of the temple, waiting for this promised deliverance, when fire was set to that building. Not one escaped. All were consumed in the conflagration of the sacred edifice! What multitudes are by false prophets plunged in eternal fire!

The place of the temple now presented a vast pile of ruins. Here terminated the glory and existence of this stupendous building, this type of the body of Christ and of his church; this type of the Millennium, and of heaven. Here it reached its close, after the period of one thousand and thirty years, from the time of its dedication by Solomon; and of six hundred and thirty-nine years, from its being rebuilt in the days of Haggai, after the seventy years captivity. It is singular, that it should be reduced to ashes not only soon after the feast of the passover, which convened so many thousands of Jews to Jerusalem to meet the ruins of their city and nation; but that it should be consumed on the same month, on the same day of the month, on which the Babylonians had before destroyed it by fire.

Josephus records another striking event, which seemed a sign of the destruction of Jerusalem. He says; (addressing the Jews who survived this ruin) "The fountains flow copiously for Titus, which to you were dried up. For before he came, you know that both Siloam and all the springs without the city failed; so that water was brought by the amphora, (a vessel.) But now they are so abundant to your enemies, as to suffice for themselves and their cattle. This wonder you also formerly experienced, when the king of Babylon laid siege to your city."

The priests of the temple, after the destruction of their sacred edifice, betook themselves (those who had thus far escaped the general slaughter) to the top of one of its broken walls, where they sat mourning and famishing. On the fifth day necessity compelled them to descend, and humbly to ask pardon of the Roman general. But Titus at this late period rejected their petition, saying; "As the temple, for the sake of which I would have spared you, is destroyed; it is but fit the priests should perish also." All were put to death.

The obstinate leaders of the great Jewish factions, beholding now the desperateness of their cause, desired a conference with Titus. One would imagine they would at least now lay down their arms. Their desiring an interview with the triumphant Roman general, appeared as though they would be glad to do this. But righteous Heaven designed their still greater destruction. Titus, after all their mad rebellions, kindly offered to spare the residue of the Jews, if they would now submit. But strange to relate, they refused to comply. The noble general then, as must have been expected, was highly exasperated; and issued his general order that he would grant no further pardon to the insurgents. His legions now were ordered to "*ravage and destroy.*" "With the light of the next morning, arose the tremendous flame of the castle of Antonio, the council chamber, register's office, and the noble palace of the queen Helena. These magnificent piles were reduced to ashes. The furious legions, (executioners of divine vengeance, Ezek. ix. 5,6) then flew through the lower city, of which they soon became masters, slaughtering and burning in every street. The Jews themselves aided the slaughter. In the royal palace, containing vast treasures, eight thousand four hundred Jews were murdered by their seditious brethren. Great numbers of deserters from the furious leaders of faction, flocked to the Romans; but it was too late. The general order was given, all should be slain. Such therefore fell.

The Roman soldiers however, being at length weary with butchery, and more than satisfied with blood, for a short time sheathed their swords, and betook themselves to plunder. They collected multitudes of Jews, -husbands, wives, children, and servants; formed a market; and set them up at vendue for slaves. They sold them for any trifle; while purchasers were but few. Their law-giver, Moses, had forewarned them of this; Deut. xxviii. 68: "And ye shall be sold for bond men, and bond women; and no man shall buy you." Tremendous indeed must the lot of those be, who reject the Messiah, and are found fighting against the Son of God. Often had these Jews heard read (but little it seems did they understand the sense of the tremendous passage) relative to the Jewish rejectors of Christ, "He that sitteth in the Heavens shall laugh; the Lord shall have them in derision. Then shall he speak unto them in his wrath, and vex them in his sore displeasure. Yet have I set my king upon my holy hill of Zion. Thou shalt break them with a rod of iron; thou shalt dash them in pieces like a potter's vessel." "Thus saith the Lord, say, A sword, a sword is sharpened, and also furbished: it is sharpened to make a sore slaughter; it is furbished that it may glitter; (said God by the prophet, Ezek. xxi. alluding to this very event;) the sword is sharpened, and it is furbished to give it into the hand of the slayer. Cry and howl, son of man; smite upon thy thigh; smite thy hands together, and let the sword be doubled a third time; the sword of the slain. I have set the point of the sword against all their gates, that their hearts may faint, and their ruins be multiplied: Ah, it is made bright! it is wrapped up for the slaughter." -Such, and much more, were the divine denunciations of this very scene, which the infidel Jews would not escape, but would incur! And even a merciful God shrunk not from the execution! Let antichristian powers, yea. let all infidels and gospel despisers, consider this and tremble!

The whole lower city now in the possession of the Roman legions, (after the respite noted,) was set on fire. But the insolence of the devoted Jews in a part of the higher city remained unabated. They even insulted and exasperated their enemies, as though afraid the work of vengeance might not be sufficiently executed.

The Romans brought their engines to operate upon the walls of this higher branch of the city, still standing; which soon gave way before them. Before their demolition, Titus reconnoitred the city, and its fortifications; and expressed his astonishment that it should ever fall before his arms. He exclaimed, "Had not God himself aided our operations, and driven the Jews from their fortresses, it would have been absolutely impossible to have taken them. For what could men and the force of engines have done against such towers as these?" Yes, unless their Rock had sold them for their iniquities, no enemy could have prevailed against Jerusalem. Josephus, who was an eye witness of all the scene, says; "All the calamities, which ever befel any nation, since the beginning of the world, were inferior to the miseries of the Jews at this awful period."

The upper city too fell before the victorious arms of the Roman conquerors. Titus would have spared all who had not been forward in resisting the Romans; and gave his orders accordingly. But his soldiers, callous to all the feelings of humanity, slaughtered the aged and sick, as well as the mass of the people. The tall and most beautiful young men, however, were spared by Titus to grace his triumph at Rome. Of the rest, many above the age of seventeen were sent in chains to Egypt to be disposed of as slaves. Some were reserved to be sacrificed on their amphitheatres, as gladiators; to be slain in sham fights, for the sport of their conquerors. Others were distributed through the empire. All who survived, under the age of seventeen, were exposed for sale.

The triumphant general commanded what remained of the city, to be razed to its foundation, except three of the most stately towers, Mariamne, Hippocos, and Phasael. These should stand as monuments of the magnificence of the place and of his victory. A small part of the wall of the city at the west also, he commanded should be spared, as a rampart for his garrison. The other parts of the city he wished to have so effectually erased, as never to be recognized to have been inhabited. The Talmud and Mamonides relate that the foundations of the temple were so removed, that the site of it was ploughed by Terentius Rufus. Thus our Saviour predicted, that " there should not be left one stone upon another."

One awful occurrence is noted as transpiring during these scenes; that eleven thousand Jews, under the guard of one Fronto, a Roman general, were (owing to their own obstinacy, and to the scarcity of provisions) *literally starved to death*!

Josephus informs that eleven hundred thousand Jews perished in this siege of Jerusalem; that two hundred and thirty-seven thousand perished in that last war in other sieges and battles; besides multitudes who perished by famine and pestilence: making a total of at least fourteen hundred thousand. Some hundreds of thousands, in sullen despair, laid violent hands on themselves. About ninety-seven thousand were captured, and dispersed. Relative to the two great leaders of the Jewish factions, Simon and John, they were led to Rome, to grace the triumph of Titus; after which Simon was scourged and executed as a malefactor; and John was committed for life to dungeon. Thus ended their violent factious contentions.

The Roman army, before they left Jerusalem, not only demolished the buildings there, but even dug up their foundations. How fatal was the divine judgment on this devoted city. Five months before it was the wonder of the world; and contained, at the commencement of the siege, more than a million and a half of Jews, natives and visiters; now it lay in total ruins, with not "one stone upon another;" as Christ had denounced. These ruins Eusebius informs us he beheld. And Eleazer is introduced by Josephus as exclaiming; "Where is our great city, which it was believed God inhabited." The prophet Micah had predicted; "Therefore shall Zion for your sakes be ploughed as a field, and Jerusalem shall become heaps, and the mountain of the Lord's house as the high places of the forest." A captain of the army of Titus, did in fact plough where some part of the foundation of the temple had stood, as the Talmud records, and thus fulfilled this prediction.

Jesus Christ had foretold of this destruction, that "there should be great tribulation, such as was not since the beginning of the world." And of the event Josephus says; "If the misfortunes of all nations from the beginning of the world, were compared with those which befel the Jews, they would appear far less." Again; "No other city ever suffered such things; as no other generation from the beginning of the world, was ever more fruitful in wickedness."

Other parts of Judea were still to be subdued. Macherus was attacked. Seventeen hundred Jews surrendered and were slain; also three thousand fugitives taken in the woods of Jardes. Titus at Caesarea celebrated in great splendour the birth day of his brother Domitian. Here a horrid scene, according to the bloody customs of those times, was presented. To grace this occasion, more than two thousand five hundred Jews fell; some by burning; some by fighting with wild beasts; and some by mutual combat with the sword.

Massada was besieged. The Jewish commander, in despair, induced the garrison first to destroy their stores, and then themselves. They (nine hundred and sixty in number) consented to the horrid proposal. Men, women, and children took their seats upon the ground, and offered their necks to the sword. Ten men were selected to execute the fatal deed. The dreadful work was done. One of the ten was then chosen to execute the nine, and then himself. The nine being put to death, and fire being set to the place, the last man plunged his dagger into his own heart.

Seven persons, (women and children,) found means to conceal themselves, and escape the ruin. When the Romans approached, these seven related to them these horrid events.

Most of the remaining places now, through sullen despair, gave up all opposition, and submitted to the conquerors. Thus Judea became as a desolate wilderness; and the following passage in Isaiah had at least a primary accomplishment; "Until the cities be wasted without inhabitant; and the houses without man; and the land be utterly desolate; and the Lord have removed man far away, and there be a great forsaking in the midst of the land."

A line of prophecies is found in the sacred oracles, which relate to a signal temporal destruction of the most notorious enemies of the kingdom of Jesus Christ. Those were to have a two-fold accomplishment; first upon the Jews; and secondly upon the great Antichrist of the last days, typified by the infidel Jews. Accordingly those prophecies in the Old Testament are ever found in close connexion with the Millennium. The predictions of our Saviour, in Matt. xxiv. Mark xiii. and Luke xxi. are but a *new edition* of these sacred prophecies. This has been noted as *"the destruction of the city and temple foretold."* It is so indeed, and *more.* It is also a denunciation of the destruction of the great Antichrist of the last days. The certainty of this will appear in the following things, as New Testament writers decide. The Thessalonians, having heard what our Lord denounced, that all those things he had predicted should take place on *that generation,* were trembling with the apprehension, that the *coming* of Christ predicted, would then very soon burst upon the world. Paul writes to them, (2 Thes. ii.) and beseeches them by this coming of Christ, not to be shaken in mind, or troubled with such an apprehension. For *that day,* (that predicted coming of Christ, as it related to others beside the Jews.) was not to take place on that generation. It was not to come till the Antichristian apostacy come first; that man of sin was first to be revealed. This long apostacy was to be accomplished before the noted coming of Christ in its more important sense be fulfilled. After the Roman government, which hindered the rise of the man of sin, should be taken out of the way, Paul says, "Then shall that wicked one be revealed whom the Lord shall consume with the spirit of his mouth, and destroy with the brightness of *his coming.*" Here then is the predicted *coming of Christ,* in its more interesting sense, in the battle of that great day, which introduces the Millennium. Here is a full decision that these noted denunciations of Christ alluded more especially (though not primarily) to a coming which is still future.

The same is decided by Christ himself, in Rev. xvi. After the sixth vial, in the drying up of the Turkish Euphrates, three unclean spirits of devils, like frogs, go forth to the kings of the earth, and of all the world, to gather them to the great battle. The awful account is interrupted by this notice from the mouth of Christ; verse 15, "Behold, I come as a thief. Blessed is he that watcheth and keepeth his garments; lest he walk naked, and they see his shame." This is as though our Lord should say; now the time is at hand, to which my predictions of *coming as a thief,* principally alluded. Now is the time when my people on earth shall need to watch, as I directed, when predicting my *coming* to destroy first the type of Antichrist, and secondly the antitype.

The predictions in the prophets, which received an incipient fulfilment in the destruction of Jerusalem, were to receive a more interesting fulfillment in Christ's coming to destroy his antichristian foes. Hence it is that the seventh vial is called (Rev. xvi. 14,) "the battle of that great day of God Almighty;" clearly alluding to that great day noted through the prophets. And of the same event it is said, Rev. x. 7; "the mystery of God shall be finished, as he hath declared to his servants, the prophets." Here again the allusion clearly is to the many predictions in the prophets of the destruction of the enemies of Christ's kingdom, which were to receive an incipient fulfilment in the destruction of Jerusalem; and a far more interesting one, in the sweeping from the earth the last antichristian powers, to introduce the millennial kingdom of Christ. We accordingly find those predictions through the prophets clearly alluding to the last days, and the introduction of the Millennium.

Viewing the destruction of Jerusalem then, as but a type of an event now pending upon antichristian nations, we peruse it with new interest; and it must be viewed in the light of a most impressive warning to this age of the world. -The factions, madness, and self-ruin of the former, give but a lively practical comment upon the various predictions of the latter. Three great and noted factions introduced the destruction of Jerusalem. And of the destruction of Antichrist we read (perhaps alluding to that very circumstance) Rev. xvi. 19; "And the great city was divided into three parts."

Then it follows; "and the cities of the nations fell; and great Babylon came in remembrance before God to give unto her the cup of the wine of the fierceness of his wrath." In the desolation of Gog and his bands, faction draws the sword of extermination. "I will call for a sword against him throughout all my mountains, saith the Lord God; every man's sword shall be against his brother." Exek. xxxviii. 21.

The great coalition against the Jews, in the time of Jehoshaphat, was destroyed by the sword of mutiny and faction: See 2 Chron. xx. And in allusion to this very battle which God fought for his church, the vast coalitions of Antichrist, in the last days, when the Jews are restored, is said to be gathered "to the valley of Jehoshaphat:" See Joel iii. The various circumstances of the destruction of Jerusalem afforded a lively incipient comment on the many denunciations of the battle of that great day of God Almighty, which awaits the antichristian world; while it is fully evident, that the passages more especially allude to the tremendous scenes of judgment, which shall introduce the Millennium.

II

The Certain Restoration Of Judah And Israel

The subject of this chapter is introduced with a concise view of the expulsion of the ten tribes from the promised land. The ten tribes revolted from the house of David, early in the reign of Rehoboam, son and successor of king Solomon. They received from this young prince treatment, which was considered impolitic and rough; upon which they separated themselves from that branch of the house of Israel, who, from that time, have been distinguished by the name of Jews. The revolting ten tribes submitted to another king, Jeroboam. And this breach was never after healed. Jeroboam, to perpetuate and widen this breach, and apprehending that if the Jews and ten tribes amicably met for public worship, according to the law of God, the rupture between them would probably soon be healed, set up two golden calves, one in Dan, and one in Bethel; and ordered that the ten tribes of Israel should meet there for their public worship. He thus "made Israel to sin." And would to God he had been the last who has made the professed worshippers of Jehovah "to sin," by assigning them different places of worship, from motives not more evangelical than those of Jeroboam.

The ten tribes thus went off to idolatry. A line of kings succeeded Jeroboam; but none of them, to the time of the expulsion, were true worshippers of the God of Israel. By their apostacy, folly, and idolatry, the ten tribes were preparing themselves for a long and doleful rejection, an outcast state for thousands of years. This Moses had denounced; Deut. xxviii. And this God fulfilled.

Tiglah Pilnezer, king of Assyria, captured the tribes of Reuben and Gad, and the half tribe of Manessah, who lay east of Jordan, and placed them in Halah, Harah, and Habor, by the river Gozen. 1 Chro. v. 26. About twenty years after (134 years before the Babylonish captivity of the Jews, and 725 years before Christ.) the rest of the ten tribes continuing impenitent, Shalmanezer, the succeeding king of Assyria, attacked Samaria, took the remainder of the ten tribes, in the reign of Hoshea, king of Israel, carried them to Assyria, and placed them with their brethren in Halah and Habor, by the river Gozen in Media -2 Kings xvii. This final expulsion of Israel from the promised land, was about 943 years after they came out of Egypt. The king of Assyria placed in their stead, in Samaria, people from Babylon, Cutha, Ava, Hama, and Sapharvaim. Here was the origin of the mongrel Samaritans.

From this captivity the ten tribes were never recovered. And they have long seemed to have been lost from the earth. They seem to have been indeed "outcast," from the social world, and the knowledge of civilized man. The Jews, long after, were dispersed among the nations; but have ever been known as Jews. But not so with Israel. They have seemed strangely to disappear from the world; and for 2500 years to have been utterly lost.

What are we to believe concerning the ten tribes? Are they ever again to be restored and known as the natural seed of Abraham? Are they now in existence as a distinct people? If so, where are they to be found? All parts of the world are now so well known, that one would conceive the commonwealth of Israel cannot now be found among the civilized nations.

Must we look for them in a savage state? If so, the knowledge of their descent must be derived from a variety of broken, circumstantial, traditionary evidence. Who, or where, then, are the people who furnish the greatest degree of this kind of evidence?

An answer, relative to their restoration, will be involved in this chapter; and an answer to the other questions may be expected in the chapter following.

That the Jews are to be restored to Palestine as Jews, seems evident from a variety of considerations. And that the ten tribes of Israel will there be united with them, seems also to be plainly predicted in the prophets.

Let the following things be considered:

1. The preservation of the Jews, as a distinct people, among the many nations whither they have been dispersed, now for nearly eighteen hundred years, affords great evidence, to say the least, that the many predictions which seem to foretel such a restoration are to have a literal accomplishment. This their preservation is a most signal event of providence. Nothing like it has ever, in any other instance, been known on earth; except it be the case with the ten tribes of Israel. Other dispersed tribes of men have amalgamated with the people where they have dwelt, and have lost their distinct existence. And nothing but the special hand of God could have prevented this in the case of the Jews. The event then shows, that God has great things in store for

them, as Jews. What can these things be, but the fulfilment of those many prophecies which predict their restoration to the land of their fathers, as well as their conversion to the Christian faith?

2. That people have never, as yet, possessed all the land promised to them; nor have they possessed any part of it so long as promised. Hence their restoration to that land is essential to the complete fulfilment of those ancient promises. They were to possess the land to the river Euphrates, and forever; or to the end of the world. God promised to Abraham, Gen. xv. 18 -"Unto thy seed have I given this land, from the river of Egypt, unto the great river, the river Euphrates." Exod. xxiii. 31 -"And I will set thy bounds from the Red Sea, even unto the sea of the Philistines, and from the desert unto the river (Euphrates;) for I will deliver the inhabitants of the land into your hands, and thou shalt drive them out before thee." -Deut. xi. 21- "Every place wheron the sole of thy feet shall stand, shall be yours, from the wilderness and Lebanon, from the river, the river Euphrates, even unto the uttermost sea, shall your coast be." Here then, are the boundaries of this ancient divine grant to Abraham and his natural seed. Beginning at the river of Egypt, (a river not far from the north-east corner of the Red Sea, and running into the Mediterranean.) Thence northward, on the shore of the said sea, as far as the point due west of Mount Lebanon. Thence eastward, over said mountain, away to the river Euphrates. Thence southward, as far as the north line of Arabia. Thence westward, to the first named river. The whole of this territory, the natural seed of Abraham were to possess "for ever." The inhabitants "should be driven out before them." But this people anciently possessed but a small part of this territory. There was indeed a kind of typical possession of it in the reign of Solomon; which reign was a type of the Millennium. (See Psalm lxxii.) David, in his wars which were typical of the wars that will introduce the Millennium, subdued and put under tribute the Syrians, Moabites, Ammonites, and most of the nations dwelling in the above named territories. And they continued in subjection in the reign of Solomon. (See 1 Kings iv. 21.) But those nations were not then driven out; nor was their land possessed by the children of Abraham. They afterward threw off their yoke, and were extremely troublesome to the people of God. They were only made tributary during a part of two reigns. But God promised -Exod. xxiii. 31- "I will set thy bounds from the Red Sea even to the sea of the Philistines, and from the desert unto the river (Euphrates.) For I will deliver the inhabitants of the land into

your hands, and thou shalt drive them out before thee." The land east of Canaan, and away to the river Euphrates, was never possessed by Israel. Their literal possession of that extent of territory must be an event still future.

The promised land was given to Israel "for an everlasting possession;" Gen. xvii. 8. Surely this must mean a longer time than they did in ages past possess it. This promise remains then to be yet fulfilled. It must mean an undisturbed possession of it, so long as the possession of it on earth may be desirable; or to the end of the world. We accordingly find that people, at the time of the introduction of the Millennium, expostulating with God, and pleading that ancient grant; Isa. lxiii. 17,18; "O Lord, why hast thou made us to err from thy way, and hardened our heart from thy fear? Return for thy servants' sake, the tribes of thine inheritance. The people of thy holiness have possessed it (thine inheritance) but a little while: our adversaries have trodden down thy sanctuary. We are thine. Thou never bearest rule over them; they are not called by thy name." Here is a plea put in the mouths of the ancient people of the Lord, at the time of their restoration, not long before the battle of the great day, with a description of which battle this chapter begins. They expostulate relative to the sovereignty of God, in the resting of the veil of blindness and hardness so long on their hearts, during their long, rejected state. They plead that they are God's servants, according to the ancient entail of the covenant. They plead for a restoration; and plead that their nation had enjoyed, that their everlasting inheritance, but a little while; but that a people not called by God's name, nor governed by his word, had trodden down the sanctuary; a description exactly fulfilled by the Turks. This fully implies the entering again of the Jews upon their ancient inheritance, in the last days.

3. I shall now adduce some of the numerous express predictions of this event. In the prophecy of Ezekiel, the restoration of the Jews and of Israel to their own land, as well as their conversion in the last days, is clearly predicted. In chapter xxxvi, we have their long dispersion, and their guilty cause of it. But God, in the last days, works for his own name's sake, and recovers them. God says, "And I will sanctify my great name, which was professed among the heathen; and the heathen shall know that I am the Lord -when I shall be sanctified in you before their eyes. For I will take you from among the heathen, and gather you out of all countries, and will bring you into your own land. And I will sprinkle clean water upon you and ye shall be

clean; from all your filthiness, and from all your idols will I cleanse you. A new heart also will I give unto you, and a new spirit will I put within you; and I will take away the stony heart out of your flesh, and I will give you an heart of flesh. And I will put my spirit within you, and cause you to walk in my statutes, and ye shall keep my judgments and do them. And ye shall dwell in the land that I gave to your fathers, and ye shall be my people, and I will be your God. Then shall ye remember your own evil ways -and shall loathe yourselves. -Not for your sakes do I this, saith the Lord God, be it known unto you. Thus saith the Lord God; in the day that I shall have cleansed you from all your iniquities, I will also cause you to dwell in the cities, and the wastes shall be builded. And the desolate land shall be tilled, whereas it lay desolate in the sight of all the heathen that passed by. And they shall say, this land that was so desolate is become like the garden of Eden; and the waste and desolate and ruined cities are become fenced and are inhabited. Then the heathen who are left round about you, shall know that I the Lord build the ruined places, and plant that which was desolate. I the Lord have spoken it, and I will do it." Here is their regeneration; having a new heart; being cleansed from all sin. And beside this, we find expressly promised their being reinstated in the land of their fathers, which had long lain waste. They rebuilid their ancient cities. That this is in the last days, connected with the introduction of the Millennium, the connexion of the whole passage, and the following chapters, fully decide. Both houses of the descendants of Abraham, (viz, Israel and Judah,) are recovered, as will be seen. Those predictions cannot be fulfilled merely by the conversion of that people. For over and above their express conversion, they are established in the land of their fathers.

The prophet proceeds further to predict and illustrate the wonderful event, by the resurrection of a valley of dry bones, chap. xxxvii. which figure God thus explains:"Son of man, these bones are the whole house of Israel. Behold, they say, our bones are dried, and our hope is lost; we are cut off for our parts. Therefore prophecy, and say unto them; thus saith the Lord God; behold, O my people, I will open your graves, and cause you to come up out of your graves, and bring you into the land of Israel. And ye shall know that I am the Lord, when I have opened your graves, O my people, and brought you up out of your graves, and shall put my spirit in you, and ye shall live, and I shall place you in your own land. Then shall ye know that I the Lord have spoken it, and performed it, saith the Lord."

The re-union of the two branches of that people follows, by the figure of the two sticks taken by the prophet. On the one he writes, "For Judah, and for the children of Israel his companions." Upon the other; "For Joseph, the stick of Ephraim, and for all the house of Israel his companions."

Lest any should say, the prediction which here seems to foretel the restoration of the ten tribes, as well as that of the Jews, were accomplished in the restoration of that few of the Israelites who clave to the Jews under the house of David, and the ten tribes are irrecoverably lost; it is here expressed that the Jews and those Israelites, their companions, were symbolized by one stick; and Ephraim, all the house of Israel, (the whole ten tribes,) by the other stick. These sticks miraculously become one in the prophet's hand; which is thus explained. "Thus saith the Lord God; Behold, I will take the children of Israel (their general ancient name, including the twelve tribes) from among the heathen, whether they be gone; and I will gather them on every side, and bring them into their own land. And I will make them one nation in the land, upon the mountains of Israel; and one king shall be king to them all; and they shall be no more two nations, neither shall they be divided into two kingdoms anymore at all. And they shall dwell in the land that I gave unto Jacob, my servant, wherein your fathers have dwelt, and they shall dwell therein, even they and their children and their children's children forever." Can a doubt here rest on the subject, whether the Jews and the ten tribes shall be re-established in Palestine? Can such divine testimony as this be done away? But similar testimonies to the point are numerous in the prophets. This passage has never yet received a primary, or partial fulfilment. The whole of it remains to be fulfilled. Some of the predictions which are to have an ultimate accomplishment in this final restoration had a primary one in the restoration from the seventy years captivity in Babylon. But even this cannot be said of the prophecy under consideration. None of those written on the second stick, in the hand of the prophet, have ever yet been recovered. The whole passage is intimately connected with the battle of that great day, which introduces the Millennium; as appears in the two following chapters. Here the house of Israel enter again upon their everlasting possession of the land of promise, which God engaged to Abraham.

A reiteration of these predictions is intermingled with the predictions concerning Gog, or the powers of Antichrist, to be collected against the Jews, after their restoration, in the two chapters succeeding. "In the latter years thou (Gog) shalt come into the land that is brought back from the sword, and gathered out of many people, against the mountains of Israel, which have been always waste, (or have lain waste for so many centuries during the dispersion of the Jews;) but it (that nation) is brought back out of the nations, and they shall dwell safely all of them. Thou shalt ascend and come like a storm; thou shalt be like a cloud to cover the land, thou and all thy bands, and many people with thee. Thus saith the Lord God; it shall also come to pass, that at the same time, shall things come into thy mind, and thou shalt think an evil thought; and thou shalt say, "I will go up to the land of unwalled villages, (the state of the Jews in Palestine, after their restoration;) I will go to them that are at rest, that dwell safely, all of them, dwelling without walls, and having neither bars nor gates; to take a spoil, and to take a prey, to turn thine hand upon the desolate places that are now inhabited, and upon the people that are gathered out of the nations, who have gotten cattle and goods, who dwell in the midst of the land." "Thou shalt fall upon the mountains of Israel, thou and all thy bands. So will I make my holy name known in the midst of my people Israel; and the heathen shall know that I am the Lord, the Holy One of Israel. Behold, it is come, it is done, saith the Lord God. This is the day whereof I have spoken. And they that dwell in the cities of Israel shall go forth, and shall set on fire and burn the weapons -seven years."

The whole account is thus divinely summed up. "Therefore, thus saith the Lord God; now will I bring again the captivity of Jacob, and have mercy upon the whole house of Israel, and will be jealous for my holy name; after that they have borne their shame, and all their trespasses whereby they have trespassed against me, when they dwelt safely in their land, and none made them afraid. When I have brought them again from the people, and gathered them out of their enemies' lands, and am sanctified in them in the sight of many nations; then shall they know that I am the Lord their God, who caused them to be led into captivity among the heathen; but I have gathered them into their own land, and left none of them there (among the heathen) any more; neither will I hide my face any more from them; for I have poured out my spirit upon the house of Israel, saith the Lord God." It seems as though this were enough, if nothing more were quoted from the prophets to prove our point. If this proof should be deemed insufficient, one would be apt to say, nothing that inspiration can assert upon the point, could be deemed sufficient!

But that it may appear that the prophetic writings unite to exhibit this as a great object of the Christian's belief, I shall note some of the other predictions of it.

In Isaiah xi. the stem from the root of Jesse is promised. The Millennium follows when the cow and the bear shall feed together, and the wolf and the lamb unite in love; and nothing more shall hurt or offend. "And it shall come to pass in that day that the Lord shall set his hand again, the second time, to gather the remnant of his people, who shall be left, from Assyria and from Egypt, and from Pathros, and from Cush, and from Elam, and from Shinar, and from Humah, and from the isles of the sea. And he shall set up an ensign for the nations, and shall assemble the outcasts of Israel, and gather together the dispersed of Judah, from the four corners of the earth." Here just before the Millennium, the Jews and ten tribes are collected from their long dispersion, by the hand of Omnipotence, set *a second time* for their recovery. A body of the Jews, and some of several other tribes, were recovered from ancient Babylon. God is going, in the last days, to make a *second*, and more *effectual* recovery from mystical Babylon, and from the four quarters of the earth. The prophet proceeds; "And the Lord shall utterly destroy the tongue of the Egyptian sea; and with his mighty wind shall he shake his hand over the river, and shall smite it in the seven streams, and make men go over dry shod. And there shall be an highway for the remnant of his people, which shall be left from Assyria; like as it was to Israel in the day that he came up out of the land of Egypt." Mr. Scott, upon this passage, says; "For the Lord will then remove all obstacles by the same powerful interposition, that he vouchsafed in behalf of Israel, when He separated the tongue, or bay of the Red Sea, and destroyed that hindrance to the departure of Israel; and with a mighty wind he will so separate the waters of the river Euphrates, in all its streams, that men may pass over dry shod. Thus an highway shall be made for Israel's return, as there was for their ancestors to pass from Egypt into Canaan. This part of the chapter contains a prophecy, which certainly remains yet to be accomplished. -"Bishop Lowth says the same; and adds, as quoted by Mr. Scott, "This part of the chapter foretels the glorious times of the church, which shall be ushered in by the restoration of the Jewish nation, when they shall embrace the gospel, and be restored to their own country. This remarkable scene of Providence is plainly foretold by most of the prophets; and by St. Paul. " We thus have the testimony of those great men, Lowth and Scott, in favour of a literal restoration of the Jews to their own land, being here predicted. And here is a drying upof a mighty river, to prepare the way for the event. A river is the symbol of a nation. When Israel were to be redeemed from Egypt, the Red Sea was to be dried up before them. When they were to be redeemed from Babylon, the Euphrates was by Cyrus to be dried or turned, to accomplish the event. And in their last restoration to Palestine, (ere long to be accomplished,) another great mystical river is to be dried up. The sixth vial dries up the mystic Euphrates, that the way of the kings of the east may be prepared. This is to be fulfilled on the Turks. Perhaps the event is now transpiring. This river is to be smitten in its *seven streams;* as stated in this prophecy of Isaiah; perhaps indicating that the Turks, be they ever so powerful in provinces and resources, as seven is a number of perfection, they yet shall fall by the remarkable hand of God, to accomodate the return of his ancient people. These prophetic hints give an interest to the present struggles in the south-east of Europe, or in Greece.

In Jeremiah, xxiii. 6,8, is the restoration of Israel. "In his days, (i.e. under the millennial reign of the righteous branch raised up to David,) Judah shall be saved, and Israel shall dwell safely; I will gather the remnant of my flock out of all countries, whither I have driven them, and will bring them again to their folds. Therefore, behold the days come, saith the Lord, that they shall no more say, The Lord liveth, who brought up the children of Israel out of the land of Egypt; but, the Lord liveth, who brought up, and who led the house of Israel out of the north country, and from all countries whither I have driven them, and they shall dwell in their own land." As this event is under the reign of Christ, so it has never yet been fulfilled. It is an event of the last days; and plants the ancient people of God in their own land.

The same comparison of the same event, we find in Jeremiah xvi. 14, 15. After denouncing their long dispersion for their sins; God says," Therefore, behold the days come, saith the Lord, that it shall no more be said, The Lord liveth that brought the children of Israel out of the land of Egypt; but the Lord liveth that brought up the children of Israel from the land of the north, and from all the lands whither I had driven them; and I will bring them into their land, that I gave unto their fathers."

In Isaiah xviii. a land shadowing with wings at the last days, is by the Most High addressed, and called to aid this restoration of that people of God. "Go, ye swift messengers, to a nation scattered and peeled, to a people terrible from the beginning hitherto; a nation meted out, and trodden down; whose land the rivers have spoiled. In that day shall the present be brought unto the Lord of hosts, of a people scattered and peeled, and from a people terrible from the beginning hitherto; a nation meted out and trodden under foot; whose land the rivers have spoiled, to the place of the Lord of hosts, the Mount Zion." The people here described, (to be brought by that land addressed, as a present to the Lord, to Mount Zion, or to Palestine,) are evidently the descendants of Abraham, and an event of the last days. A further explanation of this chapter is to be given in the last chapter of this work.

The same thing is noted in Isaiah lx. The Jewish church is called upon: "Arise, shine, for thy light is come and the glory of the Lord is risen upon thee. The gentiles shall come to thy light, and kings to the brightness of thy rising. Who are these that fly as clouds, and as doves to their windows? Surely the isles shall wait for me, and the ships of Tarshish first, to bring thy sons from far, their silver and their gold with them, unto the name of the Lord thy God, and to the Holy One of Israel, because he hath glorified thee." Here are ships conveying the Hebrews to Palestine, as clouds and as doves to their windows. Chap. lxvi. 20: "And they shall bring of your brethren for an offering unto the Lord, out of all nations, upon horses, and in chariots, and in litters, and upon mules, and upon swift beasts, to my holy mountain Jerusalem, saith the Lord, as the children of Israel bring an offering in a clean vessel unto the house of the Lord." In Zephaniah iii. 10. (connected with the battle of the great day, and the Millennium.) we read; "From the rivers of Ethiopia my suppliants (or worshippers) shall bring my offering, even the daughter of my dispersed;" as the passage should be rendered.

In Isaiah lxv. we find the sin, the dispersion, and the gathering again, at the Millennium, of the ancient tribes of the Lord. In relation to their gathering after their banishment, and "their works are measured into their bosom," it follows; "Thus saith the Lord; As the new wine is found in the cluster, and one saith, destroy it not; for a blessing is in it; so will I do for my servants' sakes that I may not destroy them all. And I will bring forth a seed out of Jacob, and out of Judah an inheritor of my mountains; and mine elect shall inherit it, and my servants shall dwell there." Here, after the long rejected state of Jacob and Judah, a blessed remnant at last shall be recovered; a seed from Jacob, (the ten tribes) and from Judah (the Jews) an inheritor of Canaan, shall come and dwell in that land. This has never yet been fulfilled. But it will be accomplished when God will (as in the following verses) "create new heavens and a new earth," in the millennial glory of the church.

In Amos ix. 14, 15, is a prediction of this event. "And I will bring again the captivity of my people Israel, and they shall build the waste cities, and inhabit them; and they shall plant vineyards, and drink the wine thereof; and I will plant them upon their land, and they shall no more be pulled up out of their land, which I have given them, saith the Lord God." This restoration is surely *future.* For after the restoration from the Babylonish captivity, they were again expelled from their land, now for many centuries. But after the restoration here promised, God says, "They shall no more be pulled up out of their land. " This shows that the restoration here promised is both future and literal. Jer. xxx. 3; "For lo, the days come, saith the Lord, that I will bring again the captivity of my people, Israel and Judah, saith the Lord; and I will cause them to return to the land that I gave to their fathers, and they shall possess it." In the restoration from Babylon, Israel was not returned; and the Jews possessed their land but a short time. Hence this prophecy remains to be fulfilled. Read the whole 31st chapter of Jeremiah, and you will find the restoration of the Jews and the ten tribes, to the land of their fathers, in the last days; and their continuance in it so long as the sun, moon and stars endure. "If those ordinances depart from before me, saith the Lord, (i.e. of the sun, moon and stars) then the seed of Israel shall cease from being a nation before me forever." God here promises "the city (Jerusalem) shall be built to the Lord; it shall not be plucked up, nor thrown down any more forever." Here God engages that as Ephraim is God's first born; so he will earnestly remember him still, and surely have mercy upon him, for his bowels are pained with his long outcast state. That he will sow the house of Israel and the house of Judah with the seed of men; and that "like as he had watched over them, to pluck up, and to break down, to throw down, and destroy and afflict; so he will watch over them to build and plant.["] That all this shall be, when the new covenant is made with the house of Israel and the house of Judah, not according to the covenant that he made with their fathers. Thus it is an event to take place under the last, the gospel dispensation; and hence it must be now future.

The prophet Joel, when foretelling the last days, and the Millennium, notes this event; chap. iii. 1. "For behold, in those days, and at that time, when I shall bring again the captivity of Judah and Jerusalem, I will also gather all nations, and will bring them down into the valley of Jehoshaphat." The battle of the great day of God follows; verse 9-17. Upon which follows the Millennium. In this series of events, God "brings again the captivity of Judah and Jerusalem."

In Zeph. iii. is the same. A new preparatory scene of judgment is predicted; verse 6, 7. The battle of the great day follows; verse 8. Then the Millennium; verse 9. To prepare the way for this, the noted restoration is promised; verse 10-18. And the scene closes thus; verse 19, 20. "Behold, at that time I will undo all that afflict thee; and I will save her that halteth, and gather her that was driven out; and I will get me praise and fame in every land where they have been put to shame. At that time I will bring you again, even in the time that I gather you; for I will make you a name and a praise among all the people of the earth, when I turn back your captivity before your eyes, saith the Lord."

The prophet Hosea most decisively predicts this event. His first son must be called Jezreel; for God would soon avenge the blood of Jezreel; "and I will cause to cease the house of Israel."

This house did cease; and has been banished and lost to this day. The name of his daughter Lo-ruhamah, is explained: "Ye are not my people; and I will not be your God." Here is their long excommunication. But he immediately proceeds to predict their restoration. Chap. i. 10, 11; "Yet the number of the children of Israel shall be as the sand of the sea, which cannot be measured nor numbered; and it shall come to pass that in the place, where it was said unto them, Ye are not my people; there shall it be said to them, Ye are the sons of the living God. Then shall the children of Israel and the children of Judah be gathered together, and appoint themselves one head; and they shall come up out of the land; (earth;) for great shall be the day of Jezreel." Here the ten tribes were to be dispersed, and again restored, together with the Jews; and their numbers and prosperity shall be immense. St. Paul quotes this passage, Rom. ix. 25, merely by way of *accomodation*, to note that the gentiles were called into the church; (a thing noted by expositors as very common in the sacred writings;) yet by no means with a view to hint, that this text is not to receive a more literal accomplishment in a future restoration of the ten tribes. In numerous scriptures the sentiment is confirmed that there shall be a literal restoration. The bringing in of the gentile church is a prelude to this. Israel were excommunicated that the gentiles might take their place. But it was to be thus only "till the fulness of the gentiles be come in," and then Israel shall be grafted in again, and their promised restoration be accomplished.

This prophet proceeds in the following chapters to predict the same event. See Hosea, 2d and 3d chapters. The account closes thus; "For the children of Israel shall abide many days without a king, and without a prince, and without a sacrifice, and without an image, and without an ephod, and without a teraphim. Afterward shall the children of Israel return and seek the Lord their God, and David, their king; and shall fear the Lord and his goodness in the latter days." Here is a description of the present rejected state of Israel; and a prediction of their national restoration, "in the latter days."

But few of the predictions of this final restoration are given. To recite them all, would be unwieldy. In Isai. xiv. is a prediction of the destruction of a power under the name of the king of Babylon; which event is evidently the same with the destruction of the mystical Babylon of the last days, -inasmuch as it is to be accomplished upon the mountains of Israel: verse 25. To prepare the way for this, we have the promised restoration of Israel, verse 1, as immediately preparatory to the event; and therefore it must in its ultimate accomplishment be still future. "For the Lord will have mercy on Jacob, and will yet choose Israel, and set them in their own land. And the strangers shall be joined with them, and they shall cleave to the house of Jacob." The stranger being joined unto Israel, restored to their own land, and what follows in the second and third verses, were events, which were not fulfilled when the Jews returned from ancient Babylon; but are just such events as are promised to take place after the final restoration of Israel, and the battle of the great day. The promised restoration is expressly applied to Israel. Judah and Israel had become two nations long before this prophecy. The event is then clearly future. Israel shall be again chosen and set in their own land.

This restoration is a great event in the prophets; and we find it in the New Testament. Paul (in his epistle to the Romans, chap. xi.) notes their being again grafted into their own olive tree, as a notable event of the last days, which shall be the "riches of the gentiles;" yea, "life from the dead" to them. See also Isaiah xlix. 18-23. One passage more I will adduce from the writings of Moses; Deut. xxx. The long and doleful dispersion of this people had been predicted in the preceding chapters. Here their final restoration follows. "And it shall come to pass, when all these things are come upon thee, and thou shalt call them to mind among all the nations whither the Lord thy God hath driven thee, and shalt return unto the Lord thy God; -that then the Lord thy God will turn thy captivity, and have compassion upon thee, and will return and gather thee from all the nations whither the Lord thy God hath scattered thee. And the Lord thy God will bring thee into the land, which thy fathers possessed, and thou shalt possess it, and he will do thee good, and multiply thee *above thy fathers."* This has never yet been fulfilled. For the Jews, returned from Babylon, were very far from being multiplied in their land *above their fathers.* This remains still to be accomplished.

          Thus the prophetic writings do clearly decide, that both Israel and the Jews shall, in the last days, before the Millennium, be literally restored to their own land of Palestine, and be converted to the Christian faith.

          4. To give a mystical import to all these prophecies, and say they will be fulfilled only in the *conversion* of these ancient people of God to Christianity is to take a most unwarrantable liberty with the word of God. Some have made such pretence; but far be it from me to follow them! Why not as well apply a mystical sense to every prediction of future events? To the predictions of the battle of that great day; of the Millennium; of the resurrection of the bodies of men; of the final judgment; of the conflagration of this world; of heaven; and of hell? Why may not those as well all be fulfilled, not by a literal, but by some mystical accomplishment? Is not this to *add* and to diminish, with a witness? Paul says, (2 Tim. ii. 16.) "But shun profane and vain babblings; for they will increase unto more ungodliness, and their words will eat as doth a canker; of whom is Hymeneas and Philetus; who concerning the truth have erred, saying, that the resurrection is past already, and overthrow the faith of some." What was the liberty taken by those arch heretics? No doubt it was this; applying to the predictions of a resurrection of the bodies of men from the 'grave, a mystical resurrection of the soul from the death of sin. But the predictions of the resurrection are far less numerous, and are not more express, than are the

predictions of the restoration of the Jews and Israel to their own land.

In various of the most remarkable of these predictions, we find it distinctly ascertained that the Jews shall be converted; shall have a new heart given them; shall have their hearts circumcised to fear the Lord. And beside this, it is said that people shall (as a distinct nation.) be restored to the land of their fathers, and shall dwell in temporal prosperity there through all following ages, and be more numerous than ever were their fathers. To say then, that all those predictions of such a restoration to Palestine, are to be accomplished only in the bringing of that people (in their dispersed state) to embrace the Messiah; is to take a most unwarrantable liberty with the word of God! Look at one passage; Ezekiel, 36th, 37th, 38th and 39th chapters. Are the new heart (the heart of flesh) there promised, and God's gathering them out of all lands into their own land, which had so long lain waste, one and the same event? What can such expositors do with the predictions of Gog and his bands, gathered against them, and falling upon the mountains of Israel? Are these (and all the predictions in Joel, Zechariah, and other prophets, of the gathering of all nations to Jerusalem.) to be explained away, so that no "gathering of the nations, and assembling of the kingdoms" must be expected? It must be a dangerous expedient thus to explain away the clear and express sentiments of revelation. The old and best expositors generally have believed in a literal restoration of Judah and Israel. And no material objections can be raised against it, which might not in its principle operate as forcibly against all predicted future events.

5. That the Hebrews are to have a literal restoration, appears from the fact, that the threatenings that God would cast them off, had their fulfillment in a literal rejection of them from the promised land. The promises of their restoration appear to be an exact counterpart of this; and hence must have their effect in restoring them again to Palestine. If such promises did not design to restore them again to the land of their fathers; why should the threatenings of their rejection of God, be designed to have their effect in expelling them literally from the land of promise? Why should one of them receive a literal, and the other a mystical construction? No account can be given of this. If there is no benefit in restoring them to Palestine; why was there any calamity in expelling them from Palestine? Why did not God let them continue there, though he withdrew his spirit and grace from them? But if, over and above this they must be expelled

from the land of promise; then surely their promised restoration must (over and above giving them the heart of flesh) bring them back to the Canaan, which was given to them for an everlasting possesion.

III

The Present State Of Judah And Israel

The present state of the Jews is so well understood in the Christian and literary world, that very little will here be said on this part of the subject. While a more particular attention will be paid to the present state of the ten tribes of Israel.

The whole present population of the Jews has been calculated at five millions. But the probability is, (as has been thought by good judges.) that they are far more numerous. [Rev. Mr. Frey says more than nine millions.] One noted character says, that in Poland and part of Turkey, there are at least three millions of this people; and that among them generally, there is an unusual spirit of enquiry relative to Christianity. Mr. Noah says, that in the States of Barbary, their number exceeds seven hundred thousand. Their population in Persia, China, India, and Tartary, is stated (in a report of the London Society for the conversion of the Jews,) to be more than three hundred thousand. In Western Asia the Jews are numerous; and they are found in almost every land.

As in Europe this remarkable people have been singularly depressed, and in ages past, made a taunt, reproach, and by word, trodden down, scattered and peeled: one would hope that quarter of the world would feel themselves obligated to be singularly active in bringing about their restoration.

Considerable has been undertaken to meliorate their condition, and prepare the way for their restoration.

It is fourteen years since a society was formed in London to aid the christianization of this people. A chapel has been erected by this society for their benefit. The New Testament they have caused to be translated into the Hebrew language; also many tracts written in Hebrew. These tracts and Testaments have been liberally distributed among the Jews, and been read by multitudes of them with no small attention. Missionaries have been sent among them; schools opened, and various means used. A seminary was opened in 1822 for the instruction of the youth of this people. Four students of the seed of Abraham entered it; one of them the celebrated Mr. Wolff a Jewish convert and missionary. In various parts of the United Kingdoms, auxillary societies have been formed; and the amount of monies received in 1822, was upwards of I.10,698 sterling, (between 40 and $50,000.) In the schools of the society are between seventy and eighty children of the Jews. In 1822 there were distributed, 2,459 Hebrew Testaments; 892 German Jewish do.; 2,597 Polish Judea do.; 800 Hebrew Psalters; 42,410 Hebrew Tracts; 30,000 English do. for the Jews; 19,300 Hebrew cards. The prophets are about to be printed in Hebrew, on stereotype plates, for the benefit of the Jews. Places of deposit of books for the Jews are established extensively in the four quarters of the world.

Other and similar societies in favour of the Jews are becoming numerous. Only several will be given in detail. One has been formed in Berlin under the sanction of his Prussian majesty. This society in an address to the public, observes; "Pious Christians in Germany seem themselves almost excluded from the work of converting the heathen; to whom seafaring nations only have an immediate access. May they be of good cheer in turning their eyes to the millions of the ancient people of God, who live among them, or in their vicinity. There is no nation provided with so effective means now to begin the work of their conversion, as protestant Germany. For this country the most glorious harvest seems to be in reserve. Let us then clear ourselves from the blame of leaving to perish these millions living among us, or near our gates, without having ever made any well regulated attempt to lead them to that cross upon which their fathers crucified the Messiah. This field is our own, and only requires labourers.

According to our best information of its state, we have no doubt but the soil will readily receive the seed of the divine word." The informations received from Poland too, are interesting. The Jews there seem to be convinced that some important change in their condition is preparing; and they seem ready to cooperate in the means of such a change. Count Von der Recke, near Westphalia, has established near Dasselsdorf an asylum for converted Jews. And numerous societies have been formed in Europe and America, to aid this great object. The American Meliorating Society, with its auxiliaries, might be noted in detail; but they are well known. The history of the Palestine mission also; the noted agency of Mr. Frey, and the mission of Mr. Wolff, the Jewish missionary to Palestine; also the remarkable conversion of many of the Jews; but this would exceed my designed limits; and these things are well known to the Christian world.

My present object is rather to attend to the present state of the ten tribes of Israel. This branch of the Hebrew family have long been "outcasts" out of sight; or unknown as Hebrews. The questions arise, are they in existence as a distinct people? If so, who or where are they?

These are queries of great moment, at this period, when the time of their restoration is drawing near. These queries may receive an answer in the following pages.

Some preliminary remarks will be made; and then arguments adduced relative to the present state of the tribes of Israel.

1. It has been clearly ascertained in the preceding chapter, that the ten tribes, as the Israel of God, are in the last days to be recovered, and restored with the Jews. The valley of dry bones, and the two sticks becoming one in the prophet's hand, have been seen clearly to ascertain this: See Ezek. xxxvii. as well as the many other passages noted in that chapter. But as this fact is essential to our inquiring after the ten tribes with confidence of their existence, I shall here note several additional predictions of the event, found in the prophets; and note some passages, which distinguish between the dispersed state of the Jews, and the outcast state of the ten tribes; which distinction will afford some light in our inquiries.

When the restoration of the Hebrews is predicted, in Isai.xi. that God will in the last days set up an ensign for the nations; it is to "assemble the *outcasts* of Israel; and gather together the *dispersed* of Judah from the four corners of the earth." Mark the distinction; the Jews are "*dispersed*;" scattered over the nations as Jews, as they have long been known to be; but Israel are " *outcast*;" cast out from the nations; from society; from the social world; from the knowledge of men, as being Hebrews. This distinction is repeatedly found in the prophets. The dispersed state of the Jews, as Jews, is a most notable idea in the prophetic scriptures. But of Israel, the following language is used; as Isai. lvi.8; "The Lord God who gathereth the *outcasts* of Israel, saith." &c. Accordingly, when Israel are recovered, and united with the Jews at last, the Jews express their astonishment; and inquire *where they had been?* They had utterly lost them, as is the fact. See Isai. xlix. 18-22. The Jews here, while "*removing to and fro*" through the nations in their dispersed state, had been "*left alone*," i.e. of the ten tribes. The latter being now restored to the bosom of the mother church, the Jews inquire, "*Who hath brought up these? Behold, I was left*

alone; these, where had they been?" Here we learn that the ten
tribes had, during the long dispersion of the Jews, been utterly
out of their sight and knowledge, as their brethren. This implies
the long *outcast state of the ten tribes.* We find the same idea in
Isai. 1xiii. The chapter is introduced with the battle of the great
day of God, which introduces the Millennium; See verse 1-6. The
events of the chapter then, are intimately connected with that
period. They involve the restoration of God's ancient people. And
we find a special branch of that ancient people pleading with
God in language clearly indicative of their antecedent outcast
state -having been lost from the knowledge of the known
descendants of Abraham, the Jews. Allusion is made to their
ancient redemption; and to their subsequent and fatal rebellion,
till God "was turned to be their enemy, and he fought against
them;" or cast them out of his sight. At last (at a period nearly
connected with the great battle) they are waking up, and
pleading; "Look down from heaven, and behold from the
habitation of thy holiness and of thy glory; where is thy zeal and
thy strength, the sounding of thy bowels and of thy mercies
toward me? Are they restrained?" Here after a long period they
awake as from the dead, and plead God's ancient love to their
nation. What follows is affectingly descriptive of the *outcast
banished state.* "Doubtless thou art our father, though Abraham
be ignorant of us, and Israel acknowledge us not; thou, O Lord,
art our Father, our Redeemer, thy name is from everlasting."
Here then is a branch of that ancient people, unknown to
Abraham; i.e. unacknowledged by the Israel that have always
been known as such, or the Jews; clearly meaning, that they
have long been unknown as being the descendants of Abraham;
and yet such they are, according to the whole context. When the
present outcast ten tribes shall be convinced, from their own
internal traditions, and by the aid of those commissioned to bring
them in, that they are the ancient Israel of God, the above
language exactly fits their case; as does the following connected
with it; "O Lord, why hast thou made us to err from thy ways, and
hardened our hearts from thy fear? Return for thy servant's sake,
the tribes of thine inheritance. The people of thy holiness have
possessed it but a little while." Or, our.ancestors in the promised
land enjoyed what thou didst engage to them for an everlasting
inheritance, but a limited period. "Our adversaries have trodden
down thy sanctuary. We are thine. Thou never bearest rule over
them. They were not called by thy name." Here is a branch of the
tribes, till now, and for a long time, unknown. But themselves

finding who they are, they plead with God the entail of the covenant, and their covenant right to Palestine; and that the Turkish possessors of it were never called by God's name; nor were they under his laws. This must be fulfilled at a time not far from the present period.

    Several additional passages will be noted, to show that both the branches of that ancient people are to be restored unto Isai. xi. after the promise that the dispersed Jews, and outcast Israel shall be restored; the prophet added verse 13. The envy also of Ephraim shall depart; Ephraim shall not envy Judah, and Judah shall not vex Ephraim. So that the mutual jealousies between the two branches of the house of Israel, which before the expulsion of the ten tribes kept them in almost perpetual war shall never again be revived; which passage assures us of the restoration of Israel as Israel.

    In Jer. iii those two branches are distinguished by "backsliding Israel and her treacherous sister Judah." Israel was already put away for her spiritual adulteries, (having then been rejected for nearly one hundred years.) But the same backsliding Israel is there again recovered in the last days. God calls after them; "Return, thou backsliding Israel; for I am married unto you saith the Lord. And I will take you, one of a city and two of a family; (or one of a village, and two of a tribe;) and will bring you to Zion." "in those days the house of Judah shall walk with the house of Israel; and they shall come together out of the land of the north, to the land that I have given to your fathers.." This has never yet had even a partial accomplishment. Its event is manifestly future.

    The entail of the covenant must as surely recover the ten tribes as the Jews. Paul shows in Romans xi. the consistency of the rejection of the Jews, with the entail of the covenant with Abraham. And he makes their final restoration in the last days essential to this consistency. But this inspired argument as forcibly attaches itself to the ten tribes, to ensure their recovery, as to the Jews. He accordingly there says, "and so all Israel shall be saved;" or both branches of the Hebrews shall be recovered. This same point is most positively decided in Jeremiah, 30th and 31st chapters, as has appeared in the preceding chapter.

    2. It inevitably follows, that the ten tribes of Israel must now have, somewhere on earth, a distinct existence in an outcast state. And we justly infer, that God would in his holy providence provide some suitable place for their safe keeping, as his outcast tribes, though long unknown to men as such. There is

no avoiding this conclusion. If God will restore them at last as his Israel, and as having been "outcast" from the nations of the civilized world for 2500 years; he surely must have provided a place for their safe keeping, as a distinct people, in some part of the world, during that long period. They must during that period, have been unknown to the Jews as Israelites; and consequently unknown to the world as such; or the Jews would not at last (on their being united to them) inquire, "These, where had they been?" Isai. xlix 21. Nor would they themselves plead at that time, "though Abraham be ignorant of us, and Israel (the Jews) acknowledge us not."

There is a passage in Hosea iv. 16, which confirms and illustrates this idea. There, after the ten tribes were utterly separated to spiritual whoredom, or idolatry, and were given up to total backsliding, God says; "Ephraim is joined to idols, let him alone." God was going to let him alone for a long period till the time of his restoration in the last days. In the preceding verse, God hints his care of this people in this long intermediate space. The hint is given in this comprehensive sentence; "Now the Lord will feed them as a lamb in a large place." Now being long rejected, and let alone, God would feed them as a lamb in a large place. He would provide a large capacious part of the world for them, to keep them distinct by themselves; and yet would have his special providential eye upon them as his lamb. Scott upon the passage says; (after noting their obstinate rebellion;) "The Lord therefore intended to disperse them throughout the Assyrian empire, where they would be as much exposed to injury and violence, as a single deserted lamb in a large wilderness to the wild beasts." Not knowing where they are, Scott supposed they must be somewhere in Assyria. The fact is they are not found there. But according to him, the text gives the fact that God was going to place them, as his "deserted lamb in a large wilderness of wild beasts." How perfectly do we here find described the long outcast state of Israel in the vast wilderness of a sequestered part of the world, where yet God would keep them in existence, (and make provision for them eventually to come to light,) as his long rejected lamb! "Is Ephraim a dear child? For since I spake against him, I do earnestly remember him still."

3. We have an account of the ten tribes, after their captivity, which accords with the ideas just stated. We receive not the books of the Apocrypha as given by Inspiration; but much credit has been given to historical facts recorded in it; as in the

wars of the Maccabees, and other places. In 2 Esdras xiii. 40, and on, we read; "Those are the ten tribes which were carried away prisoners out of their own land, in the time of Osea, the king, whom Salmanezer, the king of Assyria, led away captive, and he carried them over the waters, and so came they into another land." Here is the planting of them over the Euphrates, in Media. The writer adds; "But they took this counsel among themselves, that they would leave the multitude of the heathen, and go forth into a further country, where never man dwelt; that they might there keep their statutes which they never kept (i. e. uniformly as they ought,) in their own land. There was a great way to go, namely of a year and a half." The writer proceeds to speak of the name of the region being called Arsareth, or Ararat. He must allude here to the region to which they directed their course to go this year and a half's journey. This place where no man dwelt, must of course have been unknown by any name. But Ararat, or Armenia, lay north of the place where the ten tribes were planted when carried from Palestine. Their journey then, was to the north, or north-east. This writer says, "They entered into the Euphrates by the narrow passages of the river." He must mean, they repassed this river in its upper regions, or small streams, away toward Georgia; and hence must have taken their course between the Black and Caspian seas. This set them off north-east of the Ararat, which he mentions. Though this chapter in Esdras be a kind of prophecy, in which we place not confidence; yet the allusion to facts learned by the author, no doubt may be correct. And this seems just such an event as might be expected, had God indeed determined to separate them from the rest of the idolatrous world, and banish them by themselves, in a land where no man dwelt since the flood. But if these tribes took counsel to go to a land where no man dwelt, as they naturally would do, they certainly could not have taken counsel to go into Hindostan, or any of the old and long crowded nations of Asia. Such a place they would naturally have avoided. And to such a place the God of Israel would not have led them, to keep them in an outcast state, distinct from all other nations, as his lamb in a large wilderness.

4. Let several suppositions now be made. Suppose an extensive continent had lately been discovered, away north east from Media, and at the distance of "a year and a half's journey;" a place probably destitute of inhabitants, since the flood, till the time of the "casting out" of Israel. Suppose a people to have been lately discovered in that sequestered region, appearing as

we should rationally expect the nation of Israel to appear at this period, had the account given by the writer in Esdras been a fact. Suppose them to be found in tribes, with heads of tribes; but destitute of letters, and in a savage state. Suppose among their different tribes the following traditionary fragments are by credible witnesses picked up; some particulars among one region of them, and some among another; while all appear evidently to be of the same family. Suppose them to have escaped the polytheism of the pagan world; and to acknowledge one, and only one God, the Great Spirit, who created all things seen and unseen. Suppose the name retained by many of them for this Great Spirit, to be Ale, the old Hebrew name of God; and Yohewah, whereas the Hebrew name for Lord was Jehovah; also they call the Great First Cause, Yah; the Hebrew name being Jah. Suppose you find most of them professing great reverence for this great Yohewah; calling him "the great beneficent supreme holy spirit," and the only object of worship. Suppose the most intelligent of them to be elated with the idea that this God has ever been the head of their community; that their fathers were once in covenant with him; and the rest of the world were "the accursed people," as out of covenant with God. Suppose you find them, on certain occasions, singing in religious dance, "Hallelujah," or praise to Jah; also singing Yohewah, Shilu Yohewah, and making use of many names and phrases evidently Hebrew. You find them counting their time as did ancient Israel, and in a manner different from all other nations. They keep a variety of religious feasts which much resemble those kept in ancient Israel. You find an evening feast among them, in which a bone of the animal must not be broken; if the provision be more than one family can eat, a neighbour must be called in to help eat it, and if any of it be still left, it must be burned before the next rising sun. You find them eating bitter vegetables, to cleanse themselves from sin. You find they never eat the hollow of the thigh of any animal. They inform that their fathers practised circumcision. Some of them have been in the habit of keeping a jubilee. They have their places answering to the cities of refuge, in ancient Israel. In these no blood is ever shed by any avenger. You find them with their temples, (such as they be,) their holy of holies in their temple, into which it is utterly prohibited for a common person to enter. They have their high priests, who officiate in their temples, and make their yearly atonement there in a singular pontifical dress, which they fancy to be in the likeness of one worn by their predecessors in ancient times; with their breastplate, and various holy ornaments. The high priest, when addressing to his people what they call "the old divine speech," calls them "the beloved and holy people," and urges them to imitate their virtuous ancestors; and tells them of their "beloved land flowing with milk and honey." They tell you that Yohewah once chose their nation from all the rest of mankind to be his peculiar people. That a book which God gave, was once theirs; and then things went well with them. But other people got it from them, and then they fell under the displeasure of the Great Spirit; but that they shall at some time regain it. They inform you, some of their fathers once had a spirit to foretell future events, and to work miracles. Suppose they have their imitation of the ark of the covenant, where were deposited their most sacred things; into which it is the greatest crime for any common people to look. All their males must appear at the temple at three noted feasts in a year. They inform you of the ancient flood; of the preservation of one family in a vessel; of this man in the ark sending out first a great bird, and then a little one, to see if the waters were gone. That the great one returned no more; but the little one returned with a branch. They tell you of the confusion of languages once when people were building a great high place; and of the longevity of the ancients; that they "lived till their feet were worn out with walking, and their throats with eating."

You find them with their traditional history that their ancient fathers once lived where people were dreadfully wicked, and that nine tenths of their fathers took counsel and left that wicked place, being led by the Great Spirit into this country; that they came through a region where it was always winter, snow and frozen. That they came to a great water, and their way hither was thus obstructed, till God dried up that water; (probably it froze between the islands in Beering's Straits.) You find them keeping an annual feast, at the time their ears of corn become fit for use; and none of their corn is eaten, till a part of it is brought to this feast, and certain religious ceremonies performed. You find them keeping an annual feast, in which twelve men must cut twelve sapling poles, to make a booth. Here (on an altar made of twelve stones, on which no tool may pass) they must sacrifice. You find them with the custom of washing and anointing their dead. And when in deep affliction, laying their hand on their mouth, and their mouth in the dust. You find them most scrupulously practising a religious rite of separating their women, which almost precisely answers to the ancient law of Moses upon this subject. And many other things you find among this newly discovered people, which seem exclusively to have been derived from the ceremonial code of ancient Israel.

Suppose you should find things like these among such a people, without books or letters, but wholly in a savage state, in a region of the world lately discovered, away in the direction stated by the aforenoted writer in the Apocrypha; and having been ever secluded from the knowledge of the civilized world; would you hesitate to say you had found the ten tribes of Israel? and that God sent them to that sequestered region of the earth to keep them there a distinct people, during an "outcast" state of at least 2500 years? Would you not say, we have just such kind of evidence, as must at last bring that people to light among the nations? And would you not say, here is much more evidence of this kind, of their being the people of Israel, than could rationally have been expected, after the lapse of 2500 years in a savage state? Me thinks I hear every person whisper his full assent, that upon the suppositions made, we have found the most essential pile of the prophet Ezekiel's valley of dry bones! Ezek. xxxvii.; 1-14.

5. These things are more than mere supposition. It is believed they are capable of being ascertained as facts, with substantial evidence. Good authorities from men, who have been eye and ear witnesses, assure us that these things are facts. But you enquire, where or who are the people thus described? They are the aborigines of our own continent! Their place, their language, their traditions, amount to all that has been hinted. These evidences are not all found among any one tribe of Indians. Nor may all the Indians in any tribe, where various of these evidences are found, be able to exhibit them. It is enough, if what they call their beloved aged men, in one tribe, have clearly exhibited some of them; and others exhibited others of them; and if among their various tribes, the whole have been, by various of their beloved or wise men, exhibited. This, it is stated, has been the fact. Men have been gradually perceiving this evidence for more than half a century; and new light has been, from time to time, shed on the subject, as will appear.

The North American Reviewers, in reviewing a sermon of Doct. Jarvis. on this subject, delivered before the New York Historical Society, (in which he attempts to adduce much evidence to show that the natives of this continent are the tribes of Israel,) remark thus; "The history and character of the Indian tribes of North America, which have for some time been a subject of no inconsiderable curiosity and interest with the learned in Europe, have not till lately attracted much notice among ourselves. But as the Indian nations are now fast vanishing, and the individuals of them come less frequently under our observation, we also, as well as our European brethren, are beginning to take a more lively interest than ever, in the study of their character and history."

In the course of their remarks they add; "To the testimonies here adduced by Doctor Jarvis, (i.e. that the Indians are the ten tribes of Israel,) might have been added several of our New England historians, from the first settlement of the country." Some they proceed to mention; and then add, that the Rev. Messrs. Samuel Sewall, fellow of Harvard College, and Samuel Willard, vice president of the same, were of opinion, that "the Indians are the descendants of Israel." Doct. Jarvis notes this as an hypothesis, which has been a favourite topic with European writers; and as a subject, to which it is hoped the Americans may be said to be waking up at last.

Manasses Ben Israel, in a work entitled "The Hope of Israel," has written to show that the American Indians are the ten tribes of Israel. But as we have access to his authors, we may consult them for ourselves. The main pillar of his evidence is James Adair, Esq. Mr. Adair was a man of established character, as appears from good authority. He lived a trader among the Indians, in the south of North America, for forty years. He left them and returned to England in 1774, and there published his "History of the American Indians," and his reasons for being persuaded that they are the ten tribes of Israel. Remarking on their descent and origin, he concludes thus; "From the most accurate observations I could make, in the long time I traded among the Indian Americans, I was forced to believe them lineally descended from the Israelites. Had the nine tribes and a half of Israel, that were carried off by Shalmanezer, and settled in Media, continued there long, it is very probable by intermarrying with the natives, and from their natural fickleness and proneness to idolatry, and also from the force of example, that they would have adopted and bowed before the gods of Media and Assyria; and would have carried them along with them. But there is not a trace of this idolatry among the Indians." Mr. Adair gives his opinion, that the ten tribes, soon after their banishment from the land of Israel, left Media, and reached this continent from the north-west, probably before the carrying away of the Jews to Babylon.

But before I proceed to adduce the documents and evidences upon this subject, I shall make one more preliminary remark, and note another prediction relative to the outcast state of Israel.

6. There is a prophecy in Amos viii, 11, 12, relative to the ten tribes of Israel while in their state of banishment from the promised land, which appears exactly to accord with the account given by Esdras; and to the Indian tradition, which meets this, as will appear; and appears well to accord with the state of fact with the American natives, as will be seen. Amos was a prophet to the ten tribes of Israel. He prophesied not long before their banishment. The chapter containing the prophecy to be adduced, commences with a basket of summer fruit, which must soon be eaten, or it becomes unfit for use. The symbol is thus explained; "Then said the Lord unto me, The end is come upon my people of Israel; I 'will not pass by them any more." The prophet in the chapter announces that "they that swear by the sins of Samaria, and say, Thy God, O Dan, liveth; and, The manner of Beersheba liveth; even they shall fall." Here is a description of the idolatry of the ten tribes, and their utter banishment then just about to take place; from which they have never been recovered to this day.

As an event to be accomplished in their outcast state, the prophet gives this striking descriptive prediction. Verse 11, 12; "Behold the days come, saith the Lord God, that I will send a famine in the land, (or upon the tribes of Israel,) not a famine of bread, nor a thirst for water, but of hearing the words of the Lord. And they shall wander from sea to sea, and from the north even to the east; they shall run to and fro to seek the word of the Lord, and shall not find it." Here is an event, which when the reader shall have perused the traditions and sketches of the history of the Indians, he will perceive accurately describes their case. The prediction implies that Israel in their exilement should know that they had been blessed with the word of God, but had wickedly lost it; as a man in a famine knows he has had bread, but now has it not. They shall feel something what they have lost, and shall wander. They shall rove "from sea to sea; and from the north even unto the east." They shall set off a north course, and thence east; or shall wander in a north-east direction as far as they can wander, from sea to sea; from the Mediterranean whence they set out, to the extremest sea in the north-east direction. Should they cross the straits found there, into another continent, they may wander still from sea to sea; from the northern frozen ocean, to the southern ocean at Cape Horn; and from the Pacific to the Atlantic. They shall run to and fro through all the vast deserts between these extreme seas; retaining some correct ideas of God, and of his ancient word; they shall seek his word and will from their priests, and from their religious traditions; but shall not find it; but shall remain in their roving wretched state, till the distant period of their recovery from their exilement shall arrive.

Their blessed restoration is given in the following chapter. Verse 13-15; "Behold the days come, saith the Lord, that the ploughman shall overtake the reaper; and the treader of grapes him that soweth seed; and the mountains shall drop sweet wine; and all the hills shall melt. And I will bring again the captivity of my people Israel; and they shall build the waste cities and inhabit them; and they shall plant vineyards and drink the wine thereof; they shall build the waste cities and inhabit them; and they shall plant vineyards and drink the wine thereof; they shall also make gardens and eat the fruit of them. And I will plant them upon their land; and they shall no more be pulled up out of their land which I have given them, saith the Lord God." Here we have predicted the rapid preparatory scenes, the melting missionary events of our day. The mountains and hills of nations and communities shall flow together in this evangelical object. Blended with these missionary events, is the recovery of the long lost ten tribes. Here is the planting of them in their own land; and their permanent residence there to the end of the world. Never has this restoration had even a primary accomplishment; as was the return of the Jews from Babylon relative to their final restoration. The ten tribes have had no even typical restoration. They have been lost to the world to the present day. But the above passage implies, that in the midst of the sudden successful missionary events of the last days, which shall issue in the recovery and restoration of the ancient people of God, the ten tribes shall come to light, and shall be recovered.

Never has any satisfactory account been given of the fulfilment of this predicted famine of the word. It was to be inflicted on the ten tribes; not in the promised land, but during an awful exilement; "wandering from sea to sea, and from the north even to the east; running to and fro," from one extremity of a continent to another. The Spirit of Inspiration has here kindly given a clew by which to investigate the interesting and dark subject, -the place of the exilement of the tribes of Israel. q.d. Pursue them from Media, their place last known, north, then east; to the extreme sea. Find them roving to and fro in vast deserts between extreme seas; find a people of this description having retained some view of the one God; having their traditionary views of having lost the word of God; and seeking divine communications from Heaven; but seeking in vain; and you have the people sought. Listen to their traditions, borrowed from ancient revelation, which they have long lost; and you find the people perishing under the predicted famine of the word.

Having made these preliminary remarks, I shall attempt to embody the evidence obtained, to show that the natives of America are the descendants of the ten tribes of Israel.

A summary will be given of the arguments of Mr. Adair, and of a number of other writers on this subject. As the evidence given by Mr. Adair appears in some respects the most momentous and conclusive, I shall adduce a testimonial in his behalf. In the "Star in the West," published by the Hon. Elias Boudinot, LL. D. upon this subject, that venerable man says; "The writer of these sheets has made a free use of Mr. Adair's history of the Indians; which renders it necessary that something further should be said of him. Some time about the year 1774, Mr. Adair came to Elizabethtown, (where the writer lived,) with his manuscript, and applied to Mr. Livingston, (afterward governor of New Jersey -a correct scholar,) requesting him to correct his manuscript. He brought ample recommendations, and gave a good account of himself. Our political troubles with Great Britain then increasing, (it being the year before the commencement of the revolutionary war,) Mr. Adair, who was on his way to Great Britain, was advised not to risk being detained from his voyage, till the work could be critically examined; but to set off as soon as possible.

He accordingly took his passage in the first vessel bound to England. As soon as the war was over, (Mr. Boudinot adds of himself,) the writer sent to London to obtain a copy of this work. After reading it with care, he strictly examined a gentleman, then a member with him in congress, and of excellent character, who had acted as our agent among the Indians to the southward, during the war, relative to the points of fact stated by Mr. Adair, without letting him know the design, and from him found all the leading facts mentioned in Mr. Adair's history, fully confirmed from his own personal knowledge.

Here are the evidences of two great and good men most artlessly uniting in the leading facts stated by Mr. Adair. The character of Mr. Boudinot (who was for some time President of the American Bible Society,) is well known.

He was satisfied with the truth of Mr. Adair's history, and that the natives of our land are the Hebrews, the ten tribes. And he hence published his Star in the West; on this subject; which is most worthy of the perusal of all men.

From various authors and travellers among the Indians, the fact that the American Indians are the ten tribes of Israel, will be attempted to be proved by the following arguments:

1. The American natives have one origin.

2. Their language appears to have been Hebrew.

3. They have had their imitation of the ark of the covenant in ancient Israel.

4. They have been in the practice of circumcision.

5. They have acknowledged one and only one God.

6. The celebrated William Penn gives accounts of the natives of Pennsylvania, which go to corroborate the same point.

7. The Indians having one tribe, answering in various respects to the tribe of Levi, sheds further light on this subject.

8. Several prophetic traits of character given to the Hebrews, do accurately apply to the aborigines of America.

9. The Indians being in tribes, with their heads and names of tribes, affords further light.

10. Their having something answering to the ancient cities of refuge, seems to evince their Israelitish extraction.

11. Their variety of traditions, historical and religious, do wonderfully accord with the idea, that they descended from the ancient ten tribes.

The reader will pardon, if the tax on his patience under this last argument, exceeds that of all the rest.

1. The American natives have one origin. Their language has a variety of dialects; but all are believed by some good judges to be the same radical language. Various noted authors agree in this. Charlevoix, a noted French writer, who came over to Canada very early, and who travelled from Canada to the Mississippi, in his history of Canada, says; The Algonquin and the Huron languages, (which he says are as really the same, as the French and old Norman are the same,) have between them the language of all the savage nations we are acquainted with. Whoever should well understand both of these, might travel without an interpreter more than fifteen hundred leagues of country, and make himself understood by an hundred different nations, who have each their peculiar tongue; meaning dialect.

The Algonquin was the dialect of the Wolf tribe, or the Mohegan; and most of the native tribes of New England and of Virginia.

Doctor Jonathan Edwards. son of president Edwards, lived in his youth among the Indians; as his father was a missionary among them, before he was called to Princeton College; and he became as familiar with the Mohegan dialect, as with his mother tongue. He had also a good knowledge of the Mohawk dialect. He pronounced the Mohegan the most extensive of all the Indian dialects of North America. Dr. Boudinot asserts of him as follows. Dr. Edwards assures us, that the language of the Delawares, in Pennsylvania, of the Penobscots, bordering on Nova Scotia, of the Indians of St. Francis, in Canada, of the Shawanese, on the Ohio, of the Chippewas, to the eastward of Lake Huron, of the Ottawas, Nanticokes, Munsees, Minoniones, Messinaquos, Saasskies, Oilagamies, Kellestinoes, Mipegoes, Algonquins, Winnibagoes, and of the several tribes in New England, are radically the same. And the variations between them are to be accounted for from their want of letters and of communications. He adds (what all in the eastern states well know) Much stress may be laid on Dr. Edwards opinion. He was a man of strict integrity and great piety. He had a liberal education. -He was greatly improved in the Indian languages; to which he habituated himself from early life, having lived long among the Indians.

Herein the doctor agrees with the testimony of Charlevoix just noted. Here we find a cogent argument in favour of the Indians of North America, at least as being of one origin. And arguments will be furnished that the Indians of South America are probably of the same origin.

Doctor Boudinot (who for more than forty years was of opinion that the Indians are the ten tribes, and who sought and obtained much evidence on this subject,) assures us, that the syllables which compose the word

Yohewah (Jehovah) and Yah, (Jah) are the roots of a great number of Indian words, through different tribes. They make great use of these words, and of the syllables which compose the names of God; also which form the word Hallelujah, through their nations for thousands of miles; especially in their religious songs and dances. With beating and an exact keeping of time, they begin a religious dance thus; Hal, hal, hal; then le, le, le; next lu, lu, lu; and then close yah, yah, yah. This is their traditional song of praise to the great Spirit.

This, it is asserted, is sung in South, as well as North America. And this author says; Two Indians, who belong to far distant nations, may without the knowledge of each other's language, except from the general idiom of all their tribes, converse with each other, and make contracts without an interpreter. This shews them to have been of one origin.

Again, he says; Every nation of Indians have certain customs, which they observe in their public transactions with other nations, and in their private affairs among themselves, which it is scandalous for any one among them not to observe. And these always draw after them either public or private resentment, whenever they are broken. Although these customs may in their detail differ in one nation when compared with another; yet it is easy to discern that they have all had one origin.

Du Pratz says, in his history of Louisiania, "The nations of North America derived their origin from the same country, since at bottom they all have the same manners and usages, and the same manner of speaking and thinking. It is ascertained that no objection arises against this, from the different shades of complexion found among different tribes of Indians. The colour of the Indians generally, (says Doct. Boudinot,) is red, brown, or copper, according to the climate, and the high or low ground. Mr. Adair expresses the same opinion; and the Indians have their tradition, that in the nation from which they originally came, all were of one colour. According to all accounts given of the Indians, there are certain things in which all agree. This appears in the journals of Mr. Giddings, of his exploring tour. The most distant and barbarous Indians agree in a variety of things with all other tribes. They have their Great Spirit; their high priests; their sacrificing, when going to or returning from war; their religious dance; and their sacred little enclosure, containing their most sacred things, though it be but a sack, instead of an ark. - Messrs. Lack and Escarbotus both assert that they have often heard the Indians of South America sing Hallelujah. For thousands of miles the North American Indians have been abundant in this. Doctor Williams, in his history of Vermont, says; In whatever manner this part of the earth was peopled, the Indians appear to have been the most ancient, or the original men of America. They had spread over the whole continent, from the fiftieth degree of north latitude, to the southern extremity of Cape Horn. And these men every where appeared to be the same race or kind of people. In every part of the continent, the Indians are marked with a similarity of colour, features, and every circumstance of external appearance. Pedro de Cicca de Leon, one of the conquerors of Peru, and who had travelled through many provinces of America, says of the Indians; "The people, men and women, although there are such a multitude of tribes or nations, in such diversities of climates, appear nevertheless like the children of one father and mother."

Ulloa (quoted by Doct. Williams,) had a great acquaintance with the Indians of South America, and some parts of North America. Speaking of the Indians of Cape Breton in the latter, he declared them to be "the same people with the Indians in Peru." "If we have seen one American, (said he) we may be said to have seen them all." These remarks do not apply to all the people in the northern extremities of America. The Esquimaux natives appear to be a different race of men. This race are found in Labrador, in Greenland, and round Hudson's Bay. All these appear evidently the same with the Laplanders, Zemblans, Samoyeds and Tartars in the east. They probably migrated to this western hemisphere at periods subsequent to the migration of the Indians. They, or some of them, might have come from the north of Europe; from Norway to Iceland, then to Greenland, and thence to the coasts of Labrador, and farther west. But the consideration of those different people, does not affect our subject.

2. Their language appears clearly to have been Hebrew. In this, Doctor Edwards, Mr. Adair, and others were agreed. Doctor Edwards, after having a good acquaintance with their language, gave his reasons for believing it to have been originally Hebrew. Both, he remarks, are found without prepositions, and are formed with prefixes and suffixes; a thing probably known to no other language. And he shows that not only the words, but the construction of phrases, in both, have been the same. Their pronouns, as well as their nouns, Doctor Edwards remarks, are manifestly from the Hebrew. Mr. Adair is confident of the fact, that their language is Hebrew. And their laconic, bold and commanding figures of speech, he notes as exactly agreeing with the genius of the Hebrew language. He says, that after living forty years among them, he obtained such knowledge of the Hebrew idiom of their language, that he viewed the event of their having for more than two millenaries, and without the aid of literature, preserved their Hebrew language so pure, to be but little short of a miracle.

Relative to the Hebraism of their figures, Mr. Adair gives the following instance, from an address of a captain to his warriors, going to battle, "I know that your guns are burning in your hands; your tomahawks are thirsting to drink the blood of your enemies; your trusty arrows are impatient to be upon the wing; and lest delay should burn your hearts any longer, I give you the cool refreshing word; join the holy ark; and away to cut off the devoted enemy!"

A table of words and phrases is furnished by Doct. Boudinot, Adair, and others, with several added from good authority, to show how clearly the Indian language is from the Hebrew. Some of these Indian words are taken from one tribe, and some from another. In a long savage state, destitute of all aid from letters, a language must roll and change. It is strange that after a lapse of 2500 years, a single word should, among such a people, be preserved the same. But the hand of Providence is strikingly seen in this, perhaps to bring that people to light.

The following may afford a specimen of the evidence on this part of the subject.

English. - Indian. - Hebrew, or Chaldaic.
Jehovah Yohewah Jehovah
God Ale Ale, Aleim
Jah Yah or Wah Jah
Shiloh Shilu Shiloh
Heavens Chemim Shemim
Father Abba Abba
Man Ish, Ishte Ish
Woman Ishto Ishto
Wife Awah Eweh, Eve
Thou Keah Ka
His Wife Liani Libene
This man Uwoh Huah
Nose Niehiri Neheri
Roof of a house Taubana-ora Debonaour
Winter Kora Korah
Canaan Canaai Canaan
To pray Phale Phalac
Now Na Na
Hand part Kesh Kish
Do Jennais Jannen
To blow Phaubac Phauhe
Rushing wind Rowah Ruach
Ararat, or high mount Ararat Ararat

Assembly Kurbet Grabit
My skin Nora Ourni
Man of God Ishto allo Ishda alloah
Waiter of the high priest Sagan Sagan

PARTS OF SENTENCES.
    English. - Indian. - Hebrew.
    Very hot Heru bara or hala Hara bara
    Praise to the First Cause Halleluwah Hallelujah
    Give me food Natoni boman Natour bamen
    Go thy way Bayou boorkaa Boua bouak
    Good be to you Halea tibou Ye hali ettouboa
    My necklace Yene kali Vongali
    I am sick Nane guaete Nance heti

Can a rational doubt be entertained whether the above Indian words, and parts of sentences, were derived from their corresponding words and parts of sentences in Hebrew? If so, their adoption by savages at this distant time and place, would appear miraculous. Some one or two words might happen to be the same, among distant different nations. But that so many words, and parts of sentences too, in a language with a construction peculiar to itself, should so nearly, and some of them exactly correspond, is never to be admitted as resulting from accident.

And if these words and parts of sentences are from their corresponding Hebrew, the Indians must have descended from the ten tribes of Israel.

Some of the Creek Indians called a murderer Abe; probably from Abel, the first man murdered, whose name in Hebrew imports, mourning. And they called one who kills a rambling enemy, Noabe; probably from Noah, importing rest, and Abe. -He thus puts his rambling enemy to rest. The Caribbee Indians and the Creeks had more than their due proportion of the words and parts of sentences in the above table.

Rev. Dr. Morse, in his late tour among the western Indians, says of the language; "It is highly metaphorical; and in this and other respects, they resemble the Hebrew. This resemblance in their language, (he adds) and the similarity of many of their religious customs to those of the Hebrews, certainly give plausibility to the ingenious theory of Dr. Boudinot, exhibited in his interesting work, the Star in the West."

Dr. Boudinot informs that a gentleman, then living in the city of New York, who had long been much conversant with the Indians, assured him, that being once with the Indians at the place called Cohocks, they shewed him a very high mountain at the west, the Indian name of which, they informed him, was Ararat. And the Penobscot Indians, the Dr. informs, call a high mountain by the same name.

Doctor Boudinot assures us that he himself attended an Indian religious dance. He says ; "They danced one round; and then a second, singing hal-hal-hal,· till they finished the round. They then gave us a third round, striking up the words, le-le-le. On the next round, it was the words, lu-lu-lu, dancing with all their might. During the fifth round was sung, yah-yah-yah. -Then all joined in a lively and joyful chorus, and sung halleluyah; dwelling on each syllable with a very long breath, in a most pleasing manner." The Doctor adds; "There could be no deception in all this. The writer was near them -paid great attention- and every thing was obvious to the senses. Their pronunciation was very guttural and sonorous; but distinct and clear." How could it be possible that the wild native Americans, in different parts of the continent, should be found singing this phrase of praise to the Great First Cause, or to Jah -exclusively Hebrew, without having brought it down by tradition from ancient Israel? The positive testimonies of such men as Boudinot and Adair, are not to be dispensed with, nor doubted. They testify what they have seen and heard. And I can conceive of no rational way to account for this Indian song, but that they brought it down from ancient Israel, their ancestors.

Mr. Faber remarks; "They (the Indians) call the lightning and thunder, Eloha; and its rumbling, Rowah, which may not improperly be deduced from the Hebrew word Ruach, a name of the third person of the Holy Trinity, originally signifying, the air in motion, or a rushing wind." Who can doubt but their name of thunder, Eloha, is derived from a Hebrew name of God, Elohim? Souard, (quoted in Boudinot,) in his Literary Miscellanies, says of the Indians in Surinam, on the authority of Isaac Nasci, a learned Jew residing there, that the dialect of those Indians, common to all the tribes of Guiana, is soft, agreeabie, and regular. And this learned Jew asserts, that their substantives are Hebrew. The word expressive of the soul (he says) is the same in each language, and is the same with breath.

"God breathed into man the breath of life, and man became a living soul."

This testimony from Nasci, a learned Jew, dwelling with the Indians, must be of signal weight.

Dr. Boudinot from many good authorities says of the Indians; "Their language in their roots, idiom, and particular construction, appears to have the whole genius of the Hebrew; and what is very remarkable, it has most of the peculiarities of that language; especially those in which it differs from most other languages."

Governor Hutchinson observed, that "many people (at the time of the first settlement of New England,) pleased themselves with the conjecture, that the Indians in America are the descendants of the ten tribes of Israel."

Something was discovered so early, which excited this pleasing sentiment.

This has been noted as having been the sentiment of Rev. Samuel Sewall, of vice president Willard, and others. Governor Hutchinson expresses his doubt upon the subject, on account of the dissimilarity of the language of the natives of Massachusetts, to the Hebrew. Any language in a savage state, must, in the course of 2500 years, have rolled and varied exceedingly. This is shown to be the case in the different dialects, and many new words introduced among those tribes, which are acknowedged [sic] to have their language radically the same. The following facts are enough to answer every objection on this ground.

The Indians had no written language. Hence the English scholar could not see the spelling or the root of any Indian word. And the guttural pronunciation of the natives was such as to make even the Hebrew word, that might still be retained, appear a different word; especially to those who were looking for no Hebrew language among them. And the following noted idiom of the Indian language was calculated to hide the fact in perfect obscurity, even had it been originally Hebrew, viz.; the Indian language consists of a multitude of monosyllables added together. -Every property or circumstance of a thing to be mentioned by an Indian, must be noted by a new monosyllable added to its name. Hence it was that the simple word our loves, must be expressed by the following long Indian word Noowomantammoonkanunonnash. Mr. Colden, in his history of the five nations, observes, "They have few radical words. But they compound their words without end. The words expressive of things lately come to their knowledge (he says) are all compounds. And sometimes one word among them includes an entire definition of the thing." (See the Connecticutt Magazine, Vol. III, p. 267.) These things, considered of a language among savages, 2500 years after their expulsion from Canaan, must answer every objection arising from the fact, that the Indian language appears in some things very different from the Hebrew. And they must render it little less than miraculous (as Mr. Adair says it is) that after a lapse of so long a period among savages, without a book or letters, a word or phrase properly Hebrew should still be found among them. Yet such words and phrases are found. And many more may yet be found in the compounds of Indian words. I have just now observed, in dropping my eye on a Connecticut Magazine for 1803, a writer on the Indians in Massachusetts, in its earliest days, informs, that the name of a being they worshipped was Abamocko. Here, without any perception of the fact, he furnishes a Hebrew word in compound. Abba-mocko; father-mocho. As a tribe of Indians in the south call God, Abba-mingo ishto; Father-chief man. In the latter, we have two Hebrew words; Abba, father, and Ish, man. Could we make proper allowance for Pagan pronunciation, and find how the syllables in their words ought to be spelled, we might probably find many more of the Hebrew roots in their language.

It is ascertained that the Indians make great use of the syllables of the names of God, as roots of compound words. Dr. Boudinot says; "Y-O-he-wah-yah and Ale, are roots of a prodigious number of words through their various dialects." Wah being a noted name of God with the Indians, it seems often to occur in their proper names. Major Long informs us, in his expedition to the Rocky Mountains, that the name of God with the Omawhaw tribe is Wahconda. The Indians have their Wabash river, their Wa-sasheh tribe, (of which the word Osage is but a French corruption) their Wa-bingie, Wa-ping, Wa-masqueak, Wa-shpeloag, and Wa-shpeaute tribes; also their Wa-bunk, a name of the sun. A friend of mine informs me, that while surveying in his younger life in the state of Ohio, he obtained considerable acquaintance with the Indians there. That they appeared to have a great veneration for the sun, which they called Wahbunk. If bunk is an Indian name for a bed, as some suppose, it would seem that with those Indians, the sun was Jehovah's bed, or place of residence. The Indians have had much of an idea of embodying the Great Spirit in fire. It is an idea which resulted from the scene on the fiery top of Sinai, and from ancient Hebrew figures, (as Paul informed in his epistle to the Hebrews) that "Our God is a consuming fire." No wonder then those Indians in Ohio, as did the ancient Peruvians, embodied their Great Spirit in the sun. And no wonder their veneration for that visible supposed residence of the Great Spirit should be mistaken by strangers for worship paid to the sun.

3. The Indians have had their imitation of the ark of the covenant in ancient Israel. Different travellers, and from different regions unite in this. Mr. Adair is full in his account of it. It is a small square box, made convenient to carry on the back. The never set it on the ground, but on logs in low ground where stones are not to be had; and on stones where they are to be found. This author gives the following account of it. "It is worthy of notice, (he says) that they never place the ark on the ground, not sit it on the bare earth when they are carrying it against an enemy. On hilly ground, where stones are plenty, they place it on them. But in level land, upon short logs, always resting themselves (i.e. the carriers of the ark) on the same materials. They have also as strong a faith of the power and holiness of their ark, as ever the Israelites retained of theirs. The Indian ark is deemed so sacred and dangerous to touch, either by their own sanctified warriors, or the spoiling enemy, that neither of them dare meddle with it on any account. It is not to be handled by any except the chieftain and his waiter, under penalty of incurring great evil; nor would the most inveterate enemy dare to touch it. The leader virtually acts the part of a priest of war, pro tempore, in imitation of the Israelites fighting under the divine military banner."

Doct. Boudinot says of this ark, "It may be called the ark of the covenant imitated." In time of peace it is the charge of their high priests. In their wars, they make great account of it. The leader, (acting as high priest on that occasion,) and his darling waiter, carry it in turns. They deposit in the ark some of their most consecrated articles. The two carriers of this sacred symbol, before setting off with it for the war, purify themselves longer than do the rest of the warriors. The waiter bears their ark during a battle. It is strictly forbidden for any one, but the proper officer, to look into it. An enemy, if they capture it, treat it with the same reverence. Doctor Boudinot says that a gentleman, who was at Ohio, in 1756, informed him that while he was there, he saw among the Indians a stranger who appeared very desirous to look into the ark of that tribe. The ark was then standing on a block of wood, covered with a dressed deer skin. A centinel was guarding it, armed with a bow and arrow. The centinel finding the intruder pressing on, to look into the ark, drew his arrow at his head, and would have dropped him on the spot; but the stranger perceiving his danger, fled. Who can doubt the origin of this Indian custom? And who can resist the evidence it furnishes, that here are the tribes of Israel? See Num. x. 35, 36, and xiv. 44.

4. The American Indians have practised circumcision. Doct. Beaty, in his journal of a visit to the Indians in Ohio, between fifty and sixty years ago, says that "an old Indian (in answer to his questions relative to their ancient customs, the Indian being one of the old beloved wise men,) informed him, that an old uncle of his, who died about the year 1728, related to him several customs of former times among the Indians, and among the rest, that circumcision was long ago practised among them, but that their young men made a mock of it, and it fell into disrepute and was discontinued." Mr. McKenzie informs, that in his travels among the Indians, he was led to believe the same fact, of a tribe far to the north west; as stated in the Star in the West. His words (when speaking of the nations of the Slave and Dog rib Indians,) are these; "Whether circumcision be practised among them, I cannot pretend to say; but the appearance of it was general among those I saw." The Indians cautiously conceal their special religious rites from strangers travelling among them. Mr. McKenzie then wound not be likely to learn this fact from them, by any statement of the fact, or by seeing it performed. But he says, "The appearance of it was general." Doctor Boudinot assures that the eastern Indians inform of its having been practised among them in times past; but that latterly, not being able to give any account of so strange a rite, their young men had opposed it, and it was discontinued. Immanuel de Moraez, in his history of Brazil, says it was practised among the native Brazilians. These native inhabitants of South America were of the same origin with the Indians of North America.

The Rev. Mr. Bingham of Boston informed the writer of these sheets, that Thomas Hopoo, the pious native of a Sandwich Island, informed him while in this country, before he returned with our missionaries to his native region, that he himself had been circumcised; that he perfectly remembered his brother's holding him, while his father performed upon him this rite.

Mr. Bingham also informed that the pious Obookiah, of the same race, pleased himself that he was a natural descendant of Abraham, and thought their own language radically Hebrew. It is believed by men of the best information that the Sandwich Islanders and the native Americans are of the same race. What savage nation could ever have conceived of such a rite, had they not descended from Israel?

5. The native Americans have acknowledged one, and only one God; and they have generally views concerning the one Great Spirit, of which no account can be given, but that they derived them from ancient revelation in Israel. Other nations destitute of revelation, have had their many gods.

But little short of three hundred thousand gods have existed in the bewildered imaginations of the pagan world. Every thing, almost, has been deified by the heathen. Not liking to retain God in their knowledge, and professing themselves to be wise, they became fools; and they changed the glory of the one living God, into images of beasts, birds, reptiles, and creeping things. There has been the most astonishing inclination in the world of mankind to do thus. But here is a new world of savages, chiefly, if not wholly free from such wild idolatry. Doctor Boudinot (being assured by many good witnesses,) says of the Indians who had been known in his day; "They were never known (whatever mercenary Spanish writers may have written to the contrary) to pay the least adoration to images or dead persons, to celestial luminaries, to evil spirits, or to any created beings whatever." Mr. Adair says the same, and assures that "none of the numerous tribes and nations, from Hudson's Bay to the Mississippi, have ever been known to attempt the formation of any image of God." Du Pratz was very intimate with the chief of those Indians called "the Guardians of the Temple," near the Mississippi. He inquired of them the nature of their worship. -The chief informed him that they worshipped the great and most perfect Spirit; and said, "He is so great and powerful, that in comparison with him all others are as nothing. He made all things that we see, and all things that we cannot see." The chief went on to speak of God as having made little spirits, called free servants, who always stand before the Great Spirit ready to do his will. That "the air is filled with spirits; some good, some bad; and that the bad have a chief who is more wicked than the rest." Here it seems is their traditional notion of good and bad angels; and of Beelzebub, the chief of the latter.

This chief being asked how God made man, replied, that "God kneaded some clay, made it into a little man, and finding it was well formed, he blew on his work, and the man had life and grew up." Being asked of the creation of the woman, he said, "their ancient speech made no mention of, any difference, only that the man was made first." Moses' account of the formation of the woman, it seems, had been lost.

Mr. Adair is very full in this, that the Indians have but one God, the Great Yohewah, whom they call the great, beneficent, supreme, and holy Spirit, who dwells above the clouds, and who dwells with good people and is the only object of worship. So different are they from all the idolatrous heathen upon earth. He assures that they hold this great divine Spirit as the immediate head of their community; which opinion he conceives they must have derived from the ancient theocracy in Israel. He assures that the Indians are intoxicated with religious pride, and call all other people the accursed people; and have time out of mind been accustomed to hold them in great contempt. Their ancestors they boast to have been under the immediate government of Yohewah, who was with them, and directed them by his prophets, while the rest of the world were outlaws, and strangers to the covenant of Yohewah. The Indians thus please themselves (Mr. Adair assures us) with the idea that God has chosen them from the rest of mankind as his peculiar people. This, he says, has been the occasion of their hating other people; and of viewing themselves hated by all men. These things show that they acknowledge but one God.

The Peruvians have been spoken of as paying adoration to the sun; and as receiving their race of Incas, as children of the sun, in their succession of twelve monarchies. The Indians have had much of an apprehension that their one Great Spirit had a great affinity to fire. And the Peruvians, it seems, went so far as to embody him in the sun. Here seems a shred of mixture of the Persian idolatry, with the theocracy of Israel. As the more ancient Israelites caught a degree of the idolatrous distemper of Egypt, as appears in their golden calf; so the ten tribes, the time they resided in Media, and before they set off for America, may have blended some idea of fire with their one God. But the veneration the Peruvians had for their Incas, as children of the Most High, seems but a shred of ancient tradition from Israel, that their kings were divinely anointed; and is so far from being an argument against their being of Israel, that it operates rather in favour of the fact.

Doctor Boudinot informs of the southern Indians of North America, that they had a name for God, which signifies, "the great, the beloved, holy cause." And one of their names of God, is Mingo-Ishto-Abba; -Great Chief Father. He speaks of a preacher being among the Indians at the south, before the

American revolution, and beginning to inform them that there is a God who created all things. Upon which they indignantly replied, "Go about your business, you fool! Do not we know there is a God, as well as you?"

In their sacred dances, these authors assure us the Indians sing "Halleluyah Yohewah" -praise to Jah, Jehovah. When they return victorious from their wars, they sing, Yo-he-wah; having been by tradition taught to ascribe the praise to God.

The same authors assure us, the Indians make great use of the initials of the mysterious name of God, like the tetragrammaton of the ancient Hebrews; or the four radical letters which form the name of Jehovah; as the Indians pronounce thus, Y-O-He-wah. That like the ancient Hebrews, they are cautious of mentioning these together, or at once. They sing and repeat the syllables of this name in their sacred dances thus; Yo-yo, or ho-ho-he-he-wah-wah. Mr. Adair upon the same says; "After this they begin again; Hal-hal-le-le-lu-lu-yah-yah. And frequently the whole train strike up, hallelu-hallelu-halleluyah-halleluyah." They frequently sing the name of Shilu (Shilo, Christ) with the syllables of the name of God added; thus, "Shilu-yo-Shilu-yo-Shilu-he-Shilu-he-Shilu-wah-Shilu-wah." Thus adding to the praise of Shilu, the name of Jehovah by its sacred syllables. Things like these have been found among Indians of different regions of America. Syllables and letters of the name of God have been so transposed in four different ways; and so strange and guttural has been the Indian pronunciation, that it seems it took a long time to perceive that these savages were by tradition pronouncing the names of the God of Israel. Often have people been informed, and smiled at the fact, that an Indian, hurt or frightened, usually cries out wah! This is a part of his traditional religion; O Jah! or O Lord!

Doctor Williams upon the Indians" belief of the being of God,, observes; "They denominate the deity the Great Spirit; the Great Man above; and seem to have some general ideas of his government and providence, universal power and dominion. The immortality of the soul was every where admitted among the Indian tribes."

The Rev. Ithamar Hebard, formerly minister of this place, related the following: That about fifty years ago, a number of men were sent from New England by the government of Britain into the region of the Mississippi, to form some treaty with the Indians. That while these commissioners were there, having tarried for some time, an Indian chief came from the distance of what he calls several moons to the westward. Having heard that white men were there, he came to enquire of them where the Great Being dwelt, who made all things. And being informed through an interpreter, of the divine omnipresence; he raised his eyes and hands to heaven with great awe and ecstacy, and looking round, and leaping, he seemed to express the greatest reverence and delight. The head man of these commissioners had been a profane man; but this incident cured him, so that he was not heard to utter another profane word on his tour. This was related to Mr. Hebard by one Elijah Wood, who was an eye witness of the scene, and who was afterward a preacher of the gospel. The son of Mr. Hebard, a settled minister, gives this relation.

"Let this fact of the Indians generally adhering to one, and only one God, be contrasted with the polytheism of the world of pagans, and heathen besides; with the idle and ridiculous notions of heathen gods and goddesses; and who can doubt of the true origin of the natives of our continent? They are fatally destitute of proper views of God and religion.

But they have brought down by tradition from their remote ancestors, the notion of there being but one great and true God; which affords a most substantial argument in favour of their being the ancient Israel. It is agreed that within about eighty years, a great change has been produced among the Indians. They have in this period much degenerated as to their traditional religion. Their connexions with the most degenerate part of the white people, trading among them; and their knowledge and use of ardent spirit, have produced the most deleterious effects. They have felt less zeal to maintain their own religion, such as it was; and to transmit their own traditions. Remarkable indeed it is, that they did so diligently propagate and transmit them, till so competent a number of good testimonies should be furnished to the civilized and religious world, relative to their origin. This must have been the great object of divine Providence in causing them so remarkably to transmit their traditions through such numbers of ages. And when the end is answered, the cause leading to it may be expected to cease.

This may account for the degeneracy of some Indians far to the west, reported in the journals of Mr. Giddings, in his exploring tour. He informs, "They differ greatly in their ideas of the Great Spirit; one supposes that he dwells in a buffalo, another in a wolf, another in a bear, another in a bird, another in a rattlesnake. On great occasions, such as when they go to war, and when they return; (he adds) they sacrifice a dog, and have a dance. On these occasions they formerly sacrificed a prisoner taken in the war; but through the benevolent exertions of a trader among them, they have abandoned the practice of human sacrifice. There is always one who officiates as high priest. He practises the most rigid abstinence. He pretends to a kind of inspiration, or witchcraft; and his directions are obeyed." They all believe (he adds) in future rewards and punishments; but their heaven is sensual. They differ much in their ideas of goodness. One of their chiefs told him, he did not know what constituted a good man; that their wise men in this, did not agree. "Their chiefs, and most of their warriors, have a war sack, which contains generally the skin of a bird, which has a green plumage; or some other object, which they imagine to have some secret virtue."

Here we learn that those far distant savages have (as have all the other tribes) their Great Spirit, "who made every thing," though in their bewildered opinion he dwells in certain animals. On going to war, or returning, they must sacrifice; and for victory obtained, must have their religious dance. They must have their high priest, who must practice great abstinence, and pretend to inspiration; and hence must be obeyed. They have brought down their traditional notions of these things; and of future rewards and punishments. The ark of their warlike chieftains, it seems, has degenerated into a sack! but this (like the ark of the other tribes) must contain their most sacred things; "green plumage, or some other objects which they imagine to have some secret virtue." Here these Indians furnish their quota of evidence, in these more broken traditions, of their descent from Israel.

These tribes in the west are more savage, and know less of the old Indian traditions. Mr. Giddings says, "As you ascend the Missouri and proceed to the west, the nearer to the state of nature the savages approach, and the more savage they appear." This may account for their ark's degenerating into a sack; and for their verging nearer to idolatry in their views of the Great Spirit, viewing him as embodied in certain animals.

A chief of the Delaware Indians far in the west, visited by Messrs. Dodge and Blight, Jan. 1824, from the Union Mission, gave the following information to these missionaries. The chief was said by these missionaries "to be a grave and venerable character, possessing a mind which (if cultivated) would render him probably not inferior to some of the first statesmen of our country." On being inquired of by them whether he believed in the existence of a Supreme Being? he replied; "Long ago, before ever a white man stepped foot in America, the Delawares knew there was one God; and believed there was a hell, where bad folks would go when they die; and a heaven, where good folks would go." He went on to state (these missionaries inform) that "he believed there was a devil, and he was afraid of him. These things (he said) he knew were handed down by his ancestors long before William Penn arrived in Pennsylvania. He said, he also knew it to be wrong if a poor man came to his door hungry and naked, to turn him away empty. For he believed God loved the poorest of men better than he did proud rich men. Long time ago, (he added) it was a good custom among his people to take but one wife, and that for life. But now they had become so foolish, and so wicked, that they would take a number of wives at a time; and turn them away at pleasure!" He was asked to state what he knew of Jesus Christ, the Son of God. He replied that "he knew but little about him. For his part, he knew there was one God. He did not know about two Gods." This evidence needs no comment to show that it appears to be Israelitish tradition, in relation to the one God, to heaven, hell, the devil, and to marriage, as taught in the Old Testament, as well as God's estimation of the proud, rich, and the poor. These things he assures us came down from the ancestors, before ever any white man appeared in America. But the great peculiarity which white men would naturally teach them (if they taught anything,) that Jesus Christ the Son of God is the Saviour of the world, he honestly confesses he knew not this part of the subject.

The following is an extract of a letter from Mr. Calvin Cushman, missionary among the Choctaws, to a friend in Plainfield, Mass. in 1824.

"By information received of father Hoyt respecting the former traditions, rites and ceremonies of the Indians of this region, I think there is much reason to believe they are the descendants of Abraham. -They have had cities of refuge, feasts of first fruits, sacrifices of the firstlings of the flocks, which had to be perfect without blemish or deformity, a bone of which must not be broken. They were never known to worship images, nor to offer sacrifice to any god made with hands. They all have some idea and belief of the Great Spirit. Their fasts, holy days, &c. were regulated by sevens, as to time, i.e. seven sleeps, seven moons, seven years, &c. They had a kind of box containing some kind of substance which was considered sacred, and kept an entire secret from the common people. Said box was borne by a number of men who were considered pure or holy, (if I mistake not such a box was kept by the Cherokees.) And whenever they went to war with another tribe they carried this box; and such was its purity in their view, that nothing would justify its being rested on the ground. A clean rock or scaffold of timber only, was considered sufficiently pure for a resting place for this sacred coffer. And such was the veneration of all the tribes for it, that whenever the party retaining it, was defeated, and obliged to leave it on the field of battle, the conquerors would by no means touch it." This account well accords with accounts of various others from different regions of the Indians. But it is unaccountable upon every principle except that the Indians are the descendants of Israel.

It is probable that while most of the natives of our land had their one Great Spirit, some of this wretched people talked of their different gods. Among the natives on Martha's Vineyard, in the beginning of Mayhew's mission among them, we find Mioxo, in his conversation with the converted native, Hiaccomes, speaking of his thirty-seven gods; and finally -We know not what this insulated native could mean by his thirty-seven gods. But it seems evident from all quarters, that such were not the sentiments of the body of the natives of America.

The ancient natives on Long Island talked of their different subordinate gods. Sampson Occum, the noted Indian preacher, says; "the Indians on Long Island imagined a great number of gods." But he says, "they had (at the same time) a notion of one great and good God, who was over all the rest."

Here, doubtless, was their tradition of the holy angels which they had become accustomed to call gods under the one great God. The North American Reviewers speak of the fact, that the natives of our land acknowledged one supreme God. They inquire,"If the Indians in general have not some settled opinion of a Supreme Being; how has it happened that in all the conferences or talks of the white people with them, they have constantly spoken of the Great Spirit; as they denominate the Ruler of the universe?"

Lewis and Clark inform us of the Mandans, (a tribe far toward the Pacific) thus; "The whole religion of the Mandans consists in a belief of one Great Spirit presiding over their destinies. To propitiate whom, every attention is lavished, and every personal consideration is sacrificed." One Mandan informed, that lately he had eight horses; but that he had offered them all up to the Great Spirit. His mode of doing it was this; he took them into the plains, and turned them all loose; committing them to the Great Spirit, he abandoned them forever. The horses, less devout than their master, no doubt took care of themselves.

Meckewelder (a venerable missionary among the Indians 40 years, noted in Doct. Jarvis' discourse, before the New York Historical Society, and who had a great acquaintance with the wide spread dialect of the Delaware language,) says; "Habitual devotion to the great First Cause, and a strong feeling of gratitude for the benefits he confers, is one of the prominent traits which characterize the mind of the untutored Indian. He believes it to be his duty to adore and worship his Creator and Benefactor."

Gookin, a writer in New England in 1674, says of the natives; "generally they acknowledge one great Supreme doer of good." Roger Williams, one of the first settlers of New England, says; "He that questions whether God made the world, the Indians will teach him. I must acknowledge (he adds) I have in my concourse with them, received many confirmations of these two great points; -1. that God is; 2. that He is a rewarder of all that diligently seek him. If they receive any good in hunting, fishing or harvesting, they acknowledge God in it."

Surely then, the natives of the deserts of America must have been a people who once knew the God of Israel! They maintained for more than two millenaries, the tradition of Him in many respects correct. What possible account can be given of this, but that they were descendants of Israel, and that the God of Israel has had his merciful eye upon them, with a view in his own time to bring them to light, and effect their restoration?

6. The celebrated William Penn gives accounts of the natives of Pennsylvania, which go to corroborate the same point. Mr. Penn saw the Indians of Pennsylvania, before they had been affected with the rude treatment of the white people. And in a letter to a friend in England he thus writes of those natives; "I found them with like countenances with the Hebrew race; and their children of so lively a resemblance to them, that a man would think himself in Duke's place, or Barry street in London, when he sees them." Here, without the least previous idea of those natives being Israelites, that shrewd man was struck with their perfect resemblance of them; and with other things which will be noted. He speaks of their dress and trinkets, as notable,

like those of ancient Israel; their ear rings, nose jewels, bracelets on their arms and legs, rings (such as they were) on their fingers, necklaces, made of polished shells found in their rivers, and on their coasts; bands, shells and feathers ornamenting the heads of females, and various strings of beads adorning several parts of the body.

Mr. Penn adds to his friend, "that he considered this people as under a dark night; yet they believed in God and immortality, without the help of metaphysics. For he says they informed him that there was a great king, who made them -that the souls of the good shall go to him." He adds; "Their worship consists in two parts, sacrifice and cantieo, (songs.) The first is with their first fruits; and the first buck they kill goes to the fire." Mr. Penn proceeds to describe their splendid feast of first fruits, one of which he had attended. He informs; "all that go to this feast must take a piece of money, which is made of the bone of a fish." "None shall appear before me empty." He speaks of the agreement of their rites with those of the Hebrews. He adds; "They reckon by moons; they offer their first ripe fruits; they have a kind of feast of tabernacles; they are said to lay their altars with twelve stones; they mourn a year; they have their separations of women; with many other things that do not now occur." Here is a most artless testimony given by that notable man, drawn from his own observations and accounts given by him; while the thought of this people's being actually Hebrew, probably was most distant from his mind.

7. Their having a tribe, answering in various respects to the tribe of Levi, sheds further light on this subject. (Some of the tribe probably remained with the ten tribes.) The thought naturally occurs, that if these are the ten tribes, and they have preserved so many of their religious traditions; should we not be likely to find among them some tradition of a tribe answering to the tribe of Levi? If we should find something of this, the evidence of their being the tribes of Israel would indeed be more striking. Possibly this is furnished. The Mohawk tribe were held by the other tribes in great reverence; and the other tribes round about them had been accustomed to pay them an annual tribute. Mr. Boudinot gives the following account of them. "Mr. Colden says, he had been told by old men (Indians) in New England, that when their Indians were at war formerly with the Mohawks, as soon as one (a Mohawk) appeared, the Indians would raise a cry, from hill to hill, a Mohawk! a Mohawk! upon which all would flee as sheep before a wolf, without attempting to make the least

resistance. And that all the nations around them have for many years entirely submitted to their advice, and paid them a yearly tribute. And the tributary nations dared not to make war or peace, without the consent of the Mohawks." Mr. Colden goes on to state an instance of their speech to the governor of Virginia, in which it appears the Mohawks were the correctors of the misdoings of the other tribes.

Now, could any thing be found in their name, which might have an allusion to the superiority of the tribe of Levi, we should think the evidence very considerable, that here are indeed the descendants of the part of that tribe which clave to the house of Israel. And here too evidence seems not wholly wanting. The Hebrew word Mhhokek, signifies an interpreter of the law, superior. We have then, a new view of the possible origin of the Mohawks!

8. Several prophetic traits of character given of the Hebrews, do accurately apply to the aborigines of America. Intemperance may be first noted. Isaiah, writing about the time of the expulsion of Israel from Canaan, and about to predict their restoration, says; Isai. xxviii. 1 -"Wo to the crown of pride, the drunkards of Ephraim; (Ephraim was a noted name of the ten tribes of Israel.) The crown of pride, the drunkards of Ephraim, shall be trodden under feet. For all tables shall be full of vomit and filthiness; so that there is no place clean."

In the course of the descriptions of their drunkenness, that of their rejection and restoration is blended; that the Lord by a mighty one would cast them down to the earth; and their glorious beauty should be like that of a rich flower in a fertile valley, which droops, withers and dies. But in time God would revive it. "In that day shall the Lord of hosts be for a crown of glory, and for a diadem of beauty unto the residue of this people." None who know the character of the Indians in relation to intemperance, need to be informed that this picture does most singularly apply to them.

Doctor Williams in his history of Vermont, on this trait of Indian character, says: "no sooner had the Indians tasted of the spirituous liquors brought by the Europeans, than they contracted a new appetite, which they were wholly unable to govern. The old and the young, the sachem, the warrior, and the women, whenever they can obtain liquors, indulge themselves without moderation and without decency, till universal drunkenness takes place. All the tribes appear to be under the dominion of this appetite, and unable to govern it."

A writer in the Connecticut Magazine assures us of the Indians in Massachusetts, when our fathers first arrived there; "As soon as they had a taste of ardent spirits, they discovered a strong appetite for them; and their thirst soon became insatiable."

Another trait of Hebrew character which singularly applies to the Indians, is found in Isai. iii. "The bravery of their tinkling ornaments about their feet; their cauls, and round tires like the moon; their chains, bracelets, mufflers, bonnets, ornaments of the legs; head bands, tablets, ear rings, rings, and nose jewels; the mantles, the wimples; and the crisping pins." One would imagine the prophet was here indeed describing the natives of America in their full dress! No other people on earth probably bear a resemblance to such a degree.

This description was given just before the expulsion of Israel. And nothing would be more likely than that their taste for these flashy ornaments should descend to posterity. For these make the earliest and deepest impressions on the rising generation. And many of the Indians exhibit the horrid contrast which there follows.

Mr. Pixley of the Union Mission, being out among the Indians over Sabbath, thus wrote in his journal. "I have endeavoured to pay a little attention to the day, (the Sabbath) by building a fire in the woods, and there reading my bible. In reading the third chapter of the prophet Isaiah, I found in the latter part of the chapter a striking analogy between the situation of this people and the condition of the people about whom the prophet was speaking, which I never before discovered. They are represented by the prophet as sitting on the ground; having their secret parts discovered; having given to them instead of a sweet smell, a stench; instead of a girdle, a rent; instead of well set hair, baldness; instead of a stomacher, a girding of sackcloth; and burning, instead of beauty. In all these particulars, except that of baldness, the prediction of the prophet is amply fulfilled in this people.

And even this exception would be removed, if we might suppose that their shaving their heads with a razor, leaving one small lock on the crown, could constitute the baldness hinted. And certainly if any women in the world labour to secure their own bread and water, and yet a number of them be attached to one man to take away their reproach, you will find it among this people, whether the prediction may or may not be applied to them."

9. The Indians being in tribes, with their heads and names of tribes, affords further light upon this subject. The Hebrews not only had their tribes, and heads of tribes, as have the Indians; but they had their animal emblems of their tribes. Dan's emblem was a serpent; Issachar's an ass; Benjamin's a wolf; and Judah's a lion. And this trait of character is not wanting among the natives of this land. They have their wolf tribe; their tiger tribe; panther tribe; buffalo tribe; bear tribe; deer tribe; raccoon tribe; eagle tribe; and many others. What other nation on earth bears any resemblance to this? Here, no doubt, is Hebrew tradition.

Various of the emblems given in Jacob's last blessing, have been strikingly fulfilled in the American Indians. "Dan shall be a serpent by the way; and adder in the path, that biteth the horse heels, so that the rider shall fall backwards. Benjamin shall ravin as a wolf; in the morning he shall devour the prey; and at night he shall divide the spoil." Had the prophetic eye rested on the American aborigines, it seems as though no picture could have been more accurate.

10. Their having an imitation of the ancient city of refuge, evinces the truth of our subject. Their city of refuge has been hinted from Mr. Adair.

But as this is so convincing an argument, (no nation on earth having any thing of the kind, but the ancient Hebrews and the Indians,) the reader shall be more particularly instructed on this article. Of one of these places of refuge, Mr. Boudinot says; "The town of refuge called Choate is on a large stream of the Mississippi, five miles above where Fort Loudon formerly stood. Here, some years ago, a brave Englishman was protected, after killing an Indian warrior in defence of his property. He told Mr. Adair that after some months stay in this place of refuge, he intended to return to his house in the neighbourhood; but the chiefs told him it would prove fatal to him. So that he was obliged to continue there, till he pacified the friends of the deceased by presents to their satisfaction." In the upper country of Muskagee, (says Doctor Boudinot) was an old beloved town, called Koosah -which is a place of safety for those who kill undesignedly." "In almost every Indian nation (he adds) there are several peaceable towns, which are called old beloved, holy, or white towns. It is not within the memory of the oldest people that blood was ever shed in them; although they often force persons from them, and put them elsewhere to death." Who can read this, and not be satisfied of the origin of this Indian tradition.

Bartram informs; "We arrived at the Apalachnela town, in the Creek nation. This is, esteemed 'the mother town sacred to peace. No captives are put to death, nor human blood spilt here."

Adair assures us, that the Cherokees, though then exceedingly corrupt, yet so inviolably observed the law of refuge, at that time, that even the wilful murderer was secure while in it. But if he left it, he had no protection, but must expect death.

In a communication from Rev. Mr. Pixley, missionary in the Great Osage mission, to the Foreign Secretary, dated June 25, 1824 -among other things he says; "There is a class among the Indians called the Cheshoes, whose lodges are sacred as respects the stranger and the enemy who can find their way into them, -not very dissimilar to the ancient city of refuge.

The well known trait of Indian character, that they will pursue one who has killed any of the friends, ever so far, and ever so long, as an avenger of the blood shed, thus lies clearly open to view. It originated in the permission given to the avenger of blood in the commonwealth of Israel; and is found in such a degree probably in no other nation.

11. Their variety of traditions, historical and religious, go to evince that they are the ten tribes of Israel. Being destitute of books and letters, the Indians have transmitted their traditions in the following manner. Their most sedate and promising young men are some of them selected by what they call their beloved men, or wise men, who in their turn had been thus selected. To these they deliver their traditions, which are carefully retained. These are instead of historic pages and religious books. Some of these Indian traditions, as furnished from good authorities, shall be given. Different writers agree that the natives have their historic traditions of the reason and manner of their fathers coming into this country, which agree with the account given in Esdras, of their leaving the land of Media, and going to a land to the northeast, to the distance of a year and a half's journey. McKenzie gives the following account of the Chepewyan Indians, far to the northwest. He says, "They have also a tradition among them, that they originally came from another country, inhabited by very wicked people, and had traversed a great lake, which was in one place narrow, shallow, and full of islands, where they had suffered great misery; it being always winter, with ice, and deep snows. At the Copper Mine River, where they made the first land, the ground was covered with copper, over which a body of earth has since been collected to the depth of a man's

height." Doctor Boudinot speaks of this tradition among the Indians. Some of them call that obstructing water a river, and some a lake. And he assures us the Indian tradition is, "that nine parts of their nation, out of ten, passed over the river; but the remainder refused and staid behind." Some give account of their getting over it; others not.

What a striking description is here found of the passing of the natives of this continent, over from the north-east of Asia, to the north-west of America, at Beering's Straits. These Straits, all agree, are less than forty miles wide, at this period. and no doubt they have been continually widening. Doctor Williams, in his history of Vermont, says they are but eighteen miles wide. Probably they were not half that width 2500 years ago. And they were full of islands, the Indian tradition assures us. Many of those islands may have been washed away; as the Indian tradition says, "the sea is eating them up;" as in Dr. Boudinot.

Other tribes assure us that their remote fathers, on their way to this country, "came to a great river which they could not pass; when God dried up the river that they might pass over." Here is a traditionary notion among the Indians of God's anciently drying up rivers before their ancestors. Their fathers in some way got over Beering's Straits. And having a tradition of rivers being dried up before the fathers, they applied it to this event. Those straits, after Israel had been detained for a time there, might have been frozen over, in the narrows between the islands; or they might have been passed by canoes, or other craft. The natives of this land, be they who they may, did in fact arrive in this continent; and they probably must have come over those straits. And this might have been done by Israel as well as by any other people.

Relative to their tradition of coming where was abundance of copper; it is a fact, that at, or near Beering's Straits, there is a place called Copper Island, from the vast quantities of this metal there found. In Grieve's history we are informed that copper there covers the shore in abundance; so that ships might easily be loaded with it. The Gazetteer speaks of this and that an attempt was made in 1770 to obtain this copper, but that the ice even in July, was so abundant, and other difficulties such, that the object was relinquished. Here, then, those natives made their way to this land; and brought down the knowledge of this event in their tradition.

Doctor Boudinot gives it as from good authority that the Indians have a tradition "that the book which the white people have was once theirs. That while they had this book, things went well with them; they prospered exceedingly; but that other people got it from them; that the Indians lost their credit; offended the Great Spirit, and suffered exceedingly from the neighboring nations; and that the Great Spirit then took pity on them, and directed them to this country." There can be no doubt but God did, by his special providence, direct them to some sequestered region of the world, for the reasons which have been already given.

McKenzie adds the following accounts of the Chepewyan nation; "They believe also that in ancient times, their ancestors lived till their feet were worn out with walking, and their throats with eating. They describe a deluge, when the waters spread over the whole earth, except the highest mountains; on the tops of which they preserved themselves." This tradition of the longevity of the ancients, and of the flood, must have been from the word of God in ancient Israel.

Abbe Clavigero assures us, that the natives of Mexico had the tradition, that "there once was a great deluge; and Tepzi, in order to save himself from being drowned, embarked in a ship, with his wife and children and many animals. -That as the waters abated, he sent out a bird, which remained eating dead bodies. He then sent out a little bird, which returned with a small branch."

Doctor Beatty says that an Indian in Ohio informed, that one of their traditions was; "Once the waters had overflowed all the land, and drowned all people then living, except a few, who made a great canoe and were saved."

This Indian added, to Dr. Beatty, that "a long time ago the people went to build a high place; that while they were building, they lost their language, and could not understand each other."

Doctor Boudinot assures us that two ministers of his acquaintance informed him, that they being among the Indians away toward the Mississippi, the Indians there (who never before saw a white man,) informed him that one of their traditions was, - a great while ago they had a common father, who had the other people under him; that he had twelve sons by whom he administered his government; but the sons behaving silly, lost this government over the other people. This the two ministers conceived to be a pretty evident traditionary notion concerning Jacob and his twelve sons.

Mr. Adair informs that the southern Indians have a tradition that their ancestors once had a "sanctified rod, which budded in one night's time;" which seems a tradition of Aaron's rod.

Various traditions of the Indians strikingly denote their Hebrew extraction. Dr. Beatty informs of their feast, called the hunter's feast; answering, he thinks, to the Pentecost in ancient Israel. He describes it as follows:

They choose twelve men, who provide twelve deer. Each of the twelve men cuts a sapling with these they form a tent, covered with blankets. They then choose twelve stones for an altar of sacrifice. Some tribes, he observes, choose but ten men, ten poles, and ten stones. Here seems an evident allusion to the twelve tribes; and also to some idea of the ten separate tribes of Israel. Upon the stones of their altar they suffered no tool to pass. No tool might pass upon a certain altar in Israel.

The middle joint of the thigh of their game, Dr. Beatty informs, the Indians refuse to eat. Thus did ancient Israel, after the angel had touched the hollow of Jacob's thigh in the sinew that shrank: Gen. xxxii. 25, 31, 32. "In short, (says Dr. Beatty,) I was astonished to find so many of the Jewish customs prevailing among them; and began to conclude there was some affinity between them and the Jews."

Col. Smith, in his history of New Jersey, says of another region of Indians, "They never eat of the hollow of the thigh of any thing they kill." Charlevoix, speaking of the Indians still further to the north, says he met with people who could not help thinking that the Indians were descended from the Hebrews, and found in every thing some affinity between them. Some things he states; as on certain meals, neglecting the use of knives; not breaking a bone of the animal they eat; never eating the part under the lower joint of the thigh; but throwing it away. Such are their traditions from their ancient fathers. Other travellers among them speak of their peculiar evening feast, in which no bone of their sacrifice may be broken. No bone might be broken of the ancient paschal lamb in Israel, which was eaten in the evening.

Different men who had been eye witnesses, speak of this, and other feasts, resembling the feasts in Israel; and tell us relative to this peculiar evening feast, that if one family cannot eat all they have prepared, a neighbouring family is invited to partake with them; and if any of it be still left, it must be burned before the next rising sun. None who read the law of the passover can doubt the origin of this.

A Christian friend of mine informs me, that he some time since read in a book he now cannot name, the account of a man taken at Quebec, in Montgomery's defeat; of his being carried far to the north west by Indians; and of a feast which they kept in which each had his portion in a bowl; that he was charged to be very careful not to injure a bone of it; that each must eat all his bowl full, or must burn what was left on a fire, burning in the midst for this purpose. The object of the feast he knew not.

The Secretary of the American Board of Commissioners for Foreign Missions, in a letter to the writer of this View, says; "An officer of the British army, stationed at Halifax, has been at Boston this season; (1823;) and I am informed he has expressed a strong opinion that the Indians are of Israelitish descent. He derives this opinion from what he has seen and known of the Indians themselves."

The Rev. Mr. Frey, the celebrated Jewish preacher, and Agent for the American Meliorating Society, upon reading the View of the Hebrews, and warmly approving of this sentiment in it, with the others (that the American Indians are the ten tribes, informed the writer of these sheets, that he owned a pamphlet, written by the earl of Crawford and Linsey, (England,) entitled "The Ten Tribes."

In this the author gives a variety of reasons why he is convinced that the American Indians are the descendants of the ten tribes. The earl was a British officer in America during the Revolutionary war; and was much conversant with the Indians. And his arguments in favor of their being the very Israel, are from what he himself observed and learned while among them. The pamphlet was where Mr. Frey could not at present obtain it. The writer regrets that he could not have access to this document before this edition went to the press.

The Indians have their feasts of first ripe fruits, or of green corn; and will eat none of their corn till a part is thus given to God. The celebrated Penn, Mr. Adair, and Col. Smith, with others, unite in these testimonies. In these Indian feasts they have their sacred songs and dances; singing Halleluyah, Yohewah, in the syllables which compose the words. What other nation, besides the Hebrews and Indians ever in this manner attempted the worship of Jehovah? The author of the Star in the West; says; "May we not suppose that these Indians formerly understood the psalms and divine hymns? Otherwise, how came it to pass that some of all the inhabitants of the extensive regions of North and South America have, and retain, these very expressive Hebrew words, and repeat them so distinctly; using them after the manner of the Hebrews, in their religious acclamations?"

The Indian feast of harvest, and annual expiation of sin, is described by these writers; and in a way which enforces the conviction that they derived them from ancient Israel. Details are given in the Star in the West. My limits will permit only to hint at them. The detailed accounts are worth perusing.

An Indian daily sacrifice is described. They throw a small piece of the fattest of their meat into the fire, before they eat. They draw their newly killed venison through the fire. The blood they often burn. It is with them a horrid abomination to eat the blood of their game. This was a Hebrew law.

A particular or two of their feasts shall be noted. Doctor Beatty gives an account of what he saw among the Indians north west of the Ohio. He says; "Before they make use of any of the first fruits of the ground, twelve of their old men meet; when a deer and some of the first fruits are provided. The deer is divided into twelve parts; and the corn beaten in a mortar, and prepared for use by boiling or baking under the ashes, and of course unleavened. This also is divided into twelve parts. Then these (twelve) men hold up the venison and fruits, and pray, with their faces to the east, acknowledging (as is supposed) the bounty of God to them. It is then eaten. After this they freely enjoy the fruits of the earth. On the evening of the same day, (the Doctor adds) they have another public feast which looks like the passover. A great quantity of venison is provided, with other things dressed in their usual way, and distributed to all the guests; of which they eat freely that evening. But that which is left is thrown into the fire and burned; as none of it must remain till sun rise the next day; nor must a bone of the venison be broken."

Mr. Boudinot says, "It is fresh in the memory of the old traders, (among the Indians) as we are assured by those who have long lived among them, that formerly none of the numerous nations of Indians would eat, or even handle any part of the new harvest, till some of it had been offered up at the yearly festival by the beloved man (high priest) or those of his appointment at the plantation; even though the light harvest of the past year should almost have forced them to give their women and children of the ripening fruits to sustain life." Who that reads the laws of Moses, can doubt the origin of these Indian traditions?

The Hebrews were commanded to eat their passover with bitter herbs; Exod. xii. 8. The Indians have a notable custom of purifying themselves with bitter herbs and roots. Describing one of their feasts, the writer says, "At the end of the notable dance, the old beloved women return home to hasten the feast. In the mean time every one at the temple drinks plentifully of the Cussena, and other bitter liquids, to cleanse their sinful bodies, as they suppose."

The Indians have their traditionary notion clearly alluding to the death of Abel, by the murderous hand of Cain; as well as one alluding to the longevity of the ancients.

More full accounts are given by some of these authors, of the Archi-magus of the Indians -their high priest. As the high priest in Israel was inducted into office by various ceremonies, and by anointing; so is the Indian high priest by purification, and by anointing. When the holy garments are put upon him, bear's oil is poured on his head. And it is stated that the high priests have their resemblances of the various ornaments worn by the ancient high priests; and even a resemblance of the breast plate. These men have been called by the white people, ignorant of Indian customs, jugglers. But they are now ascertained by good witnesses, as a manifest though corrupt succession of the high priesthood in ancient Israel. Bartram says, those, with inferior priests and prophets, have been maintained in most if not all the tribes.

The Indian high priest makes his yearly atonement for sin. He appears at their temple, (such as it is) arrayed in his white deer skin garments, seeming to answer to the ancient ephod. Entering on his duty, the waiter spreads a white seat with a white dressed buckskin, close by the holiest apartment of their temple; and puts on his white beads offered by the people. A variety of curious things are described in this dress, by Mr. Adair, as pretty evidently designed imitations of the parts of ancient pontifical dress. This dress is left in the holy place of their temple, till the high priest comes to officiate again. His breast-plate is made of a white conch shell, through which two straps of otter skin pass in two perforations; while white buttons of buck's horn are superadded, as though in imitation of the precious stones on the ancient breastplate. A swan skin wreath adorns his head, instead of the ancient plate of gold, and for the ancient tiara, the Archi-magus has his tuft of white feathers. His holy fire he obtains by rubbing two sticks together; and his golden bells and pomegranates are formed of the dried spurs of wild turkies, strung so as to rattle on his fine moccasins.

Mr. Adair assures us, when the Indian Archi-magus (high priest) is addressing his people, and enforcing "the divine speech," that he calls them "the beloved and holy people," according to the language concerning ancient Israel. He urges them "to imitate their virtuous ancestors," and "flourishes upon their beloved land, flowing with milk and honey."

Mr. Adair describes the Indian feasts, and speaks of them as bearing a very near resemblance of the stated feasts in ancient Israel. He gives accounts that when the Indians are about to engage in war, they have their preparatory sacrifices, purifications, and fastings. He speaks of their daily sacrifice, their ablutions, marriages, divorces, burials, mournings for the dead, separations of women, and punishment of various crimes, as being in his opinion manifestly of Hebrew origin.

The purifications, fastings, abstinences, and prayers, to prepare for war, appear to be Hebrew. Adair says; "Before the Indians go to war, they have many preparatory ceremonies of purification and fasting, like what is recorded of the Israelites. When the leader begins to beat up for volunteers, he goes three times round his dark winter house, contrary to the course of the sun, sounding the war-whoop, singing the war song, and beating a drum. (The Indians have something in imitation of a drum, made of a wet deer skin drawn over a large gourd or frame of wood.) He addresses the crowd, who come about him, and after much ceremony, he proceeds to whoop again for the warriors to come and join him, and sanctify themselves for success against the common enemy, according to their ancient religious law. A number soon join him in his winter house, where they live separate from all others, and purify themselves for the space of three days and three nights, exclusive of the first broken day. On each day they observe a strict fast till sunset, watching the young men very narrowly (who have not been initiated in war titles) lest unusual hunger should tempt them to violate it, to the supposed danger of all their lives in the war, by destroying the power of their purifying, beloved physic, which they drink plentifully during that time. They are such strict observers of their law of purification, and think it so essential in obtaining health and success in war, as not to allow the best beloved trader that ever lived among them, knowingly, to enter the beloved ground appropriated to the duty of being sanctified for war, much less to associate with the camp in the woods, at such a time, though he is united with them in the same war design. They oblige him to walk and encamp separately by himself, as an impure, dangerous animal, till the leader hath purified him, according to the usual time and method, with the consecrated things of the ark."

Rev. Mr. Chapman, missionary in the west, informs us that when the Osages (with whom he was going in company to Fort Smith) had just before they arrived purified themselves, to be able to form their treaty with the Cherokees aright, and had moved on, he was about to proceed with them; but the chief forbid him on pain of death. He must for a season be separate from them, as impure. How exactly like the treatment of the stranger in the economy of Israel!

Boudinot assures us that the Indians abstain from all matrimonial intercourse three days before going to war, while purifying themselves; -also during their being out at war; and for three days after they return. The Israelites were commanded before they marched against an enemy to wash their clothes, to avoid all impurities, and to abstain from matrimonial intercourse. These Indian customs fully appear to have originated in those ancient divine orders; as do many of their rites and customs.

Their reckonings of time, Mr. Adair viewed as evidently Hebrew. They begin their year, as did Israel, at the first appearance of new moon after the vernal equinox. They reckon by the four seasons, and by the sub-divisions of the moons.

Bartram says, the Indians believe their high priests have intimate communion with the world of spirits; and that no great design is formed by the Indians without his counsel.

The Assinipoils, far to the west, we learn in Capt. Carver's travels among the western Indians, have their high priest, who pretends to great intimacy with the Great Spirit, and to be able to foretel future events; as is the case with the Killistinoes, at the Grand Portage. Certain things be thus found among different Indians, which show them to have been of the same origin.

Within about eighty years, men inform, that these rites of the high priests have been more neglected. The Indians inform, that in 1747, the high priest in the Natchez was struck dead by lightning, while using his invocation for rain. They suppose the Great Spirit to have been angry with him for some impurity; and with the "darting fire and threatening voice," took him away; and forbid them to renew the like attempt.

Bartram gives a description of a southern Indian temple. It is a square of small buildings in the centre of their Indian town. The small buildings of one story cover perhaps half an acre, more or less, according to the strength of the tribe. In one of these buildings they hold their councils.

A part of this building is shut up as a holy of holies; and it is inadmissible for any but the high priest to enter it. Here they deposit their most sacred things; as the physic-pot, rattles, chaplets, eagle's tail, and pipe of peace.

To this temple "the males (as in ancient Israel) are obliged to assemble three times a year: viz. at the feast of the first ripe fruits; at the feast for the success of hunting, about the time of the ancient pentecost; and the great feast for the expiation of sins, about the time of ripe corn." No account could be given of these things, without a complicated miracle, unless the Indians have descended from the tribes of Israel.

Mr. Boudinot informs, that "when any of their beloved people die, they soften the thought of death by saying, "he is gone to sleep with his beloved fathers." The ancient pious Hebrew dying, "fell asleep, and was gathered to his people."

The Indians, when one dies, wash and anoint the body. The Hebrews did the same.

Some of the southern Indians hire mourners to bewail and magnify the merits of the dead. Thus did the Hebrews: Jer. ix. 17. And the Indians, as had the Hebrews, have their solemn songs on such occasions. A religious procession moves round the corpse, singing, Yah (Jah.) Ho, is then sung by the procession. The leader then says, He; -all follow. Then Wah is sung by all. Thus they sing the syllables which compose Jah, Jehovah. The corpse is then buried with the face to the east.

Lewis and Clark, in their tour to the Pacific, inform that they found among the natives, in those remote regions, receptacles for the dead, always lying east and west; the door of the tomb to the east, and the bodies in the tombs lying with the face to the east.

The Indians often bury with the corpse a variety of furniture; and their best things, if the dead be a first character. The Hebrews did the same.

Josephus informs that Hyrcanus, a Maccabee, when Jerusalem was besieged by the Syrain tyrant, and money was wanted, took from king David's sepulchre 3000 talents, which had 1300 years before been buried with him.

Another noted Hebrew custom the Indians have, Doctor Boudinot informs, that a worthy minister informed him, that as he was preaching with some Indians, between the exercises, tidings were brought to an Indian woman present, that her son was suddenly drowned. In deep distress she retired to a little distance, and sat on the ground. Female friends followed, and sat around her. After sitting a season in solemn silence, the mourning mother put her hand upon her mouth, and then fell forward with her face in the dust. The rest all followed the example. The men went by themselves, and did the same. It is well known that laying the hand on the mouth, and the mouth in the dust, is a distinguished Hebraism. See Micah vii. 16; Lam. iii. 29; Prov. xxx. 32.

In the Mosaic law it was provided that the surviving brother of one deceased and childless, should marry his widow, to raise up seed to his brother. Mr. Adair informs that the Indians have a custom which appears to have originated in this law. A widow among them is bound by a strict Indian custom, to mourn the death of her husband for three years or more, unless the brother of her deceased husband wishes to take her. In that case, she is released from this law, as soon as it is known that the brother makes love to her. She may then throw off her mourning habits, and dress and paint like others. Certainly this appears to have originated in that Mosaic law.

The ceremonial law for the separation of women, the Indians appear to keep with great care. Dr. Boudinot says; "The southern Indians oblige their women in their lunar retreats to build small huts at a considerable distance from their dwelling houses -where they are obliged to stay at the risk of their lives. Should they be known to violate this ancient law, they must answer for every misfortune that the people should meet with."

"Among the Indians on the north west of the Ohio, the conduct of the women (continues the Doctor) seems perfectly agreeable (as far as circumstances will permit) to the law of Moses. A young woman, at the first change in her circumstances, immediately separates herself from the rest in a hut made at some distance from the dwelling houses, and remains there seven days. The female that brings her food, is careful not to touch her; and so cautious is she herself of touching her own food, that she makes use of a sharpened stick to take up her meat, and of a spoon for her other food.

When the seven days are ended, she bathes herself in water, washes all her clothes, and changes the vessels she has made use of. She then returns to her father's house."

Dr. Boudinot further says; "A Muskagee woman delivered of a child is separated in like manner for three moons, or eighty four days." In the ceremonial law the mother of a female child was to be separated eighty days; of a male forty days. Some of the Indian nations, Dr. Boudinot assures us, maintain a similar distinction between male and female children. Can a serious doubt remain of the origin of these Indian customs? What nation on earth beside the Jews and Israel ever maintained customs of separations and purifications like these?

Rev. Dr. Morse and Captain Carver speak of this custom among Indian women, among distant tribes where they travelled, as will appear. And many other testimonies have been borne to the same Indian rite.

Col. Smith informs that "the young women, when our people first came among them, were very modest and shame-faced; and both young and old women would be highly offended at indecent expressions."

Major Vose, at Fort Armstrong, in a letter to the secretary of the A.B.C.F.M. says; "I have been informed that in places where the Indians have had the least intercourse with the whites, there the men are the most temperate, and the women most chaste."

The traditional religion, the kind and degree of piety maintained among the Indians, are unaccountable on any other principle than that they came down by tradition from ancient Israel. Some things shall be stated from good authority, which illustrate this particular.

Rev. Dr. Mather and Rev. E. Mayhew both testify to the following fact.

Japhet Hannet was an Indian preacher on Martha's Vineyard. He was born A.D. 1638. His parents had lost, before he was born, five infant children.

Japhet was the sixth. The writer says; "The mother of this child being greatly distressed with fear lest she should lose it, as she had the former, and utterly despairing of any help from such means as had been formerly tried without any success; as soon as she was able, she took him up with a sorrowful heart, and went into a retired place, that she might there give full vent to her grief. While she was there reflecting on the insufficiency of human help, she found it powerfully suggested to her mind, that there is one Almighty God, who is to be prayed to; that this God has created all things; and that the God who had created all things, who had given being to herself and all other people, and had given her child to her, was able to preserve and continue his life. On this, she resolved that she would seek to God for that mercy; and did accordingly.

The issue was, that her child lived. And her faith in him, who had thus answered her prayer, was wonderfully strengthened. And the consideration of the divine goodness herein manifested to her, caused her to dedicate this son to the service of that God who had thus preserved his life.

She early informed her son of this her religious act; and did as far as she could educate him accordingly." Both Dr. Mather and Mr. Mayhew inform that this took place before ever the parents of Japhet were taught to know any thing of the Christian religion; -and that this mother was thus prepared to embrace the Christian religion, as soon as she heard of it from the missionary that went to the island. And when she joined the church, she gave this relation. This youth became converted, joined the church of converted Indians on the island; became a very pious and useful man; was a captain of the island, and a great friend to the English in the war with Philip; finally became a pastor of the Indian church there; and died in old age in the triumphs of faith.

How different was the religion of this native of Martha's Vineyard from that of the eastern heathen world! The knowledge she had, it seems, must have been from Hebrew tradition, and the entail of the covenant with Abraham.

In the third report of the United Foreign Missionary Society, in a letter detailing the happy things which the writer saw at Brainerd mission, he states the effects which the knowledge and conversation of the Indian children in that school had on their heathen parents, when the children visited the parents at home. The aged Indians, on hearing the children repeat the instructions given them, were pleased, and said; "Now this is good talk. It resembles the talk which the old people used to make to us when we were small children. But alas, the wicked white people (meaning the unprincipled traders among the Indians) who have come among us have rooted it out of our nation. We are glad the Great Spirit has sent these good missionaries to bring it back to us again."

It is stated on all hands that within about eighty years, the connexion of the Indians near the English with the white people has much corrupted the Indians, and extinguished much of their traditional religion. Here we find a new testimony to the fact, from the confession of those aged Cherokees.

And they discover what seems to them a resemblance between our religious instructions, and the traditional instructions given by their old people, meaning probably their old beloved wise men (the keepers of their ancient traditions) or their high priests, or both, before they knew any thing of the white people. This agrees with the other information we receive relative to the religion of the best informed natives.

In the same report of the United Foreign Missionary Society from their missionaries among the Indians at the west, they inform as follows; "It was very interesting to hear them (the natives) at the garrison joining in a kind of sacred singing. Every morning on the first appearance of light, we heard them on all sides around us, for a great distance from the camp, engaged in very earnest prayer to God, their Creator. This they did likewise on all extraordinary occasions, as when they received any distinguishing favour." This was before any mission was established among them; but while the missionaries were exploring the country to select a suitable place for a mission. They were Indians untaught by any thing but their own traditions. The missionaries add; "They are very sincere, temperate, and considerate; and appear to regard the particular providence of God with as much attention and reverence as any Christian people."

Such evidence as this hardly needs a comment. What possible account can be given for such traditional religion among a people destitute of the word of God, and of letters, who for thousands of years have been secluded from the knowledge of the civilized world; -only, that they derived it from ancient Hebrew revelation; and that they are of the tribes of Israel?

In other accounts the missionaries at the west inform as follows; "The men are generally of a lofty stature, a fine form, and a frank and open countenance. In council they are dignified; and in their speeches eloquent. Their children are numerous, and remarkably submissive to parental authority. As a people they are punctual, and apparently fervent in their morning and evening devotions. But like the ancient Athenians they address their worship to the unknown God."

Rev. Mr. Pixley, at the great Osage mission, in a tour among the wild natives says; "I asked White Hair (a chief) why he blacked his face this morning. He informed that it was that he might call upon God as we do when we sit down to eat. And I must confess (adds Mr. Pixley) their early rising, and their constancy in attending to their devotions, made me sometimes inquire, What is the power of my religion! and whether it ought not to make me, and all Christians, rise to pray, at least as early as these Indians."

Mr. Pixley in a subsequent journal says; "The Indians, although extremely singular in their way of worship, might certainly in some respects be imitated with profit by Christians. I allude particularly to their early and persevering attention to it before day, or as soon as the day dawns. Under the force of this habit, if their hearts were ever led to feel and pray aright, they will undoubtedly make most eminent Christians; especially as the heaping up of treasures, and in this sense, the love of the world, seems not to have taken possession of their minds. Let objectors inform, where these Indians learned from the heathen world such religion as they possess?

It has been stated that the Indians have a tradition that as they once, away in another country, had the old divine speech, the book of God; they shall at some time have it again, and shall then be happy. Did not the Indian deputation (noted in the sixth report of the United Foreign Missionary Society, as having come from a wild region beyond the Council Bluffs of the west) in their talk with the Board of Managers in New York, probably allude to such tradition? One of them says; "Brothers, we have long since been told, that the red men would, one day, live like white men, and have houses and food like them. These things are long coming to pass. I wish it was so. I have now grown old, and have not seen it."

In the journals of Rev. Mr. Butrick among the Cherokees, making an excursion among the Indians, he says of a certain chief; "Few men in any nation understand the art of pleasing, and of rendering their conversation agreeable, better than he. We made known to him the object of our journey.

He appeared very thankful, and told us he would lay the subject before the other chiefs, and let us know the result of their consultation. After some conversation, his wife, an old woman, told us, that when she was a small child, the old people used to say that good people would come to instruct the Cherokees at some future period; and that perhaps she and others of her age would live to see the day. And now she thought that, perhaps, we and the other missionaries had come to give them that instruction."

This traditionary opinion, among the different tribes, (noted also by Mr. Adair, Dr. Boudinot, and others,) it seems, must have been handed down from ancient prophecy of their restoration. They had indeed been seeking the word of God, (according to a prophecy in Amos, of their famine of the word,) but had not found it. God in mercy grant they may now speedily find it.

Dr. Boudinot gives an account of a speech of Cornplant, a chief in the six nations of Indians, expostulating with the head of department of our states, on account of lands taken from his people.

This chief had told his people we should not treat them thus; and they were now ready to tear him in pieces, because we had done it. After various affecting remarks, he proceeds; "Father, we will not conceal from you that the Great Spirit, and not man, has preserved Cornplant (his own name) from the hands of his own nation. For they asked continually, where is the land on which our children are to lie down? -You told us (say they) that a line drawn from Pennsylvania to Lake Ontario, would mark forever our bounds on the east; and a line from Beaver Creek to Pennsylvania, would mark it on the west. But we see that it is not so. For first one, and then another comes, and takes it away by order of that people, who you told us promised to secure it to us forever. Cornplant is silent; for he has nothing to answer. When the sun goes down, Cornplant opens his heart before the Great Spirit. And earlier than the sun appears again upon the hills, he gives thanks for his protection during the night. For he feels that among men become desperate by the injuries they sustain, it is God only that can preserve him. Cornplant loves peace. All that he had in store, he has given to those who have been robbed by your people, lest they should plunder the innocent to repay themselves."

The original peaceable and hospitable character of the Indians testifies much relative to their traditional religion as having come down from a divine origin. I might here multiply quotations; but shall content myself with two. These I shall preface with a remark, that the Indian cruelties to our people have been manifestly occasioned by the injuries they have received from various of our people, and by their own traditionary notions, which they think accord with these injuries, that the white people are out of the covenant of the Great Spirit once made with their fathers, are the accursed people, and may well be exterminated.

But let us hear the testimony of Christopher Columbus, as given in Edwards' West Indies, relative to the peaceable and hospitable temper of the natives of our land when he first discovered this continent. Writing to his royal Master and Mistress in Spain, he says; "I swear to your majesties, that there is not a better people in the world than these (natives of America;) more affectionate, affable, or mild. They love their neighbours as themselves. Their language is the sweetest, the softest, and most cheerful; for they always speak smiling." An old native approaching him with a basket of summer fruit, said, (as he seemed to have some fear of the designs of these strangers,) "If you are men subject to mortality like ourselves, you cannot be unapprized that after this life, there is another, in which a very different portion is allotted to good and bad men. If therefore you expect to die, and believe with us that every one is to be rewarded in a future state according to his conduct in the present, you will do no hurt to those who do none to you."

My other quotation is from Dr. Boudinot. He assures us he was present when Gen. Knox gave a dinner, in the city of New York, to a deputation of Indians, sachems and a chief, from Indian nations at the west, who came with a message to our President. He says; "A little before dinner, two or three of the sachems, with their chief, went into the balcony at the front of the house; the drawing room being up stairs. From this they had a view of the city, the harbour, Long Island, &c. &c. After remaining there a short time, they returned into the room, apparently dejected; -the chief more than the rest. Gen. Knox took notice of it, and said to him; Brother; what has happened to you? You look sorry!

Is there any thing to distress you? He answered; "I'll tell you brother, I have been looking at your beautiful city -the water; your fine country; and see how happy you all are. But then I could not help thinking that this fine country, and this great water were once ours. -Our ancestors lived here. They enjoyed it as their own in peace. It was the gift of the Great Spirit to them and their children. At last the white people came here in a great canoe. They asked only to let them tie it to a tree, lest the water should carry it away. We consented. They then said some of their people were sick; and they asked permission to land them and put them under the shade of the trees. The ice then came, and they could not go away. They then begged a piece of land to build wigwams for the winter. We granted it to them. They then asked for some corn to keep them from starving. We kindly furnished it to them. They promised to go away when the ice was gone. When this happened, we told them they must now go away with their big canoe. But they pointed to their big guns, round their wigwams, and said they would stay there, and we could not make them go away. Afterwards more came. -They brought spirituous and intoxicating liquors with them, of which the Indians became very fond. They persuaded us to sell them some land. Finally, they drove us back, from time to time, into the wilderness, far from the water, the fish and the oysters. They have destroyed our game. Our people are wasted away. And we live miserable and wretched; while you are enjoying our fine and beautiful country. This makes me sorry, brother; and I cannot help it."

Dr. Boudinot informs of the Indians at Yazous and Washtulu, at the south; -of their destructions by the governor of New Orleans, early the last century. The unprovoked cruelties against them are enough to break a heart of stone. They were pursued, burned, and destroyed, and their men sold at St. Domingo for slaves. Of these natives he says; "Of all the Indians they were the most polished and civilized. They had an established religion among them in many particulars rational and consistent; as likewise regular orders of priesthood. They had a temple dedicated to the Great Spirit, in which they preserved the eternal fire. Their civil polity partook of the refinement of a people apparently in some degree learned and scientific. They had kings, or chiefs, -a kind of subordinate nobility, -and the usual distinctions created by rank were well understood and preserved among them. They were just, generous, humane, and never failed to extend relief to the objects of distress and misery. They were remarkable for not deeming it glorious to destroy the human species; and therefore seldom waged any other than [defensive] war."

Col. Smith, in his history of New Jersey, gives information of the original inhabitants, which have a striking bearing on our subject. He gives an extract from the noted Indian interpreter, Conrad Wiser. He says; "I write this to give an account of what I have observed among the Indians, in relation to their belief and confidence in a divine Being, according to the observations I made from the year 1714, the time of my youth, to this day. If by religion we mean an attraction of the soul to God, whence proceed a confidence in, and a hunger after the knowledge of him; then this people must be allowed to have some religion among them. We find among them some traits of a confidence in God alone -notwithstanding their savage deportment."

This interpreter gives an account of his being sent, in 1737, by the governor of Virginia on a message to Indians five hundred miles distant, through a pathless dreary desert. Three

Indians and a Dutchman accompanied him. Climbing a steep and high mountain on the crust, one of the Indians slipped, and slid off with rapid flight down the mountain. He came to within several paces of a perpendicular precipice over the rocks of a hundred feet; and the strings of his sack caught upon something that held him. He crawled away, and saved his life. Upon this, the writer says; that "with outstretched arms, and great earnestness, he said; I thank the Great Lord and Governor of this world, that he has had mercy upon me, and has been willing that I should live a little longer."

Mr. Wiser gives an account that he himself was so fatigued and discouraged, before he got through this tour, that he sat down, unobserved by the Indians, under a tree, with a determination to die. They soon missed him, and returned. He told them his determination. After remaining silent a while, an old Indian said; "My dear companion; thou hast hitherto encouraged us. Wilt thou now quite give up? Remember that evil days are better than good days. For when we suffer much, we do not sin; and sin will be driven out of us by suffering. But good days cause men to sin; and God cannot extend his mercy to such. But when it goes evil with us, God has compassion on us." These words, Mr. Wiser assures us, made him ashamed; and he got up and went as well as he could.

The Indians murdered a Mr. Armstrong. This Mr. Wiser was sent by Gov. Shamoken to make peace by the punishment of the murderer. After the peace was established, he informs that the chief addressed his people, and "exhorted them to thankfulness to God." Again he said; "Thanks, thanks be to thee, thou Great Lord of the world, in that thou hast again caused the sun to shine, and hast dispersed the dark cloud. The Indians are thine."

Col. Smith gives account of an old Indian king, Ockanickon, who died 1681. To a proprietor of New Jersey, then with him, he said, as he was about to die; "There are two ways; a broad, and a straight way. The worst and the greatest number go in the broad way; the best and the fewest in the straight way."

It is fully evident from many sources of information that the Indians' views of the Great Spirit, and their religion, were from their own ancient tradition; and not from any thing they ever learned from the white people after the latter came to this continent. Rev. Mr. Brainerd, the noted missionary to the Indians, informs of his meeting an Indian one hundred and thirty miles from our settlements, who had a house consecrated to religious purposes. Mr. Brainerd laboured to teach him Christianity; but some of it he utterly rejected, saying, "God had taught him his religion, and he would never turn from it." He lamented that the Indians had grown so corrupt. He related that about five years before he (having before lived at ease as the Indians did) became greatly distressed, and thought he could not live among the Indians; and for some months he lived retired from them in the woods. At length, he said, the Great Spirit had comforted him. That since that time he had known the Great Spirit, and tried to serve him. That he loved all men, be they who they may, as he never did before. He treated Mr. Brainerd with great courtesy, and seemed hearty and affectionate in his religion; but so tenacious of his own traditional views, that he would not receive the peculiarities of Christianity.

Col. Smith, on a hunting tour among the Indians, informs of an aged Indian who seemed very devout, who praying to the Great Spirit would preface every petition with, "Oh, oh, oh." He would prepare himself for prayer by entering a sweat-house, and for fifteen minutes putting himself into a violent perspiration. He would then burn tobacco, and pray to the Great Spirit. Col. Smith undertook to teach him something of the way of access to God revealed in the gospel. He said "he thought he was now too old to begin to learn a new religion. He should therefore continue to worship God in the way he had been taught;" evidently meaning taught from Indian tradition. This old Indian had been informed something of the religion of the Roman Catholics; but he said, he did not believe the great and good Spirit ever taught them any such nonsense. He therefore concluded that the Indians' old way of worshipping God was better.

The exploring commissioners of the United Foreign Missionary Society reported in favour of a mission being founded among the Pawnees, high up the Missouri. They gave the following account of this tribe. "The Pawnees feel and acknowledge their dependance on God. A man who has often witnessed it informed us that in their public feasts, before they eat, a man venerable for age asks a blessing, and thanks God for success in hunting, for the meat they are about to eat, for the drink, and for the wood which makes a fire to cook their provisions." These Pawnees had never learned their religion from the whites. They were effactually out of their reach. And no straggling white traders among the western Indians were disposed to teach the Indians religion; nor would the Indians receive any instruction from them, as appears from the following.

These exploring commissioners state, as one reason why a mission should be soon established among them, thus; "They are much better prepared to receive a mission than those nations who have more intercourse with the white people. Their circumstances call on you to send the gospel among them, before the wretched hordes who are ever flying from the abodes of civilization reach their vicinity, and prejudice them against our holy religion." Their worshipping the one Great Spirit then was never learned from us. The past contiguities of the Indians to our frontiers have ever tended to subvert the religion of these natives, such as it was, and to give them a deadly prejudice against ours. No! Their religious notions (in so many respects different from all the religions of the eastern heathen world, and apparently nearly allied to the old Hebrew system) must have descended, as we have reason to apprehend, from Israel.

Listen to the religious views of the chiefs, who came to New York from beyond the Council Bluffs, in their reply to a talk with the secretary of the society, as given in the same report of the United Foreign Missionary Society which contained the reports just given. "We thank you for praying that the Great Spirit may preserve us in our long journey home." They repeat it. "Brothers; we thank you once more for praying to the Great Spirit that we may be preserved and carried home in safety to our wives and children." Such numerous instances of Indian traditions form a whole, which most powerfully evinces that the religion of our American natives is altogether of a brighter and different cast from the religion of the rest of the heathen world. What account can be given of this?

Those commissioners to the Pawnees further inform, that they invited the Pawnees to a Sabbath meeting. The commissioners prayed for those Pawnees (about to take a tour, either hunting, or for some other object) that they might go and return in safety. Two of their men were now at home sick.

After the Pawnees retired, "they expressed their apprehensions (say the commissioners) that the sick men would never return (from their proposed tour,) because they were not present to have these ministers pray for them."

Dr. Boudinot informs that a chief of the Creek nation was some time since at Philadelphia on his way to New York, with his retinue, and in company with Col. Butler, on a commission of peace with the United States. He was a chief of great note and dignity in his nation, and "of much better demeanour in his whole conduct (the Doctor remarks) than any Indian he had ever seen."

A female limner had, unobserved by the chief, taken his likeness, which she presented to him. He was astonished, and much pleased; and assured her, by his interpreter, "that he often spake to the Great Spirit; and the next time he did so, he would remember her." This chief and Col. Butler passing on, they were overset in the stage, and both wounded. After the surgeons had dressed their wounds, the chief addressed the colonel, through his interpreter, as follows. "Never mind this, brother. It will soon be well. This is the work of the evil spirit. He knows we are going to effect a work of peace. He hates peace; and loves war. Never mind it. Let us go on, and accomplish our business; we will disappoint him." He had some reason to say it was the work of the evil spirit; for the stupid stage-driver just stopped at a tavern to run in and get a glass of rum, leaving his horses loose at the door; upon which they started, ran, and upset the stage.

In the younger days of Dr. Boudinot, the following incident occurred. Two fine young missionaries were sent by the Society of Scotland (some members of which society were in our land, and the Doctor was one of them) to the natives west of Ohio. The chiefs were called to consult whether they would receive them. After some days in council, they dismissed them, most courteously, with the following answer; -that "they exceedingly rejoiced at the happiness of the whites, in being thus favoured by the Great Spirit; and felt very grateful that they had condescended to remember their red brethren in the wilderness. But they could not help recollecting that the whites here had a people among them, who because they differed in colour, the whites had made them slaves, made them suffer great hardships, and lead miserable lives; (alluding to the black slaves then in our colonies.) Now we cannot see any reason, (said they) if a people being black will entitle the whites to deal thus with them, why a red colour would not equally justify the same treatment. We therefore determine to wait to see whether all the black people among you are made thus joyful and happy, (as you tell us your religion will make us,) before we can put confidence in your promises. We think a people who have suffered so much, and so long, by your means, would be entitled to your first attention. We therefore send back the two missionaries, with many thanks; promising that when we see the black people among you restored to freedom and happiness, we will gladly receive your missionaries." Here was reasoning well worthy of the descendants of Abraham, and even of Solomon!

Mr. Herman, in his residence in the western regions of our continent, giving an account of the Chippeways, informs that in point of numbers, strength, and also attention to religious rites, they have greatly degenerated since their acquaintance with the white people. He speaks of them as having many tutelary gods. But they at the same time believe in one supreme God who governs all others, allowing the inferior gods considerable power and influence over mortals.

From various authors the following facts appear, that the better informed Indians hold to one God; and to spirits that he has made, good and bad. The bad have a leader over them worse than all the rest. Some of the tribes, it appears, have come to call these subordinate spirits (which seem but a traditionary notion of angels) gods; while yet the Great Spirit is the Creator, and is over all. This degeneracy is a most natural event among savages. Even among the ancient Hebrews, both angels and civil rulers were called gods.

Mr. Herman relates several customs, which appear like having a Hebrew origin. Among the Chippeways, each lad at the age of twelve or fifteen years, must keep a penitential fast alone in the woods for thirty or forty days; his friends carrying him, from time to time, a kind of unpalatable food, just enough to sustain life. We recollect no such rite as this in heathen mythology; but the scriptures of Israel inform of Elijah's fast of forty days.

These Indians, Mr. Herman informs, observe their solemn fasts when going to war. And each warrior has his religious symbol, which in some respects answers well to Israel's ancient ark of the covenant; and essentially the same use is made of it, as of the ark in the other tribes of Indians described. It is a sack, containing a few aromatic plants, or roots, and the feathers or skins of some rare bird, or small animal. These contents the owner imagines possess some kind of hidden virtue, which renders the owner invulnerable.

Major Long, speaking of the Omawhaws, far up the Missouri, says, they believe in one God, "the Creator and preserver of all things, the fountain of mystic medicine;" - meaning, the healer of their evils. This tribe of Chippeways, (Mr. Herman informs,) call their sacred sack, their "medicine bag." The contents appear to be essentially the same, and for the same end, with the contents of the sacred ark in other tribes; -the symbol of the presence of the Great Spirit. Hence Mr. Herman informs that the chief captain, when going to war, harangues his warriors, and exhorts them to reflect on the long fast performed in their youth; and adds; "Moreover, young men, it behoves you all to take special care of your medicine bags; for their contents ought of all things to be most precious to you, especially during such an expedition as the one on which you now embark.

Should the medicine bag of any one be placed on the ground, and any one inadvertently seat himself upon it, the first person who perceives him in that situation, ought instantly to spring up, and push the other flat on his back. This violent act will prevent any ill consequences from the unintended offence." Here it is evident their medicine bag, so called, is a religious symbol, as is the holy ark of the other tribes. And essentially the same care must be taken not to offend the Great Spirit by any improper use of it. The lapse of ages among illiterate savages scattered in unknown distant tribes, would naturally produce as great a variation among different tribes, in relation to this ancient venerable symbol -the ark of the covenant -as is this difference between these western more savage tribes, and tribes less savage farther to the south.

But they unite in the essential points. Both are sacred symbols borne to their wars. Both contain their most consecrated things; and each must be treated with the most sacred caution. No other account can be so rationally given of the origin of these Indian symbols, as the law of the holy ark in Israel.

The Rev. Dr. Morse, in his report of his tour among the Indians at the west, made under commission from our government, in 1820, to ascertain the actual state of the Indians in our country, says; "It is matter of surprise, that the Indians, situated as they have been for so many successive ages and generations, without books or knowledge of letters, or of the art of reading or writing, should have preserved their various languages in the manner they have done. Many of them are copious, capable of regular grammatical analysis, possess great strength, gracefulness, and beauty of expression. They are highly metaphorical in their character; and in this and other respects resemble the Hebrew. This resemblance in the language, and the similarity of many of their religious customs, &c. to those of the Jews, certainly give plausibility to the ingenious theory of Dr. Boudinot, exhibited in his interesting work, entitled Star in the West. A faithful and thorough examination of the various languages of the Indian tribes, would probably show that there are very few of them that are throughout radically different. The differences of these languages are mostly differences of dialect."

The various Indian tribes, visited by Dr. Morse, had their Great Spirit. Speaking of the manners and customs of the Sauks, Fox tribe, Pattowattamies, and others, he says; "Other feasts to the Great Spirit are frequently made by these Indians." Of one of these feasts, he says; "They seat themselves in a circle on the ground; when one of the guests places before each person a wooden bowl with his portion of the feast, and they commence eating. When each man's portion is eaten, the bones are collected, and put into a wooden bowl, and thrown into the river, or burnt. The whole of the feast must be eaten. If any one cannot eat his part of it, he passes his dish, with a piece of tobacco to his neighbor, and he eats it; and the guests then retire. Those who make the feast never eat any part of it themselves. They say they give their part of it to the Great Spirit." Here seems manifestly the same feast noted by other authors among other and different tribes in the different parts of the continent, and probably answering to the passover in ancient Israel. The different and distant tribes have their circumstantial differences; while yet certain things indicate that the feast is a broken tradition of the passover. In Exodus xii. 8, speaking of the passover, it is commanded; -"With bitter herbs shall ye eat it." Why does the Indian, (in this account of Dr. Morse,) accompany his portion of this singular Indian feast to his neighbor with a piece of tobacco? Is it not, probably, for the same reason that other distant tribes partake of their similar feast answering to this with bitter vegetables, as has been stated? And what heathen religion could ever have originated such a practice? This seems necessarily to have originated in the ancient law of the passover.

Another tradition from a Hebrew rite the Doctor states. He says; "The women of these nations are very particular to remove from their lodges to one erected for that particular purpose, at such seasons as were customarily observed by Jewish women, according to the law of Moses. No article of furniture ever used in this lodge, is ever used in any other; not even the steel and flint with which they strike fire. No man approaches this lodge, while a woman occupies it." The existence of this extensive Indian rite is fully ascertained. And of its origin there appears but very little room to doubt.

This writer says; "The belief of these Indians relative to their creation is not very unlike our own. Masco, one of the chiefs of the Sauks, informed me that they believed that the Great Spirit in the first place created from the dust of the earth two men; but finding that these alone would not answer his purpose, he took from each man a rib, and made two women." Of the descendants of these two pair, they say, "that they were all one nation, until they behaved so badly, that the Great Spirit came among them, and talked different languages to them; which caused them to separate and form different nations." Here are manifest broken fragments of Moses' history of creation, and of the confusion of language at Babel.

"I asked (says Dr. M.) how they supposed white men were made? He replied that Indians supposed the Great Spirit made them of the fine dust of the earth, as they know more than Indians." Dr. M. gives an account of their holding to a future state; and to some kinds of reward for the good, and of punishments for the wicked.

He informs from a Major Cummings, that the Indians are very suspicious of some evil intent, when questioned by the Americans; and that there is no way to obtain a full knowledge of their traditions and ways, but by a long residence in their country. This may account for the fact that their traditions (which seem manifestly Hebrew) were kept so long and to so great a degree, from the knowledge of our people.

Relative to their manner of transacting public business, they informed Dr. M.; "We open our council by smoking a pipe selected for the occasion; and we address the audience through a speaker chosen for the purpose; first invoking the Great Spirit to inspire us with wisdom. We open our council in the name of the Great Spirit, and close with the same."

He informs that the Indians "before attending on treaties, great councils, or any other important national business, always sacrifice in order to obtain the good will of the Great Spirit. And adds; "There are no people more frequent or fervent in their acknowledgments of gratitude to God. Their belief in him is universal; and their confidence astonishingly strong.

Speaking of their feasts, he says; "The principal festival is celebrated in the month of August; sooner or later, as the forwardness of the corn will admit. It is called the Green Corn Dance; or more properly speaking, the ceremony of thanksgiving for the first fruits of the earth.

The question continually recurs, whence came things like these among the natives of our continent, or the American savages, unless these savages are the very tribes of Israel? No evidence is furnished that such a variety of Hebrew rites is found among any other people on earth, except the Jews. And it seems morally impossible they should have derived them from any other source than the ancient Hebrew religion.

Mr. Schoolcraft, a member of the New York Historical Society, (in his Journals of travels among the western Indians, round and beyond the western lakes, and to the mouth of the Mississippi, in 1820,) gives some accounts, which confirm some of the Indian traditions already exhibited.

He speaks of attending a feast among the Sioux Indians; a feast of the first green corn. He says; "Our attention was now drawn off by the sound of Indian music which proceeded from another large cabin at no great distance; but we found the doors closed, and were informed that they were celebrating an annual feast, at which only certain persons in the village were allowed to be present; and that it was not customary to admit strangers. Our curiosity being excited, we applied to the governor, Cass, to intercede for us; and were by that means admitted. The first striking object presented was, two large kettles full of green corn, cut from the cob and boiled. They hung over a moderate fire in the midst of the cabin; and the Indians, both men and women, were seated in a large circle around them. They were singing a doleful song in a savage manner. The utmost solemnity was depicted upon every countenance. When the music ceased, as it frequently did for a few seconds, there was a full and mysterious pause, during which certain pantomimic signs were made; and it appeared as if they pretended to hold communion with invisible spirits. Suddenly the music struck up -but as we did not understand their language, it is impossible to say what they uttered, or to whom their supplications or responses were addressed. When the ceremony ceased, one of the older Indians divided out all the boiled corn into separate dishes for as many heads of families as there were present, putting an equal number of ladles full into each dish. Then while the music continued, they one by one took up their dishes, and retiring from the cabin by a backward step, so that they still faced the kettles, they separated to their respective lodges; and thus the ceremony ceased."

This writer says, "The Indians believed in the existence of a great invisible Spirit, who resides in the regions of the clouds, and by means of inferior spirits throughout every part of the earth."

Their word for spirit, he says, is manito, which he observes, "signifies the same thing among all the tribes extending from the Arkansaw to the sources of the Mississippi; and according to McKenzie, throughout the arctic regions." This word, Mr. S. remarks, with many others, strengthens the opinion "of which (he says) there appears ample grounds, that the erratic tribes of the north-western region, and of the vallies of the Mississippi, are all descended from one stock, which is presumed to have progressed from the north toward the south, scattering into different tribes, and falling from the purity of a language, which may originally have been rich and copious." Here is good testimony to some of the points, adduced in this work, viz. that all the Indians are from one origin; all originally of one language; all from the north-west, the straits of Beering, leading from the north-east of Asia to the north-west of America; all have one God, -the Great Spirit above; and the feast of the first ripe fruits is among them extensively kept.

These Indians, Mr. S. informs, "have their good and bad manitoes," or spirits. The Old Testament informs of holy and of fallen angels.

Mr. S. speaks of the best of authors allowing that great corruptions have crept into the Indian language; and that the remarks of some upon the supposed poverty of the language of these Americans, are very incorrect. He speaks of some of the Indians as looking to the people of our states for aid, and says, a council which he attended with the Sandy Lake Indians, thus closed; "The Americans (meaning the United States) are a great people. Can it be possible they will allow us to suffer?"

The Rev. Lemuel Haynes informs, that about 60 years ago, he was living in Granville, Mass. A minister by the name of Ashley, called on an old deacon, with whom he was living, being on his way from a mission among the Indians in the west, where he had been a considerable time. Mr. Ashley stated his confident belief that the Indians were the Israelites; for he said there were many things in their manners and customs, which were like those of ancient Israel. Various of these he stated. Mr. Haynes being then a boy, does not now recollect them. But the people he mentions as being impressed with the accounts; and the good old deacon long spake of them with much interest.

A brother minister informs me that his father was a lieutenant in the revolutionary war, and was long among the Indians; and that he became a firm believer that the Indians were the ten tribes of Israel from their traditions and rites; various of which he used to state; but which the minister does not now remember.

Various quotations have been given from Mr. Adair. It was thought when they were selected and inserted, they were amply sufficient. But it has occurred to the writer of these sheets that as he is a most material testimony, and his evidence fully substantiated, as has appeared, it must be desirable the reader should see more fully his arguments, and more of the facts by him stated under them.

His arguments that the natives of this continent are of the ten tribes are as follows. 1. Their division into tribes. 2. Their worship of Jehovah. 3. Their notion of a theocracy. 4. Their belief in the ministration of angels. 5. Their language and dialects. 6. Their manner of counting time. 7. Their prophets and high priests. 8. Their festivals, fasts, and religious rites. 9. Their daily sacrifice. 10. Their ablutions and anointings. 11. Their laws of uncleanness. 12. Their abstinence from unclean things. 13. Their marriages, divorces and punishments of adultery. 14. Their several punishments. 15. Their cities of refuge. 16. Their purifications and preparatory ceremonies. 17. Their ornaments. 18. Their manner of curing the sick. 19. Their burial of their dead. 20. Their mourning for their dead. 21. Their raising seed to a deceased brother. 22. Their change of names adapted to their circumstances and times. 23. Their own traditions; the accounts of English writers; and the testimonies given by Spanish and other writers of the primitive inhabitants of Mexico and Peru.

Some of his illustrations of these arguments will be here subjoined in his own words. Under the 1st argument. "As the nation hath its particular symbol, so each tribe, the badge from which it is denominated. The sachem of each tribe is a necessary party in conveyances, and treaties, to which he affixes the mark of his tribe. If we go from nation to nation among them, we shall not find one, who doth not lineally distinguish himself by his respective family. The genealogical names, which they assume, are derived either from the name of those animals, whereof the cherubims are said in revelation to be compounded, or from such creatures as are most familiar to them. The Indians, however, bear no religious respect to the animals from whence they derive their names. On the contrary, they kill them when opportunity serves. When we consider that these savages have been above twenty centuries without the use of letters to carry down their traditions, it cannot reasonably be expected that they should still retain the identical names of their primogenial tribes. Their main customs corresponding with those of the Israelites, sufficiently clears the subject. Besides, as hath been hinted, they call some of their tribes by the names of cherubinical figures that were carried on the four principal standards of Israel.

His illustrations of the second argument, blended with those of many others, have been sufficiently given.

Under the third argument, he says: "Agreeably to the theocracy or divine government of Israel, the Indians think the Deity to be the immediate head of their state. All the nations of Indians are exceedingly intoxicated with religious pride, and have an inexpressible contempt of the white people. (Within 20 years, this trait of Indian character is much meliorated.) They used to call us in their war orations, the accursed people.

-But they flatter themselves with the name of the beloved people; because their supposed ancestors, as they affirm, were under the immediate government of the Deity, who was present with them in a very peculiar manner, and directed them by prophets, while the rest of the world were aliens and outlaws to the covenant. -When the old Archimagus, or any one of their magi, is persuading the people at any one of their religious solemnities to a strict observance of the old beloved or divine speech, he always calls them the beloved or holy people, agreeably to the Hebrew epithet, Ammi (my people) during the theocracy of Israel. -It is their opinion of the theocracy, that God chose them out of all the rest of mankind as his peculiar and beloved people; which alike animates both the white, Jew, and the red American with that steady hatred against all the world except themselves; and renders them (in their opinion) hated and despised by all."

His illustrations of the 4th and 5th arguments have been given with those of other authors.

Under the 6th argument he says: "They count time after the manner of the Hebrews. They divide the year into spring, summer, autumn, and winter.

They number their year from any of those four periods, for they have no name for a year, and they subdivide these, and count the year by lunar months, like the Israelites, who counted by moons. They begin a year at the first appearance of the first new moon of the vernal equinox, according to the ecclesiastical year of Moses. Till the 70 years captivity, the Israelites had only numeral names for the solar and lunar months, except Abib and Ethamin; the former signifying a green ear of corn; and the latter robust or valiant. And by the first of these, the Indians (as an explicative) term their passover, which the trading people call the green corn dance." Mr. Adair then proceeds to show more fully the similarity between the ancient Israelites and the Indians in their counting time, as has been noted.

Under the 7th argument he says: "In conformity to, or after the manner of the Jews, the Indian Americans have their prophets, high priests, and others of a religious order. As the Jews had a sanctum sanctorum, (holy of holies) so have all the Indian nations. There they deposit their consecrated vessels; none of the laity daring to approach that sacred place. The Indian tradition says, that their fathers were possessed of an extraordinary divine spirit, by which they foretold things future, and controlled the common course of nature: and this they transmitted to their offspring, provided they obeyed the sacred laws annexed to it. Ishtoallo, (Mr. Adair says of those Indians) is the name of all their priestly order: and their pontifical office descends by inheritance to the eldest. There are some traces of agreement, though chiefly lost, in their pontifical dress. Before the Indian Archimagus officiates in making the supposed holy fire for the yearly atonement for sin, the sagan (waiter of the high priest) clothes him with a white ephod, which is a waistcoat without sleeves. In resemblance of the Urim and Thummim, the American Archimagus wears a breast plate made of a white conch shell with two holes bored in the middle of it, through which he puts the ends of an otter skin strap, and fastens a buck horn white button to the outside of each, as if in imitation of the precious stones of Urim."

In this statement Mr. Adair exhibits evidence of which himself seems unconscious. He says the general name of all their priestly order is Ishtoallo. And the name of the high priest's waiter is Sagan. Mr. Faber (remarking upon this) thinks the former word is a corruption of Ish-da-eloah, a man of God; see original of 2 Kings, iv. 21, 22, 25, 27, 40, and other places. And of the latter word he says, "Sagan is the very name by which the Hebrews called the deputy of the high priest, who supplied his office, and who performed the functions of it in the absence of the high priest. See Calmet's Dict. vox Sagan."

Here then is evidence to our purpose, that those Indians should call their order of priests, and the high priest's waiter, by those ancient Hebrew names of a man of God, and a deputy of of the high priest. How could these events have occurred, had not those natives been Hebrew, and brought down these names by Hebrew tradition?

Under the 8th argument Mr. Adair says; "The ceremonies of the Indians in their religious worship are more after the Mosaic institutions, than of pagan imitation; which could not be, if the majority of the old nation were of heathenish descent. They are utter strangers to all the gestures practised by the pagans in their religious rites. They have another appellative which with them is the mysterious essential name of God; the tetragrammaton, or great four lettered name, which they never name in common speech. Of the time and place, when and where they mention it, they are very particular, and always with a solemn air. It is well known what sacred regard the Jews had to the four lettered divine name, so as scarcely ever to mention it, but once a year, when the high priest went into the sanctuary at the expiation of sins. Might not the Indians copy from them this sacred invocation, Yo-he-wah? Their method of invoking God in a solemn hymn with that reverend deportment, and spending a full breath on each of the two first syllables of the awful divine name, hath a surprising analogy to the Jewish custom, and such as no other nation or people, even with the advantage of written records, have retained. It may be worthy of notice that they never prostrate themselves, nor bow their bodies to each other by way of salute or homage, though usual with the eastern nations; except when they are making or renewing peace with strangers, who come in the name of Yah."

Mr. Adair proceeds to speak of the sacred adjuration of the Indians by the great and awful name of God; the question being asked, and the answer given. Yah, with a profound reverence in a bowing posture of body immediately before the invocation of Yo-he-wah; this he considers to be Hebrew, adjuring their witnesses to give true evidence. He says, "It seems exactly to coincide with the conduct of the Hebrew witnesses even now on the like occasions."

Mr. Adair's other illustrations under this argument, in various feasts, fastings, their ark, and their ever refusing to eat the hollow of the thigh of their game, have been sufficiently given, in connexion with the testimonies of others to the same points. Enough has also been exhibited under the 9th, 10th, and 11th arguments.

Under the 12th he says; "Eagles of every kind they esteem unclean food; likewise ravens, crows, bats, buzzards, swallows, and every species of owl." This he considers as precisely Hebrew; as also their purifications of their priests; and purification for having touched a dead body, or any other unclean thing.

Under most of his subsequent arguments, the quotations before given have been sufficient. Under the16th he says; "Before the Indians go to war, they have many preparatory ceremonies of purification and fasting like what is recorded of the Israelites."

Under the last argument he says; "The Indian tradition says that their forefathers in very remote ages came from a far distant country, where all the people were of one colour; and that in process of time they removed eastward to their present settlements." He notes and confutes some idle fabulous stories which he says "sprung from the innovating superstitious ignorance of the popish priests to the south-west;" and speaks of the Indian tradition as being altogether more to be depended on. He says, "They, (the rambling tribes of northern Indians excepted,) aver that they came over the Mississippi from the westward, before they arrived at their present settlements. This we see verified in the western old towns they have left behind them, and by the situation of their old beloved towns or places of refuge lying about a west course from each different nation." "Ancient history (he adds) is quite silent concerning America, which indicates that it has been time immemorial rent asunder from the eastern continent. The north-east parts of Asia were also undiscovered till of. late. Many geographers have stretched Asia and America so far as to join them together; and others have divided them into two quarters of the globe. But the Russians, after several dangerous attempts, have clearly convinced the world that they are now divided, and yet have a near communication together by a narrow strait in which several islands are situated, and through which there is an easy passage from the north-east of Asia to the north-west of America. By this passage, it was very practicable to go to this new world, and afterward to have proceeded in quest of suitable climates.

Those who dissent from my opinion of the Indian American origin, (he adds) "ought to inform us how the natives came here, and by what means they found the long chain of rites and customs so similar to the usage of the Hebrew nation, and in general dissimilar to the modes of the pagan world. Their religious rites, martial customs, dress, music, dances and domestic forms of life, seem clearly to evince also, that they came to America in early times before sects had sprung up among the Jews; which was soon after their prophets ceased; also before arts and sciences had arrived at any perfection. Otherwise it is likely they would have retained some knowledge of them."

We learn in Dr. Robertson's history of America, that the Mexicans had their tradition that "Their ancestors came from a remote country situated to the north-west of Mexico. The Mexicans (he says) point out their various stations as they advanced from this into the interior provinces; and it is precisely the same rout which they must have held, if they had been emigrants from Asia." (B. 4. Page 41-2-3.)

Mr. Adair says, that though some have supposed the Americans to be descendants from the Chinese; yet neither their religion, laws or customs agree in the least with those of the Chinese, which sufficiently proves that they are not of this line. And he says the remaining traces of their religious ceremonies, and civil and martial customs, are different from those of the old Scythians. He thinks, therefore, that the old opinion that the Indians are descended from the Tartars or ancient Scythians, should be exploded as weak and without foundation. Those who have advocated the affirmative have not been able to produce much, if any evidence, that any of the religious rites found among the Indians, and resembling those of ancient Israel, have ever been found among any people in the east of Asia. Such a thing cannot be expected. Those rites were arbitrary, established only in Israel; and designed to distinguish them from all other nations. It is utterly inadmissible then, to suppose these Indian rites may be accounted for, from an idea that the Indians may have learned them from other heathen nations. With very similar propriety might the unbeliever in divine revelation say that the Jews and ancient Israel derived their religion, not from God, as the bible purports, but from the heathen nations, who at that time might for aught we know, have had just such religious customs.

If the aborigines derived these rites and customs from ancient Asiatic heathen; why have not some of those heathen themselves retained some of them, and disseminated them through some other parts of the world, besides the vast wilds of North and South America?

Capt. Carver is able to find that some of the people north-east of Asia once presented to some of the Russians their pipe of peace. The people of Israel, as they passed by that people in ancient days, may have caught this custom from them; as none pretend this was a Hebrew rite. Or, those few people thus noted in Asia may have caught this custom from the Indians over Beering's Straits. But this is nothing, compared with the many Hebrew rites found among the natives of America.

Capt. Carver, who travelled five thousand miles among the Indians of North America, states some customs observed by some of them in relation to marriage and divorce, which seem much like those of ancient Israel. He says; "When one of their young men has fixed on a young woman he approves of, he discovers his passion to her parents, who give him an invitation to come and live with them in their tent. He accepts the offer, and engages to reside in it for a whole year in the character of a menial servant.

This however is done only while they are young men, and for their first wife; and not repeated like Jacob's servitude. When this period is expired, the marriage is solemnized."

"When from any dislike (he adds) a separation takes place, for they are seldom known to quarrel, they generally give their friends a few days notice of their intention, and sometimes offer reasons to justify their conduct." Some little ceremonies follow; and he says, "The separation is carried on without any murmurings, or ill will between the couple or their relations." Probably no other nation has such a resemblance in this respect to ancient Israel.

Capt. Carver says of the Indians "wholly unadulterated with the superstitions of the church of Rome;" "It is certain they acknowledge one Supreme Being, or giver of life, who presides over all things -the Great Spirit; and they look up to him as the source of good -who is infinitely good. They also believe in a bad spirit, to whom they ascribe great power.

They hold also, that there are good spirits of a less degree, who have their particular departments, in which they are constantly contributing to the happiness of mortals." "The priests of the Indians (he adds) who are at the same time their physicians -while they heal their wounds, or cure their diseases, they interpret their dreams, and satisfy their desires of searching into futurity." But Capt. Carver unites with other authors on the subject, in speaking of the difficulty of strangers among them obtaining much knowledge of their religious rites. He says; "It is very difficult to attain to a perfect knowledge of the religious principles of the Indians. They endeavor to conceal them." It is no wonder then, that Capt. Carver, passing by them on a tour of upwards of five thousand miles, discovered but few of these many rites resembling the religion of ancient Israel, stated by Mr. Adair. He says there was "one particular female custom" bearing resemblance to the rites in the Mosaic law; alluding to the well known Indian separation of women. Speaking of their "religious principles," which he says are "few and simple," he adds, "they (the Indians) have not deviated, as many other uncivilized nations, and too many civilized ones have done, into idolatrous modes of worship." "On the appearance of the new moon they dance and sing; but it is not evident that they pay that planet any adoration."

Here then, according to this author, is their one God, infinitely good, the giver of life, and of all good, presiding over all, who is the only object of worship; though they sometimes beg of the evil spirit to avert their calamities, which in their opinion, he brings. -Here are their good angels, ministering to the good; here their priests; and a "particular female custom" inexplicable unless by the Mosaic law. Here is their firm adherence to their "few simple doctrines," or rites, less deviating to idolatry than other uncivilized, and even many civilized nations. These facts are far from being destitute of their favourable bearing on our subject. How should such things be true of those savages, were they not the descendants of ancient Israel?

It was observed in this book, that the Esquimaux natives and people round Hudson's Bay appear a different race from the American Indians, and may have come from the north of Europe. Capt. Carver notes an assertion from Grotius, that "some of the Norwegians passed into America by way of Greenland." Here may be the origin of the people of Greenland, Iceland, and round Hudson's Bay. But it gives not satisfactory account of the origin of the numerous Indian tribes of America.

Rev. Mr. Chapman, missionary of the United Foreign Missionary Society, at the Union Mission, in a letter of March 24, 1823, gives an account of some of the manners and customs of the Osage Indians.

He went with a large company of them to Fort Smith, who went to form a treaty of peace with the Cherokees. The evening before they arrived, on a hill, the chiefs informed that in the morning they must make their customary peace medicine, (a religious ceremony previous to a treaty) for the purpose of cleansing their hearts, and securing their sincerity of thinking and acting. "Ten of the principal warriors, including the priest of the Atmosphere, (a name of one of their clans) were selected and sent beneath a ledge, to dream or learn whether any error had been committed thus far -or (as they expressed it) to watch the back track."

Mr. Chapman proceeds to state their ceremonies prayers, sacred paintings, anointings, &c. -Among these he says;

"about two feet in advance, and in a line with our path, were three bunches of grass, which had been cut and piled about three feet apart, as an emblem of him whom they worshipped.

Here the priest stood with his attendants, and prayed at great length. Having finished his prayer, he again ordered the march on foot. The Indians from the right and left entered the path with great regularity; and on wheeling forward every individual was compelled to step upon each bunch of the grass." The company proceeded about forty rods; then halted and formed as before. The priest now "ordered his senior attendant to form a circle of grass about four feet in diameter, and to fix a handsome pile in the centre." By this he made another long prayer. Then stepping on the circle, and followed in this by his attendants, they passed on. The chief informed Mr. Chapman that this circle of grass too was a representation of their God. Mr. Chapman says; "It is the universal practice of these Indians to salute the dawn of every morning with their devotion." And upon the ceremonies he had described he adds; "Perhaps the curious may imagine that some faint allusion to the lost ten tribes of Israel may be discovered in the select number of dreamers (they being ten); -to the Trinity in unity, in the bunches (and the circle) of grass; -to the Jewish anointings and purifications, in their repeated paintings; -to the sacred rite of the sanctuary, in their secret consultations; -and to the prophetic office, in the office of their dreamers."

Let us look at the natives in an extreme part of South America, and see if they exhibit any evidence similar to what has been adduced of the natives of North America.

Don Alonzo de Ericilla, in his history of Chili, says of the natives there; "The religious system of the Araucanians is simple. They acknowledge a Supreme Being, the author of all things, whom they call Pillan, a word derived from Pulli, or Pilli, the soul; and signifies the Supreme Essence. They call him also, Guenupillan; the Spirit of Heaven; Bulagen, the Great Being; Thalcove, the Thunderer; Vilvemvoe, the Omnipotent; Mollgelu, the Eternal; and Avnolu, the Infinite." He adds; "The universal government of Pillan, (his Supreme Essence,) is a prototype of the Araucanian polity. He is the great Toqui of the invisible world."

He goes on to speak of his having subordinate invisible beings under him, to whom he commits the administration of affairs of less importance.

These, this author sees fit to call "subaltern divinities." We may believe they are but a traditional notion of angels, good and bad; such as is held by the Indians of North America.

This author says of this people; "They all agreed in the belief of the immortality of the soul. This consolatory truth is deeply rooted, and in a manner innate with them. -They hold that man is composed of two substances essentially different; the corruptible body and the soul, incorporeal and eternal."

Of their funerals, he says; "Their bier is carried by the principal relations, and is surrounded by women who bewail the deceased in the manner of the hired mourners among the Romans."

He also says; "They have among them a tradition of a great deluge, in which only a few persons were saved, who took refuge on a high mountain called Thegtheg, which possessed the property of moving upon the water."

Here then it seems the remote natives of Chili (a region 1260 miles south of Peru, in South America,) furnish their quota of evidence that they originated in the same family with the North American Indians, and hold some of their essential traditions.

Whence could arise the tradition of those natives, of one "Supreme Being, author of all things?" That he is the "Supreme Essence; the Spirit of Heaven; the Thunderer; the Omnipotent; the Eternal; the Infinite?" Whence their tradition of the flood, and of several persons being saved on a floating mountain, meaning no doubt the ark? Whence their ideas so correct of man's immortal soul?

This author says of those native Chilians, "Many suppose that they are indigenous to the country; while others suppose they derive their origin from a foreign stock, and at one time say, that their ancestors came from the north, and at another time from the west."

Their better informed or wise men, it seems, retain some impressions of their original emigration from a foreign land, and from the north-west, or Beering's Straits. Is it possible to give a satisfactory account of such traditions among those native Indians of Chili, short of their having received them from the Hebrew sacred Scriptures? And if from thence, surely they must be Hebrews.

The Southern Intelligencer, in extracts from the missionaries among the Chickasaws, informs us that an old Indian, stating to them some of the traditions of the Chickasaws, informs us that an old Indians, stating to them some of the traditions of the Chickasaws, (most of which were sufficiently wild and pagan) gave the following, "The Great Spirit first made the ground, and animals; afterward he made man;" "A woman was made in like manner." -"The Great Spirit drew lines on the surface of the earth with his rod; these afterward became rivers." There is an old tradition (he adds) concerning a great flood of water." He goes on to speak of its rising to the skies. "The Chickasaws came from the west," he says. -"The world is to be burned, or turned upside down; it is generally thought it will be burned." (See Isa. xxiv. 1-6) "A certain description of persons infamously wicked, will be burned with it. They will roll in fire, yet cannot die." "There are to be other signs before the end of the world; such as great shaking of the earth," This old Indian adds; "It has been said by old Indians that before that event should take place, (the burning of the world) the Indians and whites would mix, so that the tribes would be confused and lost, and not know to what nation they formerly belonged."

It appears that among abundance of trash, in Indian traditions, there are running through them some things which must have been transmitted from the Hebrew Scriptures.

This old Indian has promised the missionaries to visit them again, and relate to them more of their traditions.

In Long's expedition to the Rocky Mountains, we learn that the Omawhaw tribe of Indians (who inhabit the west side of the Missouri River, fifty miles above Engineer Cantonment,) believe in one God. They call him Wahconda; and believe him to be the greatest and best of beings; the Creator and Preserver of all things; the Fountain of mystic medicine. (sacred rites.)

Omniscience, omnipresence, and vast power are attributed to him. -And he is supposed to afflict them with sickness, poverty, or misfortune, for their evil deeds. In conversation he is frequently appealed to as an evidence of the truth of their assertions- "Wahconda hears what I say."

These Indians have many wild pagan notions of this one God. But they have brought down by tradition, it seems, the above essentially correct view of him, in opposition to the polytheistical world.

Their name of God is remarkable -Wahconda. It has been shown that various of the Indians call God Yohewah, Ale, Yah, and Wah, doubtless from the Hebrew names Jehovah, Ale, Jah. And it has been shown that these syllables which compose the name of God, are compounded in many Indian words, or form the roots from which they are formed. Here we find the fact;

while the author from whom the account is taken, it is presumed, had no perception of any such thing. Wah-conda; the last syllable of the Indian Yohewah, compounded with conda. Or Jah, Wah, their monosyllable name of God thus compounded. -Here is evidence among those children of the desert, both as to the nature and the name of their one God, corresponding with what has been exhibited of other tribes.

A religious custom, related by Mr. Long, goes to corroborate the opinion that these people are of Israel. He relates that from the age of between five and ten years, their little sons are obliged to ascend a hill fasting, once or twice a week during the months of March and April, to pray aloud to Wahconda. When this season of the year arrives, the mother informs the little son, that the "ice is breaking up in the river; the ducks and geese are migrating, and it is time for you to prepare to go in clay." The little worshipper then rubs himself over with whitish clay, and at sun rise sets off for the top of a hill, instructed by the mother what to say to the Master of Life. From his elevated position he cries aloud to Wahconda, humming a melancholy tune, and calling on him to have pity on him, and make him a great hunter, warrior, &c.

This has more the appearance of descending from Hebrew tradition, than from any other nation on earth; teaching their children to fast in clay, as "in dust and ashes;" and to cry to Jah for pity and protection. -Such are the shreds of evidence furnished, one here and another there, through the wilds of America, suggesting what is the most probable, if not evident origin, of the natives of this continent.

In the Percy Anecdotes, we have an account that the Shawano Indians in an excursion captured the Indian warrior called Old Scranny, of the Muskhoge tribe, and condemned him to a fiery torture. He told them the occasion of his falling into their hands was, he had "forfeited the protection of the Divine Power by some impurity or other, when carrying the holy ark of war against his devoted enemy.

Here he recognized the one God, his providence, speaks of his holy ark borne against enemies, alludes to the purity of those who bear it, and if they become impure, the Divine Being will forsake them. The bearing, which ideas like these have on our subject, needs no explanation.

Melvenda and Acasta (authors noted in the Star in the West) both affirm that some of the natives had a tradition of a Jubilee, according to the Jubilee in Israel. Edwards, in his West

Indies, assures us, that the striking uniformity of the prejudices and customs of the Caribbean Indians to he practices of the Jews, had not escaped the notice of historians, as Gomella, Du Testre, and others.

In Hunter's narrative of the manners and customs of the Indians, printed in Philadelphia in 1823, things are exhibited strikingly to our purpose.

This writer spent the younger part of his life among the Indians in the Arkansas territories, and up the Missouri. He was taken by the Indians when a child. He grew up among them, and lived among them many years. He seems (if I mistake not) not to be aware of any question relative to their origin. And he seems not to have undertaken to make any comparison between them and ancient Israel, as though they might be of that people. But he states many facts, which may answer for themselves. Among the many opinions and traditions of those wild natives, he gives the following. I shall give them in his own words, that all may judge for themselves. "It is certain that they acknowledge, at least as far as my acquaintance extends, one Supreme all powerful, and intelligent Being, viz. the Great Spirit, or Giver of life, who created, and governs all things." That he (the Great Spirit) often held councils and smoked with the red men (i.e. in ancient times;) gave them laws to be observed -but that in consequence of their disobedience, he withdrew from and abandoned them to the vexations of the bad spirit, who had since been instrumental of all their degeneracy and sufferings." "They believe that notwithstanding the offences of his red children, he continues to shower down on them all the blessings they enjoy. In consequence of this his parental regard for them they are truly filial and sincere in their devotions, and pray to him for such things as they need; and return thanks for such good things as they receive." Mr. Hunter goes on to speak of these Indians believing the Great Spirit to be present, and invisible, and being eternally unchangeable. And he adds; "They believe in a future state of existence." As to their devotions, he says: "At the breaking up of winter, having supplied themselves with such things as were necessary, we offered up our orisons (devotions) to the Great Spirit for having preserved us, and supplied all our wants. This (he adds) is the constant practice of the Osages, Kansas, and many other nations of Indians west of the Mississippi. -You then witness (he says) the silent but deep, impressive communication the native of the forest holds with his Creator."

Mr. H. goes on to assure us that the natives have their particular times "set apart for devotional purposes, -such as the declaration of war; the restoration of peace; and extraordinary visitations." He adds; They have also rejoicings which assume something of the pious form; such as their harvests, and the return of the new moon. In general, however, a day seldom passes with an elderly Indian, or others who are esteemed wise and good, in which a blessing is not asked, or thanks returned, to the Giver of life."

"Shortly after a council have determined on war, all who are able to walk, and the old men sometime borne by others, assemble in a grove, or some place rendered sacred, and offer up their prayers to the Great Spirit for success against their enemies. Some one of the old men, or prophets, addresses the assembly; states the cause of their grievances; and enjoins on the warriors to merit success by being brave, and placing their confidence in the great Giver of life." "Similar meetings (he adds) are generally held on the conclusion of peace; or the attainment of victory.

When triumphant, they dance and sing songs of victory, in which the name of the Great Spirit is frequently introduced with great reverence." How exactly do these accounts accord with those of Messrs. Boudinot, Adair, and others, of the natives in other regions! Who can doubt but these Indians have all one origin? and who can doubt the origin of their religion?

On the occurrence of an epidemic, such meetings are holden; and some old man, or a prophet (if one be present) addresses the Indians, and assures them that the calamity is a visitation from the Great Spirit, to chastise them for their ill spent lives, and wilful offences against him. He then commands them to be penitent for what has passed, and to reform. Silent prayers are then offered, with promises to become more obedient to their Great Father. -All amusements and recreations cease; and individual prayers and fastings are frequently observed for many successive days. -All their various devotions are performed in a standing posture."

"At the ingathering of corn, (he adds) they observe general rejoicings; at which all who are able join in appropriate dances, songs, and feasts, and in thanks to the Great Spirit for his munificence toward them." -He goes on to state that on those occasions, and at new moons, they keep lamps burning all night before and after the occasion: but for what purpose neither he nor they can tell; "as the Indians themselves conform to it only in obedience to usage." Possibly the nightly lamps burning in the temple of ancient Israel, may best explain the origin of this custom. The writer says; "They in general on discovering the new moon utter a short prayer to the Great Spirit." In all the tribes I have visited, (he adds) a belief of a future state of existence; and of future rewards and punishments, is maintained; though this in many respects is various, and generally confused and indistinct." "This belief of their accountability to the Great Spirit, (he adds) makes the Indians generally scrupulous and enthusiastic observers of all their traditionary dogmas. -This conduct with most of the Indians is founded on a perfect conviction that the cultivation and observance of good and virtuous actions in this life, will in the next entitle them to the perpetual enjoyment of ease and happiness -where they will again to be restored to the favour and enjoy the immediate presence, counsel and protection of the Great Spirit; while dereliction from it -will as assuredly entail on them endless afflictions." The writer continues -"Every Indian of any standing has his sacred place, such as a tree, rock, fountain, &c. to which he resorts for devotional exercise. Sometimes many resort to the same place. Preceding any public meeting held either for religious or festive purposes, or the assembling of a counsel, they uniformly retire to their respective places of private worship, and solicit the counsel and protection of the Great Spirit. Those who omit (these meetings) are thought less of, and their conduct is ascribed to an indifference to holy things, and want of solicitude for the national welfare."

"The religious opinions entertained, and modes of worship observed by the several Indian tribes, with which I have any acquaintance, (says Mr. Hunter) vary in their general character but little." "I have several times heard the chief of the Great Osages observe, both in public and private meetings, that all good actions would be rewarded, and all bad actions punished by the Great Spirit."

"At first (says Mr. Hunter) one might be led to suppose that this belief was a modification of doctrines taught by some of the missionaries; but such is not the case." He goes on to state reasons to show that "these things are from Indian tradition previous to their having any knowledge of white people."

In stating his attendance at a sacrifice at the Rickara villages, where the ceremony was performed on an altar and in a holy place, where none might tread but the priest, Mr. Hunter says; "The only thing farther connected with this circumstance, and worthy of remark, was the dress or habiliment of the priest. His cap was very high, and made of a beaver's skin, the tail of which was curiously ornamented with stained porcupine quills, and hung down on his back. His robe was a buffalo skin singularly decorated with various coloured feathers, and dyed porcupine quills. And he wore on his breast, suspended from his neck, a dressed beaver skin stretched on sticks, on which were painted various hieroglyphic figures in different colours." "The Indians speak of similar characters being among some other tribes."

Here, as in Mr. Adair's account, is their high priest's robe and breast plate. "On ordinary occasions, they retire secretly (Mr. H. adds) to their sacred places, and invoke the assistance of the Great Spirit, and make the most solemn vows to him, which they never fail to perform, should events correspond to their prayers. But at times more momentous, such as the declaration of war, conclusion of peace, or the prevalence of epidemics, &c. they impose on themselves long fastings, and severe penance, take narcotics and nauseating drugs." Mr. Hunter gives a long description of the Indian green corn feast; also of the harvest feast; and the feast of the new moon. None of their green corn may be eaten, till permission is given by well known order and a feast is celebrated; after which they are permitted (he says) to gather without restraint whatever their wants require. But the Indians both old and young look upon it, as upon their game, as the gift of the Great Spirit, and never wantonly destroy either."

"Murder (he adds) is punished blood for blood, according to the Mosaic law, by the relations of the deceased."

"Their mode of reckoning time (says Mr. Hunter) is very simple. Their year begins about the vernal equinox; and their diurnal reckoning from sunset to sunset." (This is perfectly Mosaic.) Upon their determining on war, he says: "Then follow the ceremonials of fasts, ablutions, anointings, and prayers to the Great Spirit, to crown their undertaking with success. They take drastic cathartics, bathe repeatedly, and finally anoint themselves with bear's grease." Relative to their returning from the war with prisoners, near their village they meet with their connexions and friends, who sally forth to congratulate them. Mr. Hunter says; "Every village has a post planted near the council lodge. It is the prisoner's place of refuge. On arriving within a short distance of it, the women and children, armed with clubs, switches, and missiles, and sometimes even with firebrands, place themselves in two ranks, between which the warriors (prisoners) one by one are forced to pass. It is in general a flight for life. Those who reach it, (the place of refuge) are afterwards treated kindly, and permitted to enjoy uninterrupted repose, till a general council determines their fate."

Had Mr. Hunter been an enthusiastic believer in the Hebrew origin of the Indians, and had he undertaken to [forge] accounts to favour the hypothesis; what could he have said more direct to the purpose? But in stating these facts, he seems to have had no idea of such an hypothesis; but artlessly states facts from his own knowledge. And he had been brought up among them from his childhood. Instead of commenting on the accounts he gives of their one God, their views of him, their worship and devotions, God's anciently giving them his law, then rejecting them yet continuing to preserve them; their fasts and feasts so similar to those in Israel; their reckoning of time, years and days; the official dress of their high priests, and his resemblance of the breastplate; and other things; I would only ask the reader to reperuse the quotations from this author; and compare them with the accounts given by Boudinot, Adair, and others, of other and distant tribes of Indians; yea, with the laws of Moses; and then say whether he can give any rational account of these things short of the American natives being the descendants of Israel?

May it not with some confidence be asked, among what other people on earth can such evidence be found of their being the ten tribes of Israel? Where are those ancient people of God, who have long been lost from the knowledge of the world; but who must soon come to light, and be recovered?

Whence came the natives of our continent? They certainly found their way hither, and no doubt over Beering's Straits from the north east of Asia. And the tribes of Israel might have found their way hither in that direction, as well as any other people. Our natives are here, and have brought down all these Israelitish traditions, and ceremonial observances, which it seems as though could be furnished from no other quarter than from the Mosaic law, the commonwealth of Israel.

Let the inquirer then, before he concludes that some other kind of evidence must be obtained, before the proposition can be adopted, consider, that the divine manner of affording evidence is not always such as human wisdom would dictate. The Jews had their strong objections against the evidences which God saw fit to furnish of the Divinity of Christ, of his resurrection, and ascension to glory. These were not such as they would have chosen. In the midst of such evidence as God saw fit to afford, the Jews required something besides. "What sign showest thou?" "How long dost thou make us to doubt?" "If he be Christ, let him descend from the cross, that we may see and believe." Naaman had formed his expectation how his cure should be effected. "I thought he would come out, and lay his hand on the sore, and call upon his God, and heal the leprosy." For want of this, he turned and was going very unpleasantly to retire.

Many things may be fancied concerning the kind and degrees of evidence, which shall bring to light the ten tribes. But Providence may adopt a different method. The methods adopted by the Most High, relative to the affairs of men, have usually been such as to baffle human wisdom, and to stain the pride of all glory.

We are to expect no new revelation from heaven. And the days of miracles are thought to be past. We probably must look for just such evidence, to exhibit to the world that people so long lost, as is in fact exhibited by the natives of America. And can we expect to find more evidence of this kind among any other people who have been for more than two millenaries lost from the world, and without records or letters? Could we well have expected to find so much? Consider, our aborigines have remained essentially distinguished from all the heathen on earth, in the uniform belief of most of them at least, of one God; and their freedom from false gods and gross idolatry.

Should it even be ascertained that some customs and habits are found among the American natives similar to what is found in the north east of Asia; this may be accounted for, without supposing these Indians to have descended from those Asiatics. For the Indians must have passed through their regions, to reach this country. They might have caught some of their manners. Some of those Asiatics might have mingled with them in their migration to this country; and though they here amalgamated with Israel, they may have perpetuated some of their own customs and manners. This is much more naturally and easily accounted for, than to account for those northern Asiatics being possessed of so much of the religious traditions of the Hebrews. If the Indians be not Hebrews, but of the wild Asiatics, their traditions are utterly unaccountable. The heathen nations, and the corrupt feelings of men, were not so fond of the laws and knowledge of God, as that the ancient, far distant, and savage Scythians of the north-east should learn and retain so much of the religion of the Israel of God, and transmit it for thousands of years to the distant ramifications of their descendants over the vast continent of North and South America. Those who can believe the affirmative, (when no account can be given how the religion and traditions of the Jews could ever have been disseminated through the far distant wilds of Scythia,) ought never to complain that the believers in the Indians being descendants from Israel, are wild and conjectural. Their solution of the difficulty is far more wild, and every way improbable! That various heathen nations bordering on ancient Israel, should have learned something of their names of the true God, and of their theology; -and that various heathen nations should have brought down some traditionary notions of the creation, of the deluge, and Noah's ark, and of some general accounts of early events taught. in ancient tradition and revelation, (as Grotias de Veritate asserts) is nothing strange. And it furnishes an incontestible argument in favour of the divinity of our bible. But that the northern roving savages of ancient Scythia should learn and adopt so much of the special rites of Israel's ceremonial law, as has in fact been found among the American Indians, and that they should so firmly embrace them as to transmit them to their posterity for thousands of years, peopling a continent so distant from their own, and of the vast dimensions of this new world, is not only incredible, but attended with moral impossibility! It is in no sense to be placed on a par with the fact of some heathen nations retaining a tradition of the flood, the ark, &c. These were general facts anciently known to all; while the ceremonial laws of Moses were revealed and practised only in one nation, in after days, when men had become scattered over the eastern world, and had fallen into a state of gross idolatry and paganism. It was an economy designed to distinguish the tribes of Israel from all other nations; and it did distinguish and insulate them; and other nations did not receive Israel's ceremonial code as their religion. Hence we are not to expect to find any traditionary observances of the ancient ceremonial law among any of the nations of the earth, at this day, except among the descendants of that ancient people of God; any more than we are to expect to find the doctrines of Confucius among the coloured race of Guinea. If some of the Arabs have practised circumcision; this makes nothing against us.

Circumcision was long antecedent to the ceremonial code. And Ishmael, the father of the Arabians, being himself a son of Abraham, was circumcised. How naturally would his descendants follow him in this rite, at least for some time. And the heathen nations being in the practice of offering sacrifices, furnishes no argument against us. For sacrifices had been offered by the progenitors of all the nations from the beginning, and were not at all peculiar to the ceremonial code. All heathen nations then, derived this their practice from their remote ancestors. But when we now find a race of men in the conscientious practice of many of the ceremonial laws in Israel; and cautiously maintain those traditions, merely because they descended from their remote ancestors; we certainly have found considerable of that very kind of evidence, which must eventually (and at a period not far from the present) bring to light the descendants of ancient Israel. And however many difficult questions may attach themselves to the subject, they are all less difficult, than to account for the origin of these traditions on any other principle, than that they are of Israel.

Some have felt a difficulty arising against the Indians being the ten tribes, from their ignorance of the mechanic arts, of writing, and of navigation. Ancient Israel knew something of these; and some imagine, that these arts being once known, could never be lost. But no objection is hence furnished against our scheme. The knowledge of mechanic arts possessed in early times has been lost by many nations. Noah and his sons must have known considerable of these arts, as appears in their building of the ark. And his early posterity must have known something considerable of them, as appears in their building of Babel. But how many of the descendants of those ancient mechanics lost this knowledge. And Israel in an outcast state might as well have lost it. It seems a fact that Israel have lost it, let them be who or where they may. Otherwise, they must have been known in the civilized world.

But that the people who first migrated to this western world did possess some knowledge of the mechanic arts, (as much doubtless, as was possessed by Israel when they disappeared in the east) appears from incontestible facts, which are furnished in Baron Humbolt, and in the American Archaeology, such as the finding of brick, earthen ware, sculptures, some implements of iron, as well as other metals, and other tokens of considerable improvement; which furnish an argument in favour of the Indians having descended from the ten tribes. For the ancient Scythians, and people of the north east of Asia, had no such degree of civilization at the time the Indians must have reached this land. Hence they could not have been from them.

The probability then is this; that the ten tribes, arriving in this continent with some knowledge of the arts of civilized life; finding themselves in a vast wilderness filled with the best of game, inviting them to the chase; most of them fell into a wandering idle hunting life.

Different clans parted from each other, lost each other, and formed separate tribes. Most of them formed a habit of this idle mode of living, and were pleased with it. More sensible parts of this people associated together, to improve their knowledge of the arts; and probably continued thus for ages. From these the noted relics of civilization discovered in the west and south, were furnished. But the savage tribes prevailed; and in process of time their savage jealousies and rage annihilated their more civilized brethren. And thus, as a holy vindictive Providence would have it, and according to ancient denunciations, all were left in an "outcast" savage state. This accounts for their loss of the knowledge of letters, of the art of navigation, and of the use of iron. And such a loss can no more operate against their being of the ten tribes, than against their being of any other origin. Yea, we cannot so well account for their evident degeneracy in any other way, as that it took place under a vindictive Providence, as has been noted, to accomplish divine judgments denounced against the idolatrous ten tribes of Israel.

It is highly probable that the more civilized part of the tribes of Israel, after they settled in America, became wholly separated from the hunting and savage tribes of their brethren; that the latter lost the knowledge of their having descended from the same family with themselves; that the more civilized part continued for many centuries; that tremendous wars were frequent between them and their savage brethren, till the former became extinct.

This hypothesis accounts for the ancient works, forts, mounds, and vast enclosures, as well as tokens of a good degree of civil improvement, which are manifestly very ancient, and from centuries before Columbus discovered America. These magnificent works have been found, one near Newark in Licking county, Ohio; one in Perry county, Ohio; one at Marietta; one at Circleville; one on Paint Creek; one on the eastern bank of the Little Miami river, Warren county; one on Paint Creek near Chillicothe; one on the Scioto river; and other places.

These works have evinced great wars, a good degree of civilization, and great skill in fortification. And articles dug from old mounds in and near those fortified places, clearly evince that their authors possessed no small degree of refinement in the knowledge of the mechanic arts.

These partially civilized people became extinct. What account can be given of this, but that the savages extirpated them, after long and dismal wars.

And nothing appears more probable than that they were the better part of the Israelites who came to this continent, who for a long time retained their knowledge of the mechanic and civil arts; while the greater part of their brethren became savage and wild. No other hypothesis occurs to mind, which appears by any means so probable. The degrees of improvement, demonstrated to have existed among the authors of those works, and relics, who have ceased to exist, far exceed all that could have been furnished from the north-east of Asia, in those ancient times.

But however vindictive the savages must have been; however cruel and horrid in extirpating their more civilized brethren; yet it is a fact that there are many excellent traits in their original character. There is in the minds of the native Americans a quality far superior to what is found in the minds of most other heathen on earth; and such as might have been expected from the descendants of the ancient Israel of God; as appears from numerous testimonies, such as the following.

A Rev. Mr. Cushman, in a sermon preached at Plymouth in 1620, says, upon the base slanders uttered against the Indians; "The Indians are said to be the most cruel and treacherous people -like lions; but to us they have been like lambs; so kind, and submissive, and trusty, that a man may truly say, many Christians are not so kind and sincere. When there were not six able persons among us, and the Indians came daily by hundreds to us, with their sachems or kings, and might in one hour have made dispatch of us; yet they never offered us the least injury, in word or deed."

Governor Hutchinson says of them; "The natives showed courtesy to the English at their first arrival; -were hospitable; and made such as would eat their food welcome to it; and readily instructed them in planting and cultivating the Indian corn. Some of the English who lost themselves in the woods, they relieved and conducted home."

William Penn spake and wrote in the highest terms of the kindness and benevolence of this people. Col. Smith, in his history of New Jersey, says; "For near a century, the Indians of that state had all along maintained an intercourse of great cordiality and friendship with the inhabitants, being interspersed among them, and frequently receiving meat at their houses, and other marks of good will and esteem."

Charlevoix, who early travelled from Quebec to New Orleans, had a great opportunity to learn the true Indian character; and he speaks highly in their favour. He says; "They rarely deviate from certain maxims and usages founded on good sense alone, which holds the place of law. They manifest much stability in the engagements they have entered upon, patience in affliction, as well as submission in what they apprehend to be the appointment of Providence. In all this, (he adds) they manifest a nobleness of soul, and constancy of mind, at which we rarely arrive with all our philosophy and religion.

Du Pratz says; "I have studied these Indians a considerable number of years; and I never could learn that there ever were any disputings or boxing matches among either the boys or men. I am convinced (he adds) that it is wrong to denominate them savages. They have a degree of prudence, faithfulness and generosity exceeding that of nations who would be offended at being compared with them. No people are more hospitable and free.

Bartram, of a part of the Creek nation, says; "Joy, contentment, love, and friendship without guile or affectation, seem inherent in them, or predominant in their vital principle; for it leaves them but with the last breath of life."

Bartram missed his way, and got lost among them. He saw an Indian at the door of his habitation beckoning to him to come in. He complied. Of himself and horse were taken the best care. When he wished to go, the Indian led him to his right way. This Indian proved to be the chief of Whotoga. Would an Indian receive such treatment among us? Bartram was a considerable time among them; and says; "they are just, honest, liberal, hospitable to strangers, considerate, loving and affectionate to their wives and relations, fond of their children, frugal, and persevering; charitable, and forbearing."

Col. Smith speaks of their "living in love, peace, and friendship, without disputes; and in this respect being an example to many who profess Christianity."

These things were said of the Indians, who were not demoralized and corrupted by a connexion with the unprincipled whites. Too many of the latter description become sufficiently hateful."

Their doleful cruelties to their prisoners of war, was a religious custom among them, which they performed with savage firmness; as was their pursuit and slaughter of one who had killed a relative. So the ancient law in Israel directed. "The avenger of blood himself shall slay the murderer; when he meeteth him he shall slay him." Numbers, xxxv. 18, 19. -Aside from these cruelties of principle, the Indians are faithful and kind.

When the Pequods were destroyed in the early days of the old colony, the noble wife of a Sachem who had before herself rescued from the Indians the maidens of Weathersfield, and returned them home, -made two requests; that her chastity might not be violated; -and that her children might not be torn from her. "The amiable sweetness of her countenance (says a writer,) and the modest dignity of her deportment, were worthy of the character she supported for innocence and justice." Whether her requests were granted, the historian neglects to inform.

De Las Casas, who spent much time in New Spain, says of the natives; "Did they not receive the Spaniards, who first came among them, with gentleness and humanity? Did they not show more joy in proportion, in lavishing reasures upon them, than the Spaniards did greediness in receiving them?

But our avarice was not yet satisfied. Though they gave up to us their lands, and their riches; we would take from them also their wives, their children, and their liberties. To blacken the characters of these people, their enemies assert that they are scarce human. But it is we (adds the author) who ought to blush for having been less men, and more barbarous than they." The natives are said to be free from the European vices of blasphemy, swearing, treachery in peace, and similar vices.

Columbus, enamoured with what he saw among this people, declared in a communication to the king and queen of Spain, that "there is not a better people in the world than these; - more affectionate, affable, or mild. They love their neighbour as themselves -They always speak smiling."

These are a few of innumerable testimonies to the same point, relative to the moral character of the natives of America. Certainly then they have deserved better treatment than they received from the whites. And these things furnish a rich quota of evidence that they probably had as good an origin as from the ancient people from Israel.

Some testimonies furnished by Baron Humbolt, in his Political Essays on the Kingdom of New Spain, will here be added. Relative to this noted author, -his translator, John Black, in his preface says; "It is observed by a popular French writer, that by far the most valuable and entertaining part of modern literature is the department filled up by travellers." He adds; "M. de Humbolt belongs to a higher order of travellers, to whom the public have of late been very little accustomed. We would place him beside a Nieubahr, a Pallas, a Bruce, a Chardin, a Barrow; and his works will probably be long consulted as authorities, respecting the countries which he describes. He seems to be a stranger to few departments of learning, or science; and his fortune enabled him to provide himself with every thing which could most advance his pursuits, and lead him to make that appearance among persons of rank and authority necessary to remove obstacles in the way of the traveller in every country."

"M. de Humbolt (his translator adds) has brought forward a great mass of information relative to New Spain; a country of which we before knew very little indeed." He compares his information with that of Robertson, and gives him the decided preference.

The Baron de Humbolt was a native of Germany, and a most celebrated character. His works were published in New York, in 1811. His travels in New Spain were in the early part of the present century. He ventures no opinion on the origin of the natives of America. He probably was a stranger to the sentiment of their having descended from Israel. Whatever evidence may be collected from him relative to this point, will hence be deemed the more precious, when he viewed it as having no such bearing.

The object, in exhibiting some things from this author will be, to show the far greater probability that our natives descended from Israel, than that they descended from the Scythians, or Tartars. -That they all had one origin.- That many of them had made such improvements in knowledge and arts, as to indicate that they had had the advantages enjoyed in the commonwealth of Israel. -And some things may be given more directly evidential of the fact. Relative to our natives having one origin, our author says: "The Indians of New Spain bear a general resemblance to those who inhabit Canada, Florida, Peru, and Brazil. They have the same swarthy and copper colour; flat and smooth hair; small beards; long eyes, with the corner directed upward; and prominent cheek bones. -The American race occupies the greatest space on the globe. Over a million and a half of square leagues, from the Terra del Fuego islands, to the river St. Lawrence, and Beering's Straits, we are struck at the first glance with the general resemblance in the features of the inhabitants. We think we perceive that they all descended from the same stock." He goes on to note some who are of a different opinion. But he adds; "In the faithful portrait which an excellent observer (M. Volney) has drawn of the Canada Indians, we undoubtedly recognize the tribes scattered in the meadows of the Rio Apure, and the Corona. The same style of features exists no doubt in both Americas."

As to the improvements of some of the natives, M. Humbolt, speaking of the Mexicans before the Spanish conquests, says; "When we consider that they had an almost exact knowledge of the duration of the year; that they intercalated at the end of their great cycle of 104 years, with more accuracy than did the Greeks, Romans, and Egyptians, we are tempted to believe that this progress is not the effect of the intellectual development of the Americans themselves; but that they were indebted for it to their communications with some very cultivated nations of central Asia." But how improbable is it that these nations of Mexico could have any communication with people in central Asia, on the other side the globe from them, when vast oceans, or many thousands of leagues of pathless deserts, lay between them! How could they, in periods subsequent to their emigration to this continent, have traversed back and forward round the world, and learned from central Asia the arts and sciences? Had this been the case, this continent and its inhabitants would have been known in the eastern world. Such an hypothesis is vastly improbable at least. But they retained and might have made progress in arts and some degree of science brought down from ancient Israel. Our author says; "The Taultees appeared in New Spain in the seventh, and the Aztees in the twelfth centuries, (as he learned from the hieroglyphical tables of the Aztees) who drew up the geographical map of the country traversed by them; constructed cities, highways, dikes, canals, and immense pyramids very accurately designed, of a base of 1416 feet in length." How striking the view here given of their historical hieroglyphics ancient dates, and emigrations! as well as geographical and mechanical improvements! Can such improvements be imputed to a northern Scythian origin? Striking evidence follows.

Our author proceeds to describe the pyramids of New Spain, -those signal Indian antiquities. The pyramid of Cholula is

177 feet in height. Its base is 1416 feet. It has four great stages, or stories. It lies exactly with the meridian, north and south; the width nearly equal to the length; (439 metres; a metre being nearly 3 1/4 feet.) This stupendous pile is composed, he tells us, "of alternate strata of brick and clay." Various other similar pyramids this author notes and describes in those regions, as being of the same construction. And of their construction he says;

"They suffice to prove the great analogy between these brick monuments -and the temple of Belus at Babylon, and the pyramids of Menschich-Dashour, near Sackhara in Egypt." On the pyramid of Cholula is a church surrounded with cypress. This pyramid M. Humbolt informs is "ten feet higher than the Mycerinus, or the third of the great Egyptian pyramids of the group of Ghize." The length of the base (he informs) is greater by almost half than that of the great pyramid Cheops; and exceeds that of all the pyramids known on the old continent. And he adds, "If it be allowed to compare with the great Egyptian monuments, it appears to have been constructed on an analogous plan."

I ask, can such pyramids be ascribed to ancient barbarous Scythians? Israel knew the pyramids of Egypt. It is with great probability supposed, that during their servitude there, they aided in building those stupendous monuments. They thus served a long apprenticeship to the art of making brick, and pyramids. Did the ancient Scythians ever serve such an apprenticeship? If the advocates for a Scythian descent of the Indians could present the fact, that the whole Scythian nation had, in former times, served an apprenticeship of a number of centuries in making just such brick pyramids as are found in America; how much would they make of this solitary argument to show, that the authors of those American pyramids must surely have been of Scythian descent? And I confess there would be, in my opinion, ten times as much argument in it, in favour of their position, as I have ever perceived in any other arguments adduced. Various authors unite, as will appear, in stating the great similarity; between those Mexican pyramids, and those of Egypt. And our noted author M. Humbolt exclaims; "We are astonished to see, in regions the most remote, men following the same model in their edifices." This is here claimed as a great argument in favour of the Israelitish extraction of those Indians. Other arguments this author unintentionally furnishes. He says; "We have examples of theocratic forms of government in South

America. For such were those of Zac, of Bogota, and of the Incas of Peru, -two extensive empires, in which despotism was concealed under the appearance of a gentle and patriarchal government.- The empire of the Zac (he adds in a note) which comprehends the kingdom of New Grenada, was founded (i.e. in their tradition) by a mysterious personage called Idacanzas, or Bochira; -who, according to the tradition of the Mozcas, lived in the temple of the sun, at Sogamozo, rising of 2000 years." Here tradition had given this people an ancient mysterious founder. His present votaries were the Mozcas. He lived at Sogamozo, inhabiting a temple. The government of this people, it seems, is theocratico patriarchal. Whom does all this most resemble? Israel; or the ancient barbarous Scythians? It would seem the warmest advocates for a Scythian descent, would not be fond of answering this question. But admitting that this theocratic, patriarchal government must well accord with Israelitish tradition; and it seems not unnatural to say, their ancient mysterious lawgiver was Moses, from whom the devoted Mozcas may have derived their name; and also the name of his supposed residence, Sogamozo. It is natural to view this as a tradition (something confused by rolling millenaries) of the lawgiver Moses ministering at the tabernacle in the wilderness, 2000 years (more or less) before some noted era of this tradition. Suppose Sogamozo to have been from Sagan-Moses. Sagan, Adair assures us, was a noted Indian name of the waiter of deputy of the Indian high priest. And it was the very name of the deputy of the ancient high priest in Israel; as the noted Calmet informs. Against the word Sagan, Calmet says; ";The Jews thus call the deputy of the high priest, who supplied his office, and who performed the function of it in the absence of the high priest." Calmet adds; "The Jews think that the office of Sagan was very ancient. They hold that Moses was Sagan to Aaron. I do not find the word Sagan, he says, in this sense in the scriptures; but it is frequent in the Rabbins." Here then, the old rabbinical traditions say, that Moses was Sagan to Aaron in the wilderness. How natural then that the same tradition should descend to the American Mozcas, (if they be of Israel) that Sogamozo (Sagan-Moses, mistaking the place of his residence for his name,) was their ancient legislator! We shall by and by find in another authority, a similar tradition with this, and bearing its part of a strange combination of just such evidence as must eventually present the long lost Israel of the world.

Our author proceeds; "But the Mexican small colonies, wearied of tyranny, gave themselves republican constitutions." Now it is only after long popular struggles that these free constitutions can be formed. The existence of republics does not indicate a very recent civilization. Here, like a wise politician, he was showing that the Mexicans from ancient date, were a civilized people, at least, in good degree.

He adds; "How is it possible to doubt that a part of the Mexican nation had arrived at a certain degree of cultivation, when we reflect on the care with which their hieroglyphical books were composed, and kept; and when we recollect that a citizen of Tlascala in the midst of the tumults of war, took advantage of the facility offered him by our Roman alphabet, to write in his own language five large volumes on the history of a country, of which he deplores the subjection?"

Our author further says; "To give an accurate idea of the indigenous (native) inhabitants of New Spain; it is not enough to paint them in their actual state of degradation and misery after the Spanish conquests. We must go back to a remote period, when governed by its own laws, the nation could display its proper energy. And we must consult the hieroglyphical paintings, buildings of hewn stone, and works of sculpture still in preservation; which, though they attest the infancy of the arts, bear however a striking analogy to several monuments of the more civilized people."

Again he says; "The cruelty of the Europeans has entirely extirpated the old inhabitants of the West Indies. The continent of America, however, has witnessed no such horrible result. The number of Indians in New Spain exceeds two millions and a half, including only those who have no mixture of European or African blood. What is still more consolatory is, that the indigenous population, far from declining, has been considerably on the increase for the last fifty years; as is proved by registers of capitation, or tribute. In general the Indians appear to form two fifths of the whole population of Mexico. In Guanaxuato, Valladolid, Oaxana, and La Puebla, this population amounts to three fifths.

"So great a number of indigenous inhabitants (he adds) undoubtedly proves the antiquity of the cultivation of this country. Accordingly we find in Oaxana remaining monuments of Mexican architecture, which proves a singularly advanced state of civilization. -When the Spaniards conquered Mexico, they found very few inhabitants in the countries situated beyond the parallel of 20 degrees.

Those provinces (that were beyond) were the abode of the Chichimecks and Olomites, two pastoral nations, of whom thin hordes were scattered over a vast territory. Agriculture and civilization were concentrated in the plains south of the river of Santiago. -From the 7th to the 13th century, population seems in general to have continually flowed towards the south. From the régions situated south of the Rio Gila, issued forth those warlike nations, who successively inundated the country of Anahuac. - The hieroglyphical tables of the Aztees have transmitted to us the memory of the principal epochs of the great migrations among the Americans." This traveller goes on to speak of those Indian migrations from the north, as bearing a resemblance to the inundations of the barbarous hordes of Goths and Vandals from the north of Europe, and overwhelming the Roman empire, in the fifth century. He adds; "The people, however, who traversed Mexico, left behind them traces of cultivation and civilization. The Taultees appeared first in the year 648; the Chichimecks in 1170; the Nahualtees in 1178; the Acolhues and Aztees in 1196. The Taultees introduced the cultivation of maize and cotton; they built cities, made roads, and constructed those great pyramids, which are yet admired, and of which the faces are very accurately laid out. They knew the use of hieroglyphical paintings; they could found metals, and cut the hardest stones. And they had a solar year more perfect than that of the Greeks and Romans. The form of their government indicated that they were the descendants of a people who had experienced great vicissitudes in their social state. But where (he adds) is the source of that cultivation? Where is the country from which the Taultees and Mexicans issued?"

No wonder these questions should arise in the highly philosophical mind of this arch investigator. Had he known the present theory of their having descended from ancient Israel; it seems as though his difficulties might at once have obtained relief. These accounts appear most strikingly to favour our hypothesis. Here we account for all the degrees of civilization and improvements existing in past ages among the natives of those regions.

How perfectly consentaneous are these facts stated, with the scheme presented in the preceding pages, that Israel brought into this new continent a considerable degree of civilization; and the better part of them long laboured to maintain it. But others fell into the hunting and consequent savage state; whose barbarous hordes invaded their more civilized brethren, and eventually annihilated most of them, and all in these northern regions! Their hieroglyphical records, paintings and knowledge of the solar year, (let it be repeated and remembered) agree to nothing that could have descended from the barbarous hordes of the north-east of Europe, and north of Asia; but they well agree with the ancient improvements and state of Israel.

Our author proceeds; "Tradition and historical hieroglyphics name Huehuetlapallan, Tallan, and Aztlan, as the first residence of these wandering nations. There are no remains at this day of any ancient civilization of the human species to the north of Rio Gila, or in the northern regions travelled through by Hearne, Fiedler, and Mackenzie. But on the north-west coast, between Nootka and Cook river, especially under the 57th degree of north latitude, in Norfolk Bay, and Cox Canal, the natives display a decided taste for hieroglyphical paintings." (See Voyage de Marchand, p. 258, 261, 375. Dixon, p. 332.) "A harp (says Humbolt) represented in the hieroglyphical paintings of the inhabitants of the north-west coasts of America, is an object at least as remarkable, as the famous harp on the tombs of the kings of Thebes. I am inclined to believe that on the migrations of the Taultees and Aztees to the south (the tribes noted as most improved) some tribes remained on the coasts of New Norfolk and New Cornwall, while the rest continued their course southward. "This is not the place to discuss the great problem of the Asiatic origin of the Taultees, or Aztees. The general question of the first origin of the inhabitants of the continent, is beyond the limits presented to history; and is not perhaps even a philosophical question." Thus our author declines giving any opinion on this subject. But he here gives it as his opinion that these more improved tribes in New Mexico came from the north-west coast, and left some of their half civilized brethren there.

Among the hieroglyphical paintings of the latter, it seems, the harp is found. Was not this a noted Israelitish musical instrument? How should the American Indians be led to paint the Jewish harp? The Jews in Babylon "hung their harps upon the willows." And it is as natural an event that their brethren, in the wilds of America, should place them in their silent hieroglyphical paintings. Whence could have been derived the knowledge of the accurate hieroglyphical paintings, which this most learned author exhibits as found among some of the Indians; unless they had learned them from people to whom the knowledge of hieroglyphics had been transmitted from Egypt, its original source? It appears incredible that such improvements in this art, and the knowledge of the Jewish harp, should be transmitted from the ancient barbarous people of Scythia. If any can believe it, it is hoped they will be cautious of ever taxing others with credulity. Such evidence, it is believed, weighs many times more in favour of their Israelitish extraction. M. Humbolt informs us from Mozino (of whom he speaks with great respect,) relative to Indians at Nootka, on the north-west coasts. Of the writings of this author, he says; "These embrace a great number of curious subjects; viz. the union of the civil and ecclesiastical power in the same persons of the princes -the struggle between Quaulz and Matlax, the good and bad principle by which the world is governed;- the origin of the human species at the time when stags were without horns, birds without wings, &c.; -the Eve of the Nootkians, who lived solitary in a flowery grove of Yucuatl." Here is a traditional peculiarity of Israel; -the origin in the same person of civil and ecclesiastical government. The struggles of the good and bad principle seems very congenial to ancient revelation. The mother of all men, -Eve in paradise, is most striking in their tradition. This must have been learned from the history of Moses, and has a signal weight in favour of the Israelitish extraction of those Nootkians; as has their notion of the innocence and harmlessness of the primitive state of men and beasts. Our noted author says; "The Mexicans have preserved a particular relish for painting, and for the art of carving in wood or stone. We are astonished at what they are able to execute with a bad knife on the hardest wood. They are peculiarly fond of painting images, and carving statues of saints. This is derived from a religious principle of a very remote origin." He adds, "Cortez, in his letters to the Emperor Charles V. frequently boasts of the industry which the Mexicans displayed in gardening. Their taste for flowers undoubtedly indicates a relish for the beautiful. The European cannot help being struck (our author continues) with the care and elegance the natives display in distributing the fruits which they sell in small cages of very light wood. The sapotilles, the mammea, pears, and raisins, occupy the bottom; while the top is ornamented with odoriferous flowers. This art of entwining fruits and flowers had its origin perhaps in the happy period when, long before the introduction of inhuman rites, the first inhabitants of Anahuac, like the Peruvians, offered up to the Great Spirit the first fruits of their harvest." Here was the ancient rite, in Peru, and perhaps in Anahuac, of offering to the Great Spirit their first ripe fruits; as has appeared to have been the case among the various tribes of the natives of this continent. And our author conceives that the curious art of entwining fruits and flowers must have had an ancient origin. Possibly, indeed, it had an origin as ancient and as venerable, as the alternate knop (or fruit) and flower on the brim of Israel's brazen sea; -on the shafts of the golden candlesticks; and on the hem of the high priest's garment; -bells and pomegranates. These ideas were familiar in Israel; but probably in no other nation. Our author speaks of the language of some of the Indians in the south "of which the mechanism proves an ancient civilization." Dr. Edwards (Mr. Boudinot informs) was of the same opinion of the North American Indians: and he pronounced this ancient origin of their language to have been Hebrew.

It seems the Spanish missionaries found such traces of resemblance between some of the rites of the religion of the natives of Mexico, and the religion which they wished to introduce, that our author says, "They persuaded them that the gospel had in very remote times, been already preached in America. And they investigated its traces in the Aztee ritual, with the same ardour which the learned who in our days engage in the study of Sanscrit, display in discussing the analogy between the Greek mythology and that of the Ganges and the Burrampooter." It is a noted fact that there is a far greater analogy between much of the religion of the Indians, and Christianity, than between that of any other heathen nation on earth and Christianity. The aged Indians, noted in the preceding pages, testified to this, when the children from the missionary school came home and informed what instructions they had received. The old Indian said: Now this is good talk. This is such as we used to hear when we were children from the old people, till some of the white people came among us, and destroyed it. We thank the Great Spirit that he had brought it back again!

Our author again says; "The migrations of the American tribes having been constantly carried on from north to south, at least between the sixth and twelfth centuries, it is certain that the Indian population of New Spain must be composed of very heterogeneous elements. In proportion as the population flowed toward the south, some tribes would stop in their progress and mingle with other tribes that followed them." All seem to agree that the Indians came from the north-west, and overspread the continent to the south. Our author, speaking of the conjecture of the Indians descending from a people in the north parts of

Siberia, says; "All these conjectures will acquire more probability, when a marked analogy shall be discovered between the languages of Tartary and those of the new continent; an analogy which according to the latest researches of M. Barton Smith, extended only to a very small number of words." I forbear to offer any further remarks upon these testimonies incidentally afforded by this most celebrated author. Let them be duly weighed by the judicious reader; and he surely cannot doubt but the natives of America came from the north over Beering's Straits; and descended from a people of as great mental cultivation, as were the ancient family of Israel. He must abandon the idea of their being of Scythian descent. He will find much evidence of their being all from one origin; and also much evidence in favour of the hypothesis, that some of the original inhabitants laboured to retain their knowledge of civilization; but that an overwhelming majority abandoned it for the idle hunting life.

In the Archaeologia Americana, containing Transactions and Collections of the American Antiquarian Society," published at Worcester, Mass. in 1820; are found antiquities of the people who formerly inhabited the western parts of the United States." Of some of these I shall give a concise view, as additional arguments in favour of my theory, that some of the people of Israel who came into this western continent maintained some degree of civilization for a long time; but that the better part of the outcast tribes of Israel here finally became extinct, at least in North America, under the rage of their more numerous savage brethren. I shall present also from this interesting publication, some new and striking arguments in favour of the American natives as being of Israel.

Relative to the ancient forts and tumuli, the writer of the Archaeology says; "These military works, -these walls and ditches cost so much labour in their structure; those numerous and sometimes tasty mounds, which owe their origin to a people far more civilized than our Indians, but far less so than Europeans; are interesting on many accounts to the antiquarian, to the philosopher, and the divine. Especially when we consider the immense extent of country which they cover; the great labour which they cost their authors; the acquaintance with the useful arts which that people had, when compared with our present race of Indians; the grandeur of many of the works themselves; and the total absence of all historical records, or even traditionary accounts, respecting them. They were once forts, cemeteries, temples, altars, camps, towns, villages, race grounds, and other places of amusement, habitations of chieftains, videttes, watch towers, and monuments." These certainly are precisely such remains as naturally might have been expected to be furnished by a better part of Israel placed in their "outcast" state, in a vast wilderness, with the degree of civilization which they possessed when banished from Canaan; and were situated in the midst of savage tribes from their race, who had degenerated to the hunting life, and were intent on the destruction of this better part of their brethren. Thus situated, and struggling to maintain their existence, and to maintain their religious traditions, they would naturally form many of the very things above enumerated, walled towns, forts, temples, altars, habitations of chieftains, videttes, and watch towers. These cannot be ascribed to a people of any other origin, with any thing like an equal degree of probability. The whole process of the hypothesis stated in relation to these two branches of the descendants of Israel, when finding themselves lodged in this vast wild continent, is natural and easy.

The above publication of the American Antiquarian Society, decides that these Indian works must have been very ancient, and long before this continent was discovered by Columbus. French forts and works in the west, are also discovered; and many articles on or near the site of those old forts, evidently European and modern. But these are clearly distinguished from those ancient forts and remains. Of the authors of those many ancient remains, this publication says; "From what we see of their works, they must have had some acquaintance with the arts and sciences. They have left us perfect specimens of circles, squares, octagons, and parallel lines, on a grand and noble scale. And unless it can be proved that they had intercourse with Asia or Europe; we now see that they possessed the art of working metals." If they had been favoured with intercourse with any civilized parts of Asia or Europe, this thing must have been ascertained; and this western continent would not have been unknown to the literary eastern world. Such intercourse then is inadmissible. They probably must have derived their art of working metals, from the commonwealth of ancient Israel. They professed something of this knowledge. But none of the barbarous hordes in the north east of Asia, in these ancient days, did possess the knowledge of such arts. Speaking of the wells of those ancient works, the writer observes; "These wells, with stones at their mouths, resemble those described to us in the patriarchal age." Surely this is not unfavourable to the idea of the authors of those wells having been the descendants of Jacob.

To throw light on my hypothesis, I shall add a concise description of several of those ancient works in the west and south; and of a few of the articles there found. These are largely given with their drawings or plates in the publication of the American Antiquarian Society, published at Worcester in 1820; - a book worthy of the perusal of all.

Near Newark in Licking county, Ohio, between two branches of the Licking river, at their junction, is one of the most notable remains of the ancient works. There is a fort including forty acres, whose walls are ten feet high. It has eight gateways, each of the width of about fifteen feet. Each gateway is guarded by a fragment of a wall, placed before, and about nine feet within the gate, of the bigness of the walls of the fort, and about four feet longer than the width of the gateway. The walls are as nearly perpendicular as they could be made with earth. Near this fort is another round fort containing twenty-two acres, and connected with the first fort by two parallel walls of earth about the size of the other walls. At the remotest part of this circular fort, and just without a gateway, is an observatory so high as to command a view of the region to some distance. A secret passage was made under this observatory to an ancient watercourse. At some distance from this fort (but connected by a chain of internal works, and parallel walls) is another circular fort of about twenty-six acres, with walls from twenty-five to thirty feet in height, with a ditch just under them. Connected with these forts is another square fort of about twenty acres, whose walls are similar to those of the fort first described. These forts were not only connected with each other (though considerable distance apart) by communications made by parallel walls of five or six rods apart; -but a number of similar communications were made from them by parallel walls, down to the waters of the river. All these works stand on a large plain, the top of which is almost level, but is high land by a regular ascent from near the two branches of the river, to a height of forty or fifty feet above the branches of the river. At four different places at the ends of these internal communications between the forts and down to the river, are watch towers on elevated ground, and surrounded by circular walls. And the points selected for these watch towers, were evidently chosen with great skill, to answer their design. These forts and chains of communications between them, were so situated as nearly to enclose a number of large fields, which it is presumed were cultivated, and which were thus far secured from hostile invaders. From these works are two parallel walls leading off probably to other similar places of fortifications at a distance. They have been traced a mile or two, and are yet clearly visible. The writer says; "I should not be surprised if these parallel walls (thus leading off) are found to extend from one work of defence to another for the space of thirty miles -such walls have been discovered at different places, probably belonging to these works, for ten or twelve miles at least." He apprehends this was a road between this settlement, and one on the Hockhocking river. And he says; the planning of these works of defence "speaks volumes in favour of the sagacity of their authors."

Some small tumuli, probably for burying the dead, and other purposes, were found here. And the writer says of articles there discovered; "Rock crystals, some of them very beautiful, and hornstone, suitable for arrow and spear heads, and a little lead, sulphur, and iron, were all that I could ascertain." Four or five miles southerly from this is a stone fort enclosing forty acres or upwards. This contains two stone tumuli; "Such (says the author) as were used in ancient times as altars, and as monuments." -He adds; "I should rather suspect this to have been a sacred enclosure, or "high place," which was resorted to on some great anniversary." He deemed its design religious. At the mouth of the Muskingum, in Marietta, are notable instances of these ancient works. They stand on an elevated plain, on the east side of the mouth of the Muskingum, half a mile from its junction with the Ohio. Here are walls and mounds, in direct lines, in circular forms, and in squares. A square fort, called the town, encompasses forty acres by a wall of earth, from six to ten feet in height; and some of the wall thirty-six feet in thickness at the base. Each side has at equal distances three gates. From the middle and largest gateway next the Muskingum, was a covert way, secured by two parallel walls of earth about sixteen rods apart. The highest part of these two walls is about twenty-one feet; and of forty-two feet thickness at the base. This extends about twenty-two rods, to where the river is supposed then to have run.

Within, and at a corner of this fort, in an oblong elevated square, upwards of eleven rods in length, and between eight and nine rods in breadth. Its top forms a level, nine feet in height. The sides are nearly perpendicular. At another side of the fort is another elevated square, nearly as large. And at a third place is a third, still a little smaller.

Near the centre of this fort is a circular mound, thirty feet in diameter and five feet high. At a corner of the fort is a semi-circular parapet, guarding the gateway, and crowned with a mound. South-east of this fort is a smaller fort of twenty having a gateway in the centre of each side, and at each corner; each gateway being defended by a circular mound. On the outside of this smaller fort is a kind of circular pyramid, like a sugar loaf; it is a regular circle, one hundred and fifteen feet diameter at the base; and thirty feet in height. It is guarded by a ditch four feet deep, and fifteen wide; also by a parapet four feet in height. These works are attended with many minor walls, mounds, and excavations. One of these excavations is sixty feet in diameter at the surface; and was when first discovered twenty feet deep.

Another within the fort is twenty five feet in diameter; and poles have been pushed down into its waters and rotten substances, thirty feet. Its sides project gradually toward its centre; and are found to be lined with a layer of very fine clay, eight or ten inches in thickness. It is supposed to contain hundreds of loads of manure. Old fragments of potter's ware have been picked up in this fort. This ware was ornamented with lines on the outside, curious and ingenious; and had a glazing on the inside.

This ware seems to have been burned, and capable of holding water. The fragments when broken are black, and present shining particles when held to the light. Pieces of copper have at various times been found among these ancient works. One piece was in the form of a cup, with low sides, and the bottom thick and strong.

Tools of iron not being found in these works, is no sign the authors did not possess them. For had they been there, they would, no doubt, long since have been dissolved by rust. Some remains of iron articles however are found, as will be seen.

On the waters of the Scioto, at Circleville, Ohio, is a notable instance of these military works. Here are two forts adjoining; one an exact circle; the other a square. The former has two walls, with a ditch between them. These walls were twenty feet in height. The inner wall was of clay; the outer of earth taken from the ditch between the walls. The walls of the square fort are ten feet in height; with eight gateways, besides the one leading into the adjoining circular fort. Each of these gateways is defended on the inside with a mound of earth four feet high, and forty feet diameter at the base. Each mound is two rods within the gateway, and direct in front of it, no doubt for defence. The square and the circle of these forts are said to be most exact; and are thought to indicate much mathematical skill; as not the least error can be detected in their device.   In the centre of the round fort was a mound ten feet in height, and several rods in diameter at the base. On its eastern side, and extending six rods, was a pavement, a half circle composed of pebbles. The top of this tumulus was about thirty feet in diameter, with a way like a modern turnpike leading to it from the east.

This mound has been removed and its contents explored. Some things found in it shall be noted. Two human skeletons. A great quantity of heads, either for arrows or spears. They were so large as to induce a belief they must have been the latter. The handle of a small sword, or large knife, made of an elk's horn, was here found, and is now in a museum at Philadelphia. A silver ferrule encompassed the end containing the blade; which silver ferrule, though black, was not much injured by rolling ages. The blade was gone by rust. But in the hold of the handle, there was left the oxide, or rust of the iron, of similar shape and size of the shank formerly inserted. Some bricks well burnt were here found. And a large mirror of the length of three feet, half a foot in breadth, and one inch and a half thick, formed of isinglass, and on it a plate of iron "which (says the writer who was an eye witness) had become an oxyde;" or plate of rust. "The mirror (he adds) answered the purpose very well for which it was intended."

About forty rods from this round fort, was another tumulus, "more than ninety feet in height," says the writer in the Archaeology; which was placed on an artificial hill. It appears to have been a burying place; and probably was a high place for worship. Immense numbers of human bones, of all sizes, were here found. Here were found also with those bones, stone axes and knives, and various ornaments.

Not far from this tumulus was a semi-circular ditch. The informer remarks it was six feet deep when he first discovered it. At the bottom lay "a great quantity of human bones." These are supposed to be the remains of men slain in some great battle. They were all of the size of men, and lay in confusion, as though buried in a pile, and in haste. Here might have been about the last of those more civilized people who inhabited that station; thus entombed in a ditch by a small residue of their brethren spared; or by their savage enemies, if all in the fortress were cut off.

The articles discovered in the great tumulus were numerous; something seemed to have been buried with every corps.

On the river Scioto, mounds are frequently found, usually on hills with fair prospects to the east. Near Chilicothe are some interesting ones. In Chilicothe, Rev. Dr. Wilson of that place gives a description of one. It was fifteen feet high; sixty feet in diameter at the base; and contained human bones. Under its base in the centre lay a skeleton on a platform of twenty feet, formed of bark; and over it a mat formed of some bark. On the breast lay a piece of copper; also a curious stone five inches in length, two in breadth, with two perforations through it, containing a string of sinews of some animal. On this string were many beads of ivory, or bone. The whole appeared to have been designed to wear upon the neck, as a kind of breast-plate.

Another curious set of Indian works are found within six miles of Chilicothe, on Paint Creek, the accurate description and drawings of which are given in the Archaeology. Here the great wall encloses a hundred and ten acres; the wall twelve feet in height, with a ditch about twenty feet wide. It has an adjacent enclosure of sixteen acres, the walls like the other. In a "sacred enclosure" are six mounds. The immense labours of this place, and cemeteries filled with human bones, denote that a great people, and of some degree of civilization in ancient days dwelt here.

A stone mound was discovered in the vicinity of Licking river, near Newark, Ohio; and several others in different places. These contained human bones, and such articles as the following; "urus, ornaments of copper, heads of spears, &c. of the same metal, as well as of medals of copper." A minister of Virginia, writing to the Antiquarian Society relative to the ancient Indian monuments at Grave Creek, near the month of the Monongahela, says; "In one of the tumuli, which was opened about twenty years since, sixty copper beads were found. Of these I procured ten. -They were made of coarse wire - hammered out -cut at unequal lengths. They were soldered together in an awkward manner- They were incrusted with verdigrise; but the inside was pure copper. This fact shows that these ancient American inhabitants were not wholly unacquainted with the use of metals." There are many indications that their improvements were equal to those of Israel when expelled from Canaan; as will be seen by any who will peruse the Archaeoldgy. Several hints of them shall here be added.

Says the writer; "Along the Ohio, some of it (their pottery) is equal to any thing of the kind now manufactured." - "It is well glazed or polished; and the vessel well shaped." Many ornaments of silver and copper were found. Many wells were dug through the hardest rocks.

A crucible was found in a tumulus near Chilicothe, which is now in the hands of S. Williams, Esq. of that place. It will bear an equal degree of heat with those now used in glass manufactories; and appears made of the same materials.

A stone pipe is noted as found six feet in the alluvial earth; the brim of which is curiously wrought in high relief, and on the front side a handsome female face.

In removing a large mound in Marietta bones of a person were found. "Lying immediately over, or on the forehead of the body, were found three large circular bosses, or ornaments for a sword belt, or a buckler; they are composed of copper, overlaid with a thick plate of silver. The fronts of them are slightly convex, with a depression, like a cup, in the centre, and measure two inches and a quarter across the face of each. On the back side, opposite the depressed portion, is a copper rivet or nail, around which are two separate plates, by which they were fastened to the leather.

Two small pieces of the leather were found lying between the plates of one of the bosses. "Near the side of the body was found a plate of silver, which appears to have been the upper part of a sword scabbard, it is six inches in length and two inches in breadth, and weighs one ounce; it has no ornaments or figures, but has three longitudinal ridges, which probably correspond with the edges or ridges of the sword; it seems to have been fastened to the scabbard by three or four rivets, the holes of which yet remain in the silver."

"Two or three broken pieces of a copper tube, were also found, filled with iron rust. These pieces, from their appearance, composed the lower end of the scabbard, near the point of the sword. No sign of the sword itself was discovered, except the appearance of rust above mentioned. Near the feet was found a piece of copper, weighing three ounces. From its shape it appears to have been used as a plumb, or for an ornament, as near one of the ends is a circular crease, or groove, for tying a thread; it is round, two inches and a half in length, one inch in diameter at the centre, and half an inch at each end. It is composed of small pieces of native copper, pounded together; and in the cracks between the pieces are stuck several pieces of silver; one nearly the size of a four penny piece, or half a dime. This copper ornament was covered with a coat of green rust, and is considerably corroded. A piece of red ochre, or paint, and a piece of iron ore, which has the appearance of having been partially vitrified, or melted, were also found. The ore is about the specific gravity of pure iron."

Surely these things indicate some good degree of improvement in some of the arts of life. Multitudes of other things are noted in this most valuable publication, in which these things are given.

The great antiquity of these works of the natives is proved beyond a doubt. Trees of the third growth are found standing on them, whose annular rings show them to have been more than four hundred years of age.

And the hugeness of those works indicates a vast population. The clergyman writing from Virginia to the Antiquarian Society, of the works at Grave Creek, says of a vast tumulus in that neighborhood, called "the Big Grave;" "It is certainly one of the most august monuments of remote antiquity any where to be found. Its circumference is three hundred feet at the base -Its altitude from measurement is ninety feet, and its diameter, at the summit, is forty five feet. This lofty and venerable tumulus has been so far opened as to ascertain that it contains many thousands (probably) of human skeletons, but no farther. Of the numerous Indian works of this region the writer says; "A careful survey of the above mentioned works would probably show that they were all connected, and formed but parts of a whole, laid out with taste."

These ancient works continued all the way down the Ohio river to the Mississippi, where they increased and were far more magnificent. They abound at the junctions of rivers, in most eligible positions, and in most fertile lands. The number of tumuli on that river exceeds three thousand; "the smallest not less than twenty feet in height, and one hundred in diameter at the base. The largest are of huge magnitude. The informer in the Archaeology says; "I have been sometimes induced to think that at the period when these were constructed, there was a population as numerous as that which once animated the borders of the Nile or of the Euphrates, or of Mexico. Brackenridge calculates that there were 5000 cities at once full of people. I am perfectly satisfied that cities similar to those of ancient Mexico, of several hundred thousand souls, (says the writer) have existed in this country. Nearly opposite St. Louis there are traces of two such cities in the distance of five miles. One of the mounds is eight hundred yards in circumference at the base, (about fifty rods in diameter) the exact size of the pyramid of Asychis; and one hundred feet in height."

(See Archaeologia Americana, page 189.) The author says, in speaking of many of those pyramids of the west; there is "one near Washington, Mississippi state, of one hundred and forty-six feet in height!" "Articles found in and near these works show the improvement of the arts among those who erected them." Though these tumuli were used as places to bury their dead, and places for temples, altars and religious worship; they were no doubt places also for the last resort when likely to be overcome by an enemy. Solis, a writer noted in the Archaeology, when describing the destruction of the Mexicans by the Spaniards, speaks of them as fleeing to their Teocalli. (The Teocalli were high places, formed for the site of their temples, for altars, and places for entombing the dead. The name Teocalli, Humbolt informs, was given these sacred places from the name of the god, to whom the place was dedicated.) Solis informs that in the time of the conflicts of the Mexicans with the Spaniards, their Teocalli appeared like living hills covered with warriors, determined to defend their sacred places, where were their temples, altars, and the tombs of their fathers. Here they fought with desperation.

The high places and great tumuli of the natives on the Mississippi, no doubt were for the same purposes with those of South America. The writer of the Archaeology remarks, that had temples been built on any of their high places, probably no vestige of them would now be visible.

These ancient works of the natives Americans may well remind us of what was said in the Old Testament writings of the ancient "high places" of Israel. Psalm lxxviii. 58; "For they provoked him to anger with their high places."

How abundantly are these noted through their sacred writings. In scores of texts we read of them. Such a king built their high places. Such a reformer destroyed them. Such a vile king rebuilt them. Such a good king again destroyed them, and so on. Here was a train of the most common events. The hearts of Israel were long and most perfectly inured to the religious use of their high places, though it was forbidden. Scott remarks that these high places were "both for idolatry; and for the irregular worship of Jehovah." Solomon had used these high places. I Kings iii. 3, 4; "And Solomon loved the Lord, walking in the statutes of David his father; only he sacrificed and burned incense in high places. And the king went to Gibeon to sacrifice there; for that was the great high place. A thousand burnt offerings did Solomon offer upon that altar." Scott upon the passage says; "Until the temple was builded, the irregularity of sacrificing to the God of Israel in high places -was in some degree connived at. But the people proceeded further in it than in the days of David; and Solomon was censurable for countenancing them." It seems they had their great high places and their smaller high places, to which that ancient people were greatly attached. These high places in Israel are sometimes alluded to in a very bad sense, as when they were the seats of idolatry; and sometimes in a sense which seems more favourable. But allusions are abundantly made to them through the sacred pages; "high places" of various altitudes and dimensions "on every high hill, and under every green tree." The children of Jacob on great occasions assembled at Gilgal. The name of this place imports "a heap." Here was a pile of stones taken from the heart of Jordan, and formed into a monument at the place of Israel's first encampment in the promised land. This circumstance and the numerous monumental piles of stone in ancient Israel, bear a near resemblance to the many piles of stones found in this country, and particularly on the waters of the Licking near Newark, and in the counties of Perry, Pickaway, and Ross, Ohio.

Israel were ever accustomed to hills and high places for their resort to transact important concerns, as well as acts of devotion. Gibeon was a great high place, as has been noted. Shiloh, a noted place of such resort, was on a high hill. This was discontinued as the place of such resort, when the loftier hill of Zion was selected in its place. The temple was located, by divine decision, on this lofty mount of Zion. Ideas like these, together with their other "high places," in ancient Israel, may account for the numerous and huge tumuli found in this continent. Alluding to the high places in ancient Israel, God denounced, Amos vii. 9; "The high places of Israel shall be desolate." And Jer. xii. 7; "I have forsaken mine house, I have left mine heritage; I have given the dearly beloved of my soul into the hand of her enemies." It then follows, verse 12; "The spoilers are come upon all high places through the wilderness; for the sword of the Lord shall devour from one end of the land to the other end of the land; no flesh shall have peace." When this was written the ten tribes had been gone from Canaan many years. God had indeed "given this branch of the beloved of his soul into the hands of her enemies;" as verse 7, just recited. The subsequent verse given may be far better understood in future days, should greater light dawn on the subject, and present our natives as the tribes of Israel. They, and we, in that case, shall better understand the passage, "The spoilers are come upon all high places through the wilderness; for the sword of the Lord shall devour from the one end of the land to the other end of the land." This seems an event then future- "The sword shall come- " though the tribes had before been banished. This, as it related to Israel, seems to be an event to be accomplished during their out-cast state. For in the second and third verses, after this, is predicted their restoration to their heritage in their own land. No supposible origin assigned to the American natives could so well account for what we find of the American high places, as the supposition of their descent from ancient Israel. The events upon this supposition are most natural and characteristic.

These American high places are striking resemblances of the Egyptian pyramids. Consult those in the region of Mexico, as already stated from Mr. Humbolt; and it seems as though they must have been made by the same people with those of Egypt. But the Egyptian pyramids were seen and well known by ancient Israel; and it has long been conjectured they were built by their labours during their bondage in Egypt. How natural then, that they should carry down to succeeding generations the deep impression of them in their minds. And what other nation on earth would be so likely to form such imitations of them, in a remote outcast region, as they, and especially after all we read of Israel's high places, piles, and monuments, their acquaintance with Gibeon, and Gilgal; their deep impression of the temple on mount Zion; and especially their high and sacred places at Bethel and Dan! No other account can more naturally be given of the American high places, than that they originated in those ancient impressions. Of the high places near Mexico, the writer of the Archaeology says; "The group of pyramids of Teotihuacan is in the valley of Mexico, eight leagues north-east from the capital, in a plain named 'the Path of the Dead.' Here are two large pyramids, surrounded by hundreds of smaller ones, which form square streets with the cardinal points of the compass." This writer says, "one of these is higher than the third of the three great pyramids of Egypt, and the length of its base nearly equal to that of Cephron. These things are much in the style of the Egyptian pyramids. Around the Cheops and the Mycerinus are eight smaller pyramids placed with symmetry, and parallel to the front of the greater," says the writer, in noting the resemblance between these and the Egyptian pyramids. And after further noting the "four principal stories" of a great Teocalli, or pyramid, near Mexico, and noting its composition, he adds; "This construction recalls to mind that of one of the Egyptian pyramids of Sackhara, which has six stories, is a mass of pebbles and yellow mortar, covered on the outside with rough stones." The two great Mexican pyramids (this author informs) had on their summit huge statues of the sun and moon, formed of stone and covered with plates of gold, which the soldiers of Cortez plundered. They did not now locate upon their high places their golden calves; but statues of the sun and moon, those brightest visible emblems of their Great Spirit. Of one of these pyramids demolished, the writer says; "We still discover the remains of a staircase built with large hewn stone, which formerly led to the platform of the Teocalli."

The Archaeology informs of a pyramid toward the Gulf of Mexico discovered by Spanish hunters about thirty years ago, in a thick forest, as though concealed. "For the Indians (says the writer) carefully conceal from the whites whatever was the object of their ancient veneration." Various authors unite in this trait of Indian character; which accounts for the fact, that so many of their Israelitish rites should remain so long concealed from us. This newly discovered pyramid was built wholly of hewn stone of vast size and very beautiful. The writer says, this pyramid "had six, perhaps seven stones." "Three staircases lead to the top. The covering of its steps are decorated with hieroglyphical sculpture, and small niches, which are arranged with great symmetry." - These niches are three hundred and eighteen.

The Teocalli, or pyramid of Cholula, near Mexico, (noted before from M. Humbolt) is given on a plain in the Archaeology, with its temple on its summit, and with its staircases of one hundred and twenty steps, leading up its lofty stories. This huge majestic place was called, "The mountain made by hand of man."

In the interiors of various of these great pyramids were found considerable cavities for repositories of the dead. A square stone house was found in one of them, containing two skeletons, some images or likenesses, and many vessels curiously painted and varnished. This room was "covered with bricks and strata of clay." Large bricks were laid, each upper layer jutting over the one next below, and strengthened by beams of cypress. The same manner of laying the bricks, instead of an arch, as "been found (says the writer) in several Egyptian edifices." In a similar cavity, he informs in the tomb of a Peruvian prince, massy gold was found to the value of "more than five millions of francs."

In the time when the Spaniards invaded the Mexicans, the Cholula was by the natives deemed a holy city. Here existed a great number of priests.

And "no spot displayed greater magnificence in the celebration of public worship, or more austerity in its penances and fasts."

It is true that similar huge ancient piles have existed in some various regions of the east. But the writer of the Archaeology says; "The pagodas of Indostan have nothing in common with the Mexican temples."

Of the pyramids of Mexico, of Egypt, and of similar piles found in some parts of Asia, he says; "their destination was altogether different." He means in relation to those of Mexico having temples, and altars, and being sacred to worship. This surely affords an argument in favour of the idea, that the occupants of those high places in Mexico, originated from Israel, where all their high places were for sacred worship.

On the pyramid of Cholula was an altar dedicated to Quetzalcoatl, or the serpent of green feathers; as the name imports. Of their tradition relative to this Quetzalcoatl, the writer says; "this is the most mysterious being of the whole Mexican mythology." An account is then given of this person, sufficiently indeed intermixed with fables; as is usual in the pagan mythologies of events, even founded on revelation. Passing over various of the immaterial fictions, I will sketch the leading points of the picture.

The character to whom their most noted altar was dedicated, whose name imported a serpent of green feathers; was at the same time (in their own description) "a white and bearded man." "He was high priest of Tula, legislator, chief of a religious sect who inflicted on themselves the most cruel penance."

"He introduced the custom of piercing the lips and ears; and lacerating the rest of the body with prickles and thorns." "He appeased by his penance divine wrath." "A great famine prevailed in the province of Culan."

"The saint (this legislator) had chosen his place of retirement on the volcano Catcitepetl, or speaking mountain , where he walked barefoot on agave leaves armed with prickles."

"The reign of Quetzalcotl was a golden age of the people of Anahuac. The earth brought forth without culture the most fruitful harvests. But this reign was not of long duration."

"The Great Spirit offered Quetzalcotl beverage, which in rendering him immortal, inspired him with a taste for travelling, and with an irresistible desire of visiting a distant country called Tlapallan."

In passing "towards the plains of Cholula and thence to the eastern coasts of Mexico and making his way from the north-west to the south-east," he yielded to the entreaties of the inhabitants, who offered him the reins of government." He dwelt twenty years among them, taught them to cast metals, ordered fasts, and regulated the intercalations of the Taltic year."

"He preached peace to men, and would permit no other offerings to the Divinity than the first fruits of the harvests."

"He disappeared, after he had declared to the Cholulans that he would return and govern them again, and renew their happiness."

The writer of the Archaeology says; "It was the posterity of this saint whom the unhappy Montezuma (the most noted and venerable Mexican chief when the Spaniards first arrived at Mexico) thought he recognized in the soldiers of Cortez, the Spanish general. "We know by our books," (said Montezuma, in his first interview with that Spanish general,) "that myself and those who inhabit this country, are not natives, but strangers, who came from a great distance. We know also, that the chief who led our ancestors hither, returned for a certain time to his primitive country. We have always believed that his descendants would one day come to take possession of this country. Since you arrive from that region where the sun rises; and as you assure me you have long known us; I cannot doubt but that the king who sent you is our natural master." (p. 263.) It has generally been the fact, that events in pagan mythology, which are founded on ancient revelation, have yet been confused, and blended with much fable. Much of the mythology of the heathen is thought to be of this character. Some of the events can easily be traced to ancient revelation; while others are so fabulous, that to reduce them to such an origin is more difficult. While considerable fable is involved in this historic tradition of the

Cholulans; it appears to offer a singular facility to trace it to the inspired records of Israel.

Though their ancient "legislator" is called by a name importing the serpent of green feathers; yet he was an ancient man, a white man and bearded; called by Montezuma, a saint who led them to this country, and taught them many things. Who could this be but Moses, the ancient legislator in Israel? The Indians in other regions have brought down a tradition, that their former ancestors, away in a distant region from which they came, were white. And the Cholulans, it seems, teach that they wore their beards; which was the fact; in opposition to the Indians, who pluck them out with their tweezers. How exactly does Moses answer to this their ancient legislator, and chief of their religious community, as may appear.

As Moses inducted into office Aaron, the high priest; so this office, in their mythology, is blended in him. I will remark upon these points in their order. This religious community, under their "legislator and chief," inflicting on themselves cruel penance, may be but a traditional notion of the strictness of the Mosaic laws and religion.

The name of the serpent of the green plumage being given to this legislator, leads the mind to Moses" brazen serpent in the wilderness; and now in Indian tradition, adorned with their most noted amulet, and article of "medicine," the green plumage. This has ever been the most precious article known in their holy ark, and their "medicine bag," through various tribes. Hence it is their most natural emblem of the healing power annexed to the ancient brazen serpent made by Moses; and thus annexed to the name given to him.

This legislator and chief's introducing the custom of "piercing the ears;" -reminds of the noted law of Moses, of boring the ear of the servant who was unwilling to leave his master.

This teaching to lacerate the body with prickles and thorns, is a striking Hebrew figure of the many self-denying services demanded in the Mosaic rituals.

His appeasing divine wrath, may have a striking allusion to the system of the Mosaic sacrifices, including also the mediation of Moses as a type of Christ, and God's turning away his fierce wrath from Israel at his intercession, as was repeatedly the case.

The great famine in Culan naturally reminds of the great famine in Canaan and its adjacent nations; which famine brought Israel into Egypt.

This legislator's retiring to the place of a volcano, and a speaking mountain, most naturally leads the mind to Moses retiring, in the land of Midian, to the backside of the wilderness, to the mount of God, where God spake to him in the burning bush, and in after days made the same mountain appear like a tremendous volcano indeed, as well as like a speaking mountain; -when from the midst of the terrible fire, and sound of the trumpet, God commanded his people in the giving of the law.

This legislator's walking barefoot; naturally alludes to Moses' putting his shoes from his feet at the divine direction, before the burning bush.

The golden age, with spontaneous harvests, naturally suggests the seven years of plenty in Egypt; and may include also (and especially) the happy period during the theocracy in Israel; and the vast fruitfulness of the land which flowed with milk and honey, while the people of Israel walked with God.

His preaching peace to men, and "offering to the Divinity the first fruits of the harvests," alludes to the preaching of the gospel under the Old Testament; and to the signal institution of the offerings of the first ripe fruits; a rite which the various tribes of Indians have most scrupulously maintained; as has been made to appear.

His yielding to the entreaties of the people who offered him the reins of government, and his teaching them useful things, may be a general traditional view of Moses' government of Israel, and the benefits resulting from it. They would naturally ascribe whatever knowledge of the useful arts, and of astronomy, they had, to this their noted chieftain.

The close of this golden age strikingly exhibits the expulsion of Israel from that happy land.

The giving of the beverage, which rendered immortal, is an impressive representation of the immortality of the human soul, as taught in ancient revelation.

And the producing of an ardent desire for transmigration to a distant region of the world, is a most natural tradition of the fact, that Israel were disposed to emigrate (and did indeed emigrate) from the station in Media where they were first lodged when carried from Canaan, to some remote and unknown part of the world, where they were outcast and lost from the knowledge of civilized man; as has been the fact.

And their coming from the north-west to Mexico, indicates to what region, and in what direction, they came; over Beering's Straits into America, and south-ward through the continent. This accords with the testimonies of Robinson, Humbolt, and all the most intelligible writers of Indian tradition. All bring them from the north-west coasts of America.

The venerable Montezuma (over whom our hearts have so often bled) was prepared to receive the blood plundering Cortez, and his armies, into his bosom; believing them to be sent by their ancient legislator (in the distant part of the world from which they came) to reign again over them, and to make them happy! Abundantly are we assured of Indian tradition which well accords with this.

Israel had read in Moses, of God's "scattering them from one end of the earth to the other;" and again recovering them. Amos, the prophet to Israel, had assured them of God's scattering them in a "famine of the word, from north to east, from sea to sea," wandering to and fro over a vast continent between those extreme seas; and had expressly predicted their being again recovered, as had some others of the prophets before their expulsion. They would then naturally carry down these ideas with them in their broken traditions.

They would retain the expectation that the Being who banished them, would again, at some time, and in some way, appear and meliorate their condition. And our native Americans generally, if not all the most intelligent among them, have (with the venerable Montezuma) retained something of this idea. Often have we had information from Indian chiefs, and others from different regions, that they have ever understood from their traditions that the time is coming which shall make them more happy.

The same tradition led the aged wife of the Indian chief (related by our missionaries) to say, after the missionaries had unfolded their object in her hearing, to the following effect. We have ever understood that at some time good people are to come and teach us the right way. How do we know but these are those good people come to teach us?

What account can be given of this expectation brought down by the natives, but that they derived it from the ancient prophets in Israel; and from the fact that God had promised them the everlasting possession of the land of Canaan; and had repeatedly recovered them in ages past from their states of bondage and captivity.

The piece of Mexican mythology, which has been explained, and which is pronounced "the most mysterious," can receive probably no rational explanation, if applied to a Tartar origin, or to any other eastern nation beside Israel. But if applied to Israel, its application is most striking;" and it contains such facts as might in such a case be expected.

If our natives be of Israel, it is natural to expect the most enlightened of them would have some tradition of their noted lawgiver Moses. These Cholulans probably were among the most enlightened. And here is their ancient lawgiver bearing a traditional assemblage of various of the distinguishing religious insignia of ancient Israel. This reminds of the testimony of Baron Humbolt, before noted, who speaking of the "theocratic forms of government" of the Zac, Bogota, and Peru, notes the tradition of the former; and of their having been founded by a "mysterious personage" who, according to the tradition of the Mozcas, (possibly followers of Moses) "lived in the temple of the sun at Sogamozo rising two thousand years." Nothing can be more natural than to view this a traditional notion of Moses" administration in Israel in the wilderness.

The place of their mysterious founder was at Sogamozo -perhaps explained by Sagan Moses as before noted.

This their tradition relative to their ancient lawgiver, and the structure of their pyramids, so similar to those of Egypt, suggest much relative to the origin of this people. Could the advocates for their Tartar descent find so much in favour of their hypothesis; could they truly exhibit the fact, that the whole Tartar race had, in ancient times, served an apprenticeship of a number of centuries to the art of making such brick and pyramids as are found in America; (as the children of Israel are supposed to have done in Egypt;) how forcibly would they adduce this argument to show that the authors of those pyramids of America must have been of Tartar descent! And indeed there would be in my humble opinion, much more force in it, in favour of their hypothesis, than in all the arguments they have ever been able to adduce.

One more argument I shall adduce from facts furnished in the Archaeology, to show that the American natives are from the tribes of Israel. The argument is a tradition of a trinity in their Great Spirit. Evidence of different kinds, and from different regions, relative to such a sentiment, is exhibited; not that the writer of the Archaeology makes this application of it. An Indian article, called by this writer a "triune vessel," and noted as a religious article, and an emblem of their gods was found on the forks of the Cumberland river, in alluvial earth, four feet below the surface. It may now be seen; and its perfect drawing is given in the Archaeology. It is composed of fine clay of light amber colour, rendered hard by fire; and parts of it painted with vermilion; which paint is very brilliant. The vessel contains about a quart, and is of the following figure. The top is a hollow stem of three inches diameter, and swelling in size downward like a gourd shell, Against the bulge, there is the accurate resemblance of three human heads, joined each one to the shell by the back of the head, and each face outward in a triangular form, and all of the same dimensions. The workmanship of the faces and features is excellent; so that (says the writer) "even a modern artist might be proud of the performance." The writer in the Archaeology conceives of it to be an emblem of three of their principal gods, and seems to think of deriving an argument from it in favour of the natives being of East Indian extraction. He says of this triune vessel; "Does it not represent the three chief gods of India, Brahma, Vishnoo, and Siva." This certainly seems very far fetched! Why should they be supposed to be a representative of those three East Indian gods, any more than three other heathen gods on earth?

Brahma, Vishnoo, and Siva are three distinct ideal gods. But this triune vessel is one entire thing. It must rather then have been designed to represent one God with something like three faces, or characters. One of the faces denotes an old person; the other two, younger persons. The vessel stands on the three necks of these three heads, each projecting from the bottom of the middle part of the vessel one inch and a half. If the writer of the Archaeology may imagine he discerns in this an affinity with the East Indian worshippers of Brahma, Vishnoo, and Siva; I may certainly be allowed in my turn to conjecture, that here may be discovered a striking affinity with the ancient worshippers of the one Jehovah in three persons; as in ancient Israel. The thought perfectly accords with the idea of our natives being the descendants of Israel,. that this triune vessel was a designed emblem of the triune God of Israel. The doctrine of a mysterious three in the one God of Israel, runs through the Bible, -Old Testament as well as New. This plurality in their one God, Israel had always read from the days of Moses. They found a plurality in God's name, and various appellations. They found him speaking in the plural, we and us. They found who this plural were - God; the Seed of the woman, and the Spirit of God; always three, and only three. They had read, "The Lord said unto my Lord, sit thou on my right hand" In the first three chapters of their Bible, they found this three in God, as well as in all subsequent parts of their sacred book.

Long had Israel read, or heard read, abundance of such sacred language as the following; which ancient critics assure us relates to a mysterious trinity in the one God; "When God, they caused me to wander," in the Hebrew. "Remember now thy Creators in the days of thy youth." "For thy Makers is thy husbands." "The knowledge of the Holy, (Hebrew plural, Holies, or Holy Ones) is understanding." Nouns, adjectives, and verbs, applied to God, they had abundantly found to be plural; and yet absolute divinity ascribed to each. Their infant to be born, was "the mighty God, the everlasting Father." And their Spirit of the Lord, they had read of, as the Being who garnished the heavens, who created the world. Of this mysterious three in one God, Israel had ever read, or heard. When the intelligent among them thought of God, this triune view of him must have been familiar. And when their distant descendants had lost (or were losing) the knowledge of reading, it is natural to suppose they would construct an emblem, to perpetuate the memory of their God. The Indians are known to make great use of hieroglyphics and figures of speech; and they never form them for no purpose. As circumstances indicated that this triune vessel was a religious emblem, as the narrator of it believes; so this affords an argument of some weight that the inventors of it were of Israel.

Another argument going to the same point is this. The writer in the Archaeology says; "One fact I will here mention; whenever there is a group of tumuli, three are uniformly larger than the rest; and stand in the most prominent places. Three such are to be seen standing in a line on the north side of Detroit. Three such are to be seen near Athens; and at a great many places along the Ohio river. There are three such near the town of Piketon. "Were they not altars, (he inquires) dedicated to their principal gods?" Permit me to reply; They were much more likely to have been emblems dedicated to the one triune God of Israel.

The numerous ancient inhabitants on the Mississippi were the same race with those of Mexico and Peru. And the latter have exhibited similar ideas of the triune God. The writer of the Archaeology says of those ancient people of the Mississippi; "Their religious rites were, it is believed, the same with those of Mexico and Peru." And he further notes, "Clavigero, who was well acquainted with the histories of the Mexicans and Peruvians, professes to point out the places from whence they emigrated; the several places they stopped at; and the times they continued to sojourn there.

According to him they arrived at Mexico in 648, and came across the Pacific not far from Beering's Straits." Thus all these people were of one stock.

And the writer of the Archaeology speaks of the native South Americans as having three principal gods. He says; "One of the three principal gods of the South Americans was called by a name, which signifies the god of the shining mirror. He was supposed to be a God who reflected his own supreme perfections, and was represented by a mirror, which was made in that country of polished obsidian, or of mica, like ours. The scarcity of obsidian, which is a volcanic production, may well account for its absence in this country. The numerous volcanoes in South America equally account for the abundance of mirrors of obsidian there. This deity was represented as enjoying perpetual youth and beauty. Other gods had images placed on pedestals in the Mexican temples; this one had a mirror on his. This divinity was held in awful veneration as the great unknown God of the universe. Who does not here discover (continues the writer) a strong trace of a knowledge of the true God, derived by tradition from the first patriarchs?" Truly we may exclaim with this writer; "Who does not discover here some knowledge of the true God of Israel and a manifest traditionary view of him?" But who does not discover also, that what the writer calls the three principal gods of the South Americans, is truly but one God? -the great unknown God of the universe! No evidence is here, or elsewhere exhibited, that those people held to three principal divinities, only that the images of the other two gods were placed on pedestals; and the mirror representing the other was not. But it is not evident from this, that they believed in three distinct gods; or that the builders of these temples designed any such thing. The view they had of the God of the mirror, shows they could not hold to three principal deities. And it has been universally testified of the great body of the Indians of America, that they hold to but one great Supreme Spirit. But yet when they represent this one God, there is something in him threefold. The South Americans must have three temples, while yet they had but one temple of the mirror or Supreme God. The North Americans must have three (and only three) huge high places or pyramids in a place. And the writer informs that only in one of these is found the mirror; as in the three temples of South America, only one has the mirror. The triune vessel explains the idea; -three heads combined in one; three faces, and but one vessel; -one of an old man; the other two younger. Here is Indian tradition relative to their one

Great Spirit -God; the Shiloh; and the Spirit. And the sentiment is further corroborated by the following fact, given also in the Archaeology. Another emblem was found in a tumulus near Nashville, Tennessee, and is now in the museum of Mr. Clifford of Lexington, Kentucky. It is formed of clay, like the triune vessel aforenoted; and is made to exhibit three views of a man's head and body to the middle with the arms cut off close to the body. It gives a side view of one of these heads, with strong and well formed features.

It gives a front view of another of them. And a view of the backside of the head and shoulders of the third. Each head has upon it a fillet and cake, with the hair plated. This too was deemed by the writer a religious emblem. The figures are given on a plate, as is the triune vessel. They are considered as three devices for the same object. As it is well ascertained the Indians hold to one Supreme Spirit; they cannot be said to hold to three principal gods. No evidence of such a thing exists, but in these various triune emblems. And these, it is contended, do not amount to any such thing; but to their ancient belief in the triune God of Israel.

Let the reader here recollect the account given by the Rev. Mr. Chapman, in the Union Mission, of the Ossage Indians. Stating their religious customs, when about to form a treaty of peace, he says; "About two feet in advance, and in a line with the path, were three bunches of grass, which had been cut and piled about three feet apart, as an emblem of him, whom they worshipped." Here was the station for the priest to stand and pray. And all the Indians must then step on each of these piles of grass.

Proceeding on about forty rods, they halted, and formed with grass another emblem of the Great Spirit; -a circle of about four feet diameter. By this was offered another long prayer. Then each one stepping on the circle, they passed on. The chief informed that both these were representations of their God. Mr. C. upon the incident remarks "Perhaps the curious may imagine that some faint allusion to the lost ten tribes of Israel may be discovered in the select number of dreamers; (which he had before stated, they being ten) and to the trinity in unity, in the bunches, and in the circle of grass!" These various Indian traditions from distant regions of the continent, and different ages, appear to form some striking evidence that the Indians had indeed brought down traditionary impressions of their one Great Spirit's consisting of a trinity in unity! Could so great an argument be found in favour of the Indians having descended from the Tartars, the advocates for such a descent would not fail on making much of this argument. No rational account can be given of these various and distinct triune emblems of their Great Spirit, but that they were derived from ancient revelation in Israel, which did throughout present the one God of Israel as God; the Lord; and the Spirit of the Lord; -God; the seed of the woman, who was likewise the "mighty God;" and the Spirit! No rational account beside this can be given of these various Indian emblems of their God.

These emblems of their one God explain the noted triune emblems of the other ancient Indians further south, and in different regions; the triune vessel of three faces; the three other faces; the three chief pyramids; -and the three temples, with one of them containing the mirror.

These three piles of grass in one of their emblems of God, are not to represent "the three chief gods of India, Brahma, Vishnoo, and Siva;" as has (without any evidence) been conjectured of southern triune emblems.

But the Indians expressly inform, they are an emblem of him, whom they worshipped." And the same one God of the Indians was in the same Indian rites denoted by three bunches of grass; and also by one grass circle, with a bunch of grass in its centre. We thus have from different Indian regions, different ages, and a variety of emblems, a complete union of evidence of an Indian tradition of trinity in unity in their God. And this is the God of whom they boast, as the head of their nation; the God exclusively in covenant with their ancient fathers. This has appeared from ample testimony; to which is added the following. The celebrated Boudinot informs, that while he was at the seat of government, at a certain time, chiefs and leading characters were present from seven different distant tribes of Indians. He says, on the Sabbath he was much pleased to see their orderly conduct. They learned that this was a day in which the white people worship the Great Spirit. An old sachem addressed his red brethren very devoutly. Mr. Boudinot asked the interpreter what he said? He replied, "The substance of it is, the great love which the Great Spirit always has manifested toward the Indians; that they were under his immediate direction; and that hence they ought gratefully to acknowledge him, obey his laws, do his will, and avoid every thing displeasing to him."

Some readers have said; If the Indians are of the tribes of Israel, some decisive evidence of the fact will ere long be exhibited. This may be the case. But what kind of evidence shall we expect? Must some miracle be wrought? It is generally thought the days of miracles are past. Probably no evidence ought to be expected in this case, but such as naturally grows from the nature of the subject, and the situation of Israel. Would evidence like the following be deemed as verging toward what would be satisfactory? Suppose a leading character in Israel - wherever they are - should be found to have had in possession some biblical fragment of ancient Hebrew writing. This man dies, and it is buried with him in such a manner as to be long preserved. Some people afterward removing that earth, discover this fragment, and ascertain what it is, -an article of ancient Israel. Would such an incident, in connexion with the traditional evidence already exhibited on this subject, be esteemed of some weight! Something like this may possibly have occurred in favour of our Indians being of Israel.

The Rev. Dr. Griffin, President of Williams College, communicated to the writer, while preparing his first edition of the View of the Hebrews, the following account, with liberty to insert it in his book, if he pleased. The late venerable Dr. Boudinot stated to Dr. Griffin that the Rev. S. Larned (who died in New Orleans) informed him that while he was living in Pittsfield, Mass. - his native place - after he left college, there was dug up in Pittsfield by one of his neighbours, probably from an Indian grave, some written parchments enclosed in a cover of skins. These parchments he obtained, took them to Boston, had them read, and found them to be the same with the parchments used in Jewish phylacteries, and well written in Hebrew. Mr. Larned added that he left them with the Rev. Dr. Elliot of Boston. Dr. Boudinot obtained leave of Mr. Larned to send and take them. He sent; but for some reason could not obtain them. Dr. Elliot soon after died; and nothing more was done upon the subject. On receiving this information from Dr. Griffin, the writer wrote to Rev. Dr. Humphrey, then minister of Pittsfield, requesting him to see what further information might be there obtained relative to this matter. He returned an answer. It was just as Mr. Humphrey was about leaving his people for the Presidency of the Amherst Collegiate Institution; and he could not pay much attention to the subject. He made considerable inquiry, however; but without much success. But he informed that he had a distinct recollection, that when he came to Pittsfield, not long after the said parchments were found, he heard considerable said upon this subject. And he found an impression on his mind that it was then said that some Jew probably lost these parchments there. The author wrote also to J. Everts, Esq. of Boston, desiring him to see if the parchments could be found. An answer was returned, that they were then in the hands of the Antiquarian Society. He stated also, the same account with that of Mr. Humphrey, that they were supposed to have been left in Pittsfield by some Jew. The writer afterward speaking of this thing to a celebrated minister in the centre of the state of New York, was by him informed that he had heard of the finding of these parchments; but that a Jew from Germany was known to have resided in Pittsfield, and probably lost them. Another supposed the Jews had a custom of burying their phylacteries; which might account for this phenomenon. The public mind had thus been laid to rest relative to the parchments. The writer concluded to pay no further attention to the subject. But being advised by one whom he highly respected, and who apprehended there might be something about this, not yet investigated, he took a journey to Pittsfield. With some of the first characters of that town he took pains to ascertain whether any Jew was ever known to have resided or been in Pittsfield? Inquiry was made of different aged people, and who it was thought would be likely to give the most correct information -one or two who had been there from within several years of the first settlement of the place. One and all answered in the negative, that no Jew was ever known in Pittsfield, as they believed, till Rev. Mr. Frey was there a few weeks before. The man was then found who first discovered the parchments under consideration. This was Joseph Merrick, Esq. a highly respectable character in the church of Pittsfield, and in the county, as the minister of the place informed. Mr. Merrick gave the following account; That in 1815, he was levelling some ground under and near an old wood shed standing on a place of his, situated on Indian Hill, (a place in Pittsfield so called, and lying, as the writer was afterward informed, at some distance from the middle of the town where Mr. Merrick is now living.) He ploughed and conveyed away old chips and earth, to some depth, as the surface of the earth appeared uneven. After the work was done, walking over the place, he discovered, near where the earth had been dug the deepest, a kind of black strap, about six inches in length, and one and a half in breadth, and something thicker than a draw leather of a harness. He perceived it had at each end a loop of some hard substance, probably for the purpose of carrying it. He conveyed it into his house, and threw it in an old tool box. He afterward found it thrown out of doors, and again conveyed it to the box. After some time he thought he would examine it. He attempted to cut it, and found it hard as a bone. He succeeded in cutting it open, and found it was formed with pieces of thick raw hide, sewed and made water tight with the sinews of some animal; and in the fold it contained four folded leaves of old parchment. These leaves were of a dark yellow, and contained some kind of writing. Some of the neighbours saw and examined them. One of these parchments they tore in pieces; the other three he saved, and delivered them to Mr. Sylvester Larned, a graduate then in town, who took them to Cambridge, and had them examined. They were written in Hebrew with a pen, in plain and intelligible writing. The following is an extract of a letter sent to Mr. Merrick by Mr. Larned, upon this subject.

"Sir; I have examined the parchment manuscripts, which you had the goodness to give me. After some time and with much difficulty and assistance I have ascertained their meaning, which is as follows; (I have numbered the manuscripts.)

No. 1 is translated by Deut. vi. 4-9 verses inclusive.

No. 2, by Deut. xi. 13-21 verses inclusive.

No. 3, Exod. xiii. 11-16 versus inclusive.

I am, &c.

SYLVESTER LARNED.

The celebrated Calmet informs that the above are the very texts of scripture which the Jews used to write on three out of four of their leaves of phylacteries; from which it is presumable that the fourth leaf, torn in pieces, contained the texts which belong to the fourth leaf. The leaves of their phylacteries were ever four. Calmet, on the article Phylactery, says; "This word from the Greek signifies a preservative.

These phylacteries were little boxes, or rolls of parchments, wherein were written certain words of the law. These (boxes or rolls, containing their four leaves of parchment on which their texts were written) they wore upon their foreheads, and upon their wrist of their left arm. They founded this custom upon Exodus xiii. 9, 16."

Various authors noted by Calmet contend that the phylacteries were used in Israel from the days of Moses.

Mr. Merrick informed that á Dr. James was living in Pittsfield when these parchments were found, and felt much interest in the event. He soon moved into New York. He afterward informed Mr. Merrick, that he had laid this matter before an aged Jew, who also felt interested in the event; and who, after considering the subject some time, concluded that he could give no account of the leaves being found in such a condition in Pittsfield from any custom of the Jews.

I asked Mr. Merrick if he had ever known of any Jew as having resided or been in Pittsfield? He said he had not; nor did he believe one had ever been there. I further inquired whether he could account for the story of some Jew having left them in Pittsfield? He said it originated as follows.

At the time the parchments were found, there were British prisoners residing in Pittsfield, taken in the late war. As much wonder was excited relative to these leaves, some neighbour expressed his conjecture that perhaps some of these British prisoners were Jews, and they had dropped or buried this thing there. Mr. Merrick viewed it wholly unlikely. But to ascertain the point, he went to the prisoners and asked if any of them were Jews? They said they were not. He inquired of their officers, and received the same assurance. He asked if any of them had any knowledge of this thing? and was answered in the negative. Mr. Merrick assured me, he had ever believed it to have been of Indian origin; and that Col. Larned (father of the late Rev. Mr. Larned) lived and died in the same belief. It seems no evidence has appeared to the contrary; notwithstanding the above groundless conjecture, which when it got abroad was magnified into a satisfactory account.

The writer conversed with the Rev. Mr. Frey (the celebrated Jewish preacher in this country) upon this subject; who could give no account of the incident from any Jewish custom. He informed that the Jews have a custom of burying their leaves of phylacteries when worn out and illegible; as they had also any old leaf of a Hebrew bible. They would roll it up in some paper, and put it under ground from respect. But these leaves were whole and good, and were sewed up (as has been stated) in thick raw hide, and with the sinews of some animal; a thing which no Jew in Christendom would have done.

The writer left Pittsfield for Boston with a view to obtain these parchments, and to have them examined by the Hebrew professor at Cambridge, and professor Stuart of Andover. In Boston the Rev. Mr. Jenks informed him the parchments were at Worcester, in the care of the Antiquarian Society. He said he had seen them; and spoke of the story of the Jew's having lost them at Pittsfield. He added that the Rev. Dr. Holmes of Cambridge had seen and examined them. On my way returning to Worcester, I called on Dr. Holmes. He said he had carefully read the three parchments under consideration, and found them to be three out of four of the leaves which compose the Jewish phylacteries, containing the very passages which have ever been selected for their phylacteries; that they were written with a pen, and in fair Hebrew. He was shown the copy of Rev. Mr. Larned's letter to Mr. Merrick, which he said was correct. Rev. Dr. Holmes is known to be a correct Hebrew scholar. His wonder (with that of others) had been laid to rest by the rumour of a Jew having been known to leave them in Pittsfield. He was asked whether upon supposition of these leaves having been of Indian origin, any thing occurred to his mind relating to the parchments or writing, which might militate against the idea of their having been written in ancient Israel? He replied in the negative.

The writer returned to Worcester with full expectation of finding the parchments; but to his no small disappointment they could not be found.

Dr. Thomas, president of the Antiquarian Society, said that such a leaf (he thought there was but one) was some years ago lodged in his care; and he presumed it was safe in some of the Antiquarian depositories. But among the many boxes of articles he knew not where to look for it. He too had received with it the rumour of its Jewish origin; and hence had not viewed it of great consequence. We searched several hours, but in vain. It is hoped the leaves may still be found, and further examined.

The Rev. Chauncey Cook of Chili, New York, at my house, gave the following information, with liberty of inserting it with his name. He has lately been credibly informed by a minister, (he cannot recollect his name, as several within six months have called on him from New England) that Rev. Dr. West of Stockbridge gave the following information. An old Indian informed him that his fathers in this country had not long since had a book which they had for a long time preserved. But having lost the knowledge of reading it, they concluded it would be of no further use to them; and they buried it with an Indian chief. The minister spoke to Mr. Cook of this information of Dr. West, as a matter of fact.

The following remarks are submitted:

1. Mr. Merrick, who found these parchments, was in the best situation to investigate their probable origin; and he was and remains of opinion they were from the Indians. He views the conjecture of their having been brought thither by some Jew, as

without foundation. Rev. Mr. Larned, who carried them to Boston for examination, being a man of letters, must have been decently qualified to investigate and judge of this matter. He it seems was fully of opinion they were Indian. His father, Col. Larned, was a man of note, and would not be likely to be imposed upon in this thing; and he lived and died in the belief they were Indian. And the writer could find no person in Pittsfield who could state any reason for believing otherwise. The conjecture of their Jewish origin gained importance by travelling abroad; but appears to have been without foundation at home.

2. Upon supposition of the Indians being descendants of Israel, there is no essential difficulty, but something very natural in the event. Calmet informs that Origen, Chrysostom and others, deemed the use of the phylacteries in Israel to have been ancient as the days of Moses. He says that Lightfoot, Sealeg and Maldon insisted that the custom of wearing them was general in the time of our Saviour; and that Christ did not reprove the Pharisees for wearing them, but for their affectation in having their phylactery cases wider than those of others. We conclude then the wearing of these phylacteries was a noted custom in Israel at the time of their final expulsion from Canaan. And it is natural to believe that Israel, being in exilement, would preserve these fragments of their better days with the utmost care. Wherever they went then, they would have these phylacteries with them. If they brought them to this country, they would keep them with diligence. They would most naturally become some of the most precious contents in their holy ark, as their nation formerly kept the holy law in the ark. Here such a phylactery would be safe through ever so many centuries. This is so far from being improbable, that it is almost a moral certainty. After their knowledge of reading had long been lost, some chief, or high priest, or old beloved wise man, (keeper of their tradition) fearing these precious leaves would get lost, or parted, might naturally sew them in a fold of raw skins with the sinews of an animal, (the most noted Indian thread,) and keep this roll still in the ark; or carry it upon his belt. All this is what might most naturally be expected in such a case. This thing might have been thus safely brought down to a period near to the time when the natives last occupied Indian Hill, in Pittsfield; perhaps in the early part of last century. Its owner then might lose it there; or (what is most probable) it was buried with some chief, or high priest; and hence was providentially transmitted to us. This I venture to say (on the supposition the Indians are of Israel) is by no means so

improbable, as that some modern Jew left it there in the situation in which it was found. The style of the preservation of these parchments appears to be Indian; but not Jewish. No modern Jew would be likely to hide his precious leaves of phylacteries in a roll of raw hide, sewed with the sinews of an animal. Nor would he leave them, had he done it, on Indian Hill under ground. Sooner would he sacrifice his life than thus rudely to profane the most sacred symbols of religion! It is incredible. Mr. Merrick observed that the colour of these parchments was dark yellow.

Doctor Thomas, of Worcester, showed me, among his Antiquarian curiosities, an Arabic parchment manuscript, which he informed was written long before the Christian era. This was dark yellow; but the parchment and writing were in good preservation. And one of these written parchments might thus long have been preserved as well as the other.

3. This view of the subject may give an intelligible view of the account of the old Indian in Stockbridge to Dr. West, that his fathers had buried, not long ago, a book which they could not read. And it may give a striking view of the vigilant care of the Watchman of Israel, who never slumbers, in relation to laying in train this singular item of evidence among many others, which should combine to bring to light that outcast people, who were to be exhibited to the world in the last days. The government and vigilance of the God of Jacob have ever been wonderful. And great things have been found to depend on a strange combination of minute events, that the unremitting care of the Most High might appear the more conspicuous. In ancient Israel many such instances might be pointed out. And when God's bowels shall yearn for Ephraim, earnestly remembering him still, and about finally to restore him, it will prove that he has not been unmindful of that providential train of evidence, which must eventually identify a people long outcast and lost from the knowledge of the literary and civilized world, with his ancient beloved children of Abraham. Show a people on earth who have a greater claim from the most natural kind of evidence, than our natives, to be received as the descendants of Israel; and it is hoped that to such claim no objection will be offered.

IV

An Address Of The Prophet Isaiah, Relative To The Restoration Of His People.

The writer might fill a chapter in illustrating the wrongs which the Indians have suffered from people in our land; in noting their reduced and deplorable situation; in pleading the cause of humanity in their behalf; and in appealing to the magnanimous feelings of the people of our nation. He might adduce many evangelical motives the most commanding, to enforce the duty of saving the remnant of the natives of our continent from extinction, and from wretchedness. The duty of sending them the gospel, and of being at any expense to teach them Christianity and the blessings of civilized life, is great and urgent on every principle of humanity and general benevolence. And this duty peculiarly attaches itself to the people, who are now in possession of the former inheritance of those natives; and from to many of whom that people have received insufferable injuries. This subject must occur with force to the mind of every well informed American. And it is devoutly to be hoped that far greater attention will henceforth be paid to it by all among us who make any pretence to humanity, not to say piety. But the object of this chapter is to examine and illustrate an interesting portion of ancient prophetic writing, which is thought to embrace this very concern.

An address is found in the eighteenth chapter of the prophet Isaiah, which is apprehended to be of deep interest to America. It is a passage which has been esteemed singularly enigmatical. This circumstance has usually attended the prophecies, in proportion to the distance of their events. And they have often been left in silence, or their true intent misapplied, till near the time of their fulfilment. Then some incidents would throw light upon them, and render their import plain and satisfactory.

The writer was affected with this passage some years ago, when writing his Dissertation on the Prophecies. He found it to be an address to some Christian people of the last days, just at the time of the final restoration of God';s ancient people; an address to such a people beheld in vision away over the mouths of the Nile, or in some region of the west; a call and solemn divine charge to them to awake and aid that final restoration. He then apprehended it might apply to Britain, though he felt the difficulty arising from the fact that Britain lies so far to the north of the direction specified in the address. It now appears to him far more probable that the Christian people of the United States of America are the subjects of the address; or at least are especially included in it. To prepare the way for the consideration of the address, let several things be premised.

1. Some of the greatest and best of divines have thought it would be strange, if nothing should be found in the prophetic scriptures having a special allusion to our western world, which by propitious Heaven was destined to act so distinguishing a part, both in the religious and political world, in the last days. They have felt as though it might be presumed that some special allusions would be had in some of the prophetic writings to so distinguishing a community of Zion, and of men. Under this impression, Mr. Edwards apprehended this passage of Isaiah might allude to America; "So shall they fear the name of the Lord from the west." Almost all other parts of the world are noted in prophecy. It certainly then is not incredible that our land should be manifestly noted.

2. The address in the eighteenth of Isaiah to be contemplated, is clearly an address to some people of these last days; and concerning events intimately connected with the battle of that great day of God, which is now future and not far distant, and is to introduce the Millennium. This is evident in verses 5 and 6; which will be noted.

3. The address then cannot have been to any ancient people or nation. This appears with certainty, from their being cotemporary with the events of that great battle, and the restoration of the Jews. The call then must be to a people of the last days; a nation now on earth; and a nation to be peculiarly instrumental in the restoration of the Hebrews in the last days. For this is the very object of the address; to go and collect the ancient people of God; because "in that time shall the present be brought unto the Lord of hosts of a people scattered and peeled, (the very people of the ancient covenant in manifest descriptions repeatedly given) to the place of the name of the Lord of hosts, the Mount Zion." This duty of the restoration assigned is in the address connected with the tremendous scenes of judgment,

which shall subvert anti-christian Europe, and her adjutors hostile to the church; as may be seen.

4. The address then seems manifestly to a nation that may seem to have leisure for the important business assigned; while the old and eastern parts of the world (engaged in anti-christian hostilities) shall be found in the effervescence of revolutions, and in those struggles which precede dissolution. This consideration seems clearly to fix the address to a people distinct, and distant from the immediate turmoils of the old anti-christian lands; and hence probably to our own nation; perhaps including Britain.

5. Should it be proved a fact, that the aborigines of our continent are the descendants of the ten tribes of Israel; it would heighten the probability to a moral certainty, that we are the people especially addressed, and called upon to restore them; or bring them to the knowledge of the gospel, and to do with them whatever the God of Abraham designs shall be done. The great and generous Christian people, who occupy much of the land of those natives, and who are on the ground of their continent, and hence are the best prepared to meliorate their condition, and bring them to the knowledge and order of the God of Israel, must of course be the people to whom this work is assigned. This one consideration would do much toward the decision of our question, Who is the nation addressed?

6. Various things are found in the predictions of the restoration of God's ancient people, which strikingly accord with the idea of a great branch of them being recovered from this land, and by the agency of the people of our states. A few of these shall be noted.

In the thirtieth and thirty-first chapters of Jeremiah, the prophet treats of the united restoration of Judah and Israel. These chapters were written about one hundred and twenty years after the expulsion of the ten tribes.

And in relation to the ten tribes, they have never yet had even a primary accomplishment or any degree of fulfilment. The restoration there predicted is to be in "the latter days;" chap. xxx. 24; and at the time near the battle of the great day; see verses 6-8, 23, 24.

Much of the substance of these chapters is appropriated to the ten tribes of Israel; though Judah is expressly to be restored with them. Of the former, (having then been outcast for an hundred and twenty years,) God says; chap. xxxi. 20; "Is Ephraim my dear son? Is he a pleasant child? For since I spake against him, (or expelled him from Canaan,) I do earnestly remember him still; therefore my bowels are troubled for him; I will surely have mercy upon him, saith the Lord." The next verse invites and predicts his final restoration. These yearnings of the divine compassion for Ephraim (one noted name of the ten tribes) are the immediate precursor of his restoration. "I will surely have mercy upon him, saith the Lord. Set them up way-marks, make thee high heaps, set thine heart toward the high-way -turn again, O virgin of Israel; turn again to these thy cities."

"I will again be the God of all the families of Israel; and they shall be my people." "For lo, the days come, saith the Lord, that I will bring again the captivity of my people Israel and Judah; and I will cause them to return to the land that I gave to their fathers, and they shall possess it." "Fear thou not, O my servant, Jacob, saith the Lord; neither be dismayed, O Israel; for lo, I will save thee from afar." "Behold, I will bring them from the north country, and gather them from the coasts of the earth." In this country "afar" off, these "coasts of the earth," they had been in an outcast state. "Because they called thee an outcast, saying; "This is Zion, whom no man seeketh after." (For more than 2000 years none sought after the ten tribes.) These ideas strikingly accord with their having been outcasts from the known world, in America. This might with singular propriety be called the land afar off, and the coasts of the earth.

In the same connexion, when God promises to gather them "from the coasts of the earth," and says, "they shall come with weeping and with supplication; for I am a father to Israel, and Ephraim is my first born; he adds; "Hear the word of the Lord, O ye nations, and declare it in the isles afar off, and say, He that scattered Israel will gather him, and keep him as the shepherd doth his flock." "Isles afar off!" "Isles in the Hebrew language, signify any lands, ever so extensive, away over great waters. Where can these "isles afar off," (these "coasts of the earth," here addressed by God in relation to the restoration of his outcast yet beloved Ephraim,) where can they be so naturally found as in America?

In Jer. xvi. 14, 15, 16. God is predicting the restoration of Israel in the last days. "Therefore behold, the days come, saith the Lord, that it shall no more be said, The Lord liveth that brought up the children of Israel out of Egypt, but the Lord liveth that brought up the children of Israel from the land of the north, and from all the lands whither he had driven them; and I will bring them again into their land that I gave unto their fathers."

Here is the greatness of their restoration. In the next verse follows the manner of it. "Behold, I will send for many fishers, saith the Lord, and they shall fish them; and after will I send for many hunters, and they shall hunt them from every mountain, and from every hill, and out of the holes of the rocks." Here is a most striking description of Israel's being recovered from a great wilderness like the sea; and from the hills, mountains, and rocks of the vast wilds of America. The description seems well to accord with their being sought in a savage state among such wilds, mountains and rocks, as the wilds of our continent present; especially the Rocky mountains, in the western regions of North America. The first missionaries fish them from the plains of the continent. Afterward missionary hunters are sent to rocky mountains and hills, more remote and savage. This prediction accords probably with no other country and its inhabitants so well, as with the wilds and natives of America. The coincidence with these seems perfect.

In other prophets the same things are found. In Isai. xliii. God promises this same restoration of Israel. "But now, thus saith the Lord, that created thee, O Jacob, and he that formed thee, O Israel; Fear not, for I have redeemed thee, I have called thee by thy name; thou art mine. When thou passest through the waters, I will be with thee. I have loved thee with an everlasting love; therefore will I give men for thee, and people for thy life. Fear not, for I am with thee. I will bring thy seed from the east, and gather thee from the west: I will say to the north, Give up; and to the south, Keep not back; bring my sons from far, and my daughters from the ends of the earth." "Thus saith the Lord, who maketh a way in the sea, and a path in the mighty waters; Behold, I will do a new thing; now it shall spring forth; shall ye not know it? I will even make a way in the wilderness and rivers in the desert." In Isai. xi. is this wonderful restoration. Ephraim and Judah are both restored, the one from his "dispersed," the other from his "outcast" state; and their mutual envies are forever healed. And the places from which they are recovered are noted; among which are "the isles of the sea;" or lands away over the sea, and "the four corners of the earth." Certainly then, from America!

This surely is one of the four corners of the earth. Of such a land away over sea, it is predicted, Isai. lx. 9; "Surely the isles shall wait for me, and the ships of Tarshish first, (or a power expert in navigation,) to bring my sons from far."

In Zechariah's prophecy is the same thing. This prophet was sent to encourage in the rebuilding of Jerusalem and the temple soon after the return from Babylon. As this return was to exhibit a primary fulfilment of the many prophecies of the restoration of the Hebrews, which are clearly to have their ultimate accomplishment in their restoration just anterior to the Millennium; so Zechariah clearly predicted the latter event, and said various things peculiar to it. Chap. ii. 6; "Ho, ho, come forth and flee from the land of the north, saith the Lord; for I have spread you abroad as the four winds of heaven, saith the Lord." This must allude to the great dispersion of Judah, and outcast state of Israel, which strewed them over the face of the earth; and could not have been fulfilled in the Babylonish captivity, which did not disperse them to all points of the compass. Verse 8; "For thus saith the Lord of hosts; After the glory hath he sent me unto the nations, which spoiled you." This must be the same with the various predictions which speak of the battle of the great day as a display of God's glory; and which speak of a subsequent going forth of missionaries (probably Jewish) to convert the nations where the Hebrews had resided. See Isai. lxvi. 18-21, &c. Verses 10, 11; "Sing and rejoice, O daughters of Zion; for lo, I come, and I will dwell in the midst of thee, saith the Lord. And many nations shall be joined to the Lord in that day, and shall be my people; and I will dwell in the midst of thee." - Many nations were not joined to the Jews upon their return from Babylon.

Nothing of this prediction then took place. It predicted an event still future, to be accomplished upon the restoration of the Hebrews to Palestine. The prophet then says, verse 13; "Be silent, O all flesh, before the Lord; for he is raised up out of his holy habitation." This verse perfectly accords with the numerous predictions of the battle of the great day, nearly associated with the final restoration of the Jews. But it received not its fulfilment in the days of Zechariah.

In chapter viii. are predictions of the same final restoration of that people. After predicting God's great jealousy and fury in behalf of his people, he says; "I am returned unto Zion, and will dwell in the midst of Jerusalem; and Jerusalem shall be called a city of truth, and the mountain of the Lord of hosts, the holy mountain." It then follows, verse 7; "Thus saith the Lord of hosts; Behold, I will save my people from the east country, and from the west country." By the west country here, we must suppose it meant America. None were saved from any west country, at the time of the restoration from Babylon. This shows then, that the thing predicted was distinct from, and future of that event. In the original, and in the margin of the great bible, the phrase is; "from the country of the going down of the sun." The going down of the sun from Palestine is over America. And as God had said in a passage just quoted from this prophet, "For I have spread you abroad as the four winds of heaven;" so America must probably be included in this description of their being spread abroad. To decide more clearly that the ultimate events here predicted are still future, the Most High says in this 8th chapter, verse 13; "And it shall come to pass that as ye were a curse among the heathen, O house of Judah, and house of Israel; so will I save you, and ye shall be a blessing." Here is the express restoration of the house of Israel, with that of Judah. But the "house of Israel" were not restored with the "house of Judah" when the latter returned from Babylon; nor have they at any time since been restored. The event then is clearly future, and was distinct and distant from any ancient restoration. It was to take place after a long and noted scattering of that people to the four winds! and their being viewed as a "curse" there by the nations. If they were to be "spread abroad as the four winds," and thence recovered, and recovered from the "coasts of the earth," and "isles afar off," and "from the west;" this surely is not unfavorable to the idea of Israel's being found in the wilds of America.

In Zech. x. 6-9, is the same event; and Ephraim is by name saved from "far countries." "And I will strengthen the house of Judah, and will save the house of Joseph, and I will bring them again to place them; for I have mercy upon them; and they shall be as though I had not cast them off; for I am the Lord their God, and will hear them. And they of Ephraim shall be like a mighty man, and their heart shall rejoice as through wine; yea, their children shall see it, and be glad; their heart shall rejoice in the Lord. I will hiss for them, and gather them; for I have redeemed them and they shall increase as they have increased. And I will save them among the people; and they shall remember me in far countries; and they shall live with their children, and turn again." "I will hiss for them." God is represented as hissing for a people, only in two texts beside this; Isai. v. 26, and vii. 18; in both of which passages, the hiss was to call distant heathen. God's hissing, in this passage then, to gather the children of Ephraim in the last days, seems to indicate his providentially calling them from a distant heathen state! And it is a mode of calling which perfectly symbolizes with the alls of American natives, a shrill significant whistling.

Such promises of the restoration of Israel from far countries, from the west or the going down of the sun, from the coasts of the earth, from the ends of the earth, from isles afar, their being brought in ships from far, making their way in the sea, their path in the mighty waters; these expressions certainly well accord with the ten tribes being brought from America. And such passages imply an agency by which such a restoration shall be effected. Where shall such an agency be so naturally found, as among a great Christian people, providentially planted on the very ground occupied by the outcast tribes of Israel in their long exilement; and who are so happily remote from the bloody scenes of Europe in the last days, as to have leisure for the important business assigned?

Surely then this business would be assigned, either tacitly or expressly, to our nation. At this conclusion we safely arrive, reasoning a priori. The circumstances of the case enforce it. And we might expect so interesting a duty, relative to an event on which the prophecies so abundantly rest, would not be left to uncertain deductions, but would be expressly enjoined.

We may then open the prophetic scriptures with some good degree of confidence, that the assignment of such a task is somewhere to be found.

And where so natural to be found as in the prophecy of Isaiah? He is the most evangelical prophet; and treats largely upon the restoration of his brethren.

The expulsion of Israel is supposed to have taken place 725 years before Christ. Isaiah is supposed to have begun his ministry about the year 760 before Christ; and 35 years before the expulsion. He lived then, it appears, to see the expulsion of the ten tribes. And his pious heart must have been deeply affected with the event. His prophecy was "in the days Uzziah, Jotham, Ahaz, and Hezekiah, kings of Judah." But in 2 Kings, xvii.

1; we learn that "in the twelfth year of Ahaz, Hoshea began to reign over Samaria." And in verse 9 we are assured; "In the ninth year of Hoshea, the king of Assyria took Samaria, and carried Israel away into Assyria, and placed them in Halah, and in Habor by the river of Gozen, and in the cities (or territories) of the Medes." This event then, must have been in the days of Isaiah. In Isai. xxxvi. 19, where Rabshakah is insulting the officers of Hezekiah, he says, "Where are the gods of Hamah, and Arpad? Where are the gods of Sepharvaim? Have they delivered Samaria out of my hand?" Here it seems Samaria, or Israel, had already fallen. Accordingly Isaiah laments, chap. v. 13; "Therefore my people are gone into captivity, because they have no knowledge."

There is one passage which seems to place the captivity of Israel just subsequent to the prophecy of this prophet, Isai. vii. 8, where Jerusalem was invaded by a coalition of the king of Syria and the king of Israel; -Isaiah, to show that this joint effort against the Jews should not prevail, predicted "within threescore and five years shall Ephraim be broken that it be not a people." But it seems from the passages just quoted, that the main body of Israel were gone before this period, or the end of sixty-five years. This prediction then, must allude to a finishing scene, which should sweep away even the gleanings of the nation of Israel.

Hence Scott says upon the passage; "It is computed to have been sixty-five years from this prediction to the time that Esarhaddon carried away the remains of the Israelites." The main body then, it seems, had been gone before, and were swept away in the days of Isaiah. This must have most deeply affected his pious heart. And it is natural to view him revolving in his anxious mind the place of their long exilement; and delighted with a view of their final restoration.

Behold this man of God, then, wrapt in the visions of the Almighty, casting an eye of faith down the lapse of time to the days of the final restoration of his long rejected brethren. He finds presented in vision, away over the Mediterranean, and the Atlantic, far in the west, or going down of the sun, the continent of their long banishment. He also beholds in vision a great nation arising there in the last days; a land of freedom and religion. He hears the whisper of the Spirit of inspiration, directing him to address that far sequestered and happy land, and call their attention to the final restoration of his people. Isaiah xviii. verse 1; "Ho, land shadowing with wings, which is beyond the rivers of Ethiopia." Our translators render this address, "Wo to the land." - But this is manifestly incorrect, as the best expositors agree. The Hebrew particle here translated Wo to, is a particle of friendly calling, as well as of denouncing. And the connexion in any given place must decide which rendering shall be given. In this place, the whole connexion and sense decide, that the word is here a friendly call, or address; as in this passage; "Ho every one that thirsteth, come ye to the waters."

The land addressed, lies "beyond the rivers of Ethiopia." It is agreed that these rivers mean the mouths of the Nile, which enter from Egypt into the south side of the Mediterranean. This probably was the farthest boundary in that direction then known to the Jews. And no doubt it was the most noted of any in that point of compass. When a landscape of a western continent then, was presented in vision to the prophet precisely in that course, he would naturally fix upon the place most notable and farthest distant, by which to describe the direction of this region of the world.

It is then as though the prophet had said; Thou land beheld in vision away over the mouths of the Nile. Where would such a line strike? It would glance over the northern edge of the States of Barbary. But could the friendly address to a people of the last days, light on those barbarous Mohammedan shores? Surely not. No land "shadowing with wings," or that would aid the restoration of the Hebrews, is found in those horrid regions. No; the point of compass and the address must have been designed for a new world, seen in that direction. This address of Heaven must be to our western continent; or to a hospitable people found here. The prophetic eye glanced beyond all lands then known; and hence no land is named. It must have been a land over the Mediterranean and the Atlantic.

Thou land "shadowing with wings." The above direction lands the prophetic vision at the point of the western continent, where the two great wings of North and South America meet, as at the body of a great eagle. This at first might furnish the prophetic imagery of a land "shadowing with wings." As though the inspiring Spirit had whispered; The continent of those two great wings shall be found at last most interesting in relation to your Hebrew brethren.

And those two great wings shall prove but an emblem of a great nation then on that continent; far sequestered from the seat of anti-christ, and of tyranny and blood; and whose asylum for equal rights, liberty, and religion, shall be well represented by such a national coat of arms, -the protecting wings of a great eagle; which nation in yonder setting of the sun, (when in the last days, judgments shall be thundering through the nations of the eastern continent,) shall be found a realm of peaceful protection to all who fly from the abodes of despotism to its peaceful retreat; even as an eagle protects her nest from all harm.

Yea, a land that, when all other lands shall be found to have trampled on the Jews, shall be found to have protecting wings for them, free from such cruelty, and ready to aid them.

Verse 2; "Who sendeth ambassadors by the sea, even in vessels of bulrushes upon the face of the waters." It is to be supposed that a great difficulty would at once present itself to the prophet's view, when beholding in vision this western continent, over the mighty waters of the Mediterranean, and the Atlantic, and about to be called to restore his people. What could be done across such mighty waters? The difficulty at once vanishes, by the prophet's being ascertained of this characteristic of the people addressed. They would be most expert in navigation. They could traverse the Atlantic and Mediterranean, and be able to send missionaries to Jerusalem, or to the ends of the earth, in those last days, or convey the Hebrews from one continent to another, with an expedition similar to that with which the Nile (beyond which this new world is beheld) used to be navigated with the skiffs made of the bulrush, or the rind of the papyrus. [Our states may claim the characteristic of expert navigation, equal at least to any people on earth. Consider our steamboat navigation, and such accounts as the following; found in Niles "Register of March 22, 1823. "Baltimore vessels, -The brig Thessalian arrived at Baltimore on Saturday evening last, in 79 days from Lima, and 24 from the sight of the city of Pernambuco, in Brazil; a distance of 12,000 miles; averaging siz and a quarter miles every hour of her passage. The vessel was, less than eight months ago, on the stocks in this city."]

Verse 2, concluded. "Saying, go ye swift messengers, to a nation scattered and peeled, to a people terrible from the beginning hitherto; a nation meted out and trodden down, whose land the rivers have spoiled." "Saying," before the command Go, is interpolated in our translation, and destroys the sense; as though the nation said this to her swift messengers; whereas it is what God says to the nation addressed. q.d. Come, thou protecting nation; I have a great business for you. Collect and restore my ancient people; that nation whose ancient history has been so remarkable and terrible; that nation so long dispersed, robbed, and insulted, in the people of the Jews; and so long outcast in the ten tribes; that people of line line, (as in the Hebrew, and in the margin of the great bible;) or, whose only hope to find their ancient inheritance must be in the line of divine promise, or the entail of the covenant. [If this characteristic allude to this people in their dispersed state, as do the other characteristics here connected with it, it must be construed, as the Hebrew well admits, as their being subjected to great terror. This has been the fact. And this well accords with ancient predictions relative to them. Lev. xxvi 16 "I will even appoint over you terror, consumption, and the burning ague, that shall consume the eyes, and cause sorrow of heart" Deut. xxviii 37 And thou shalt become an astonishment, a proverb, and a byword among all nations whither the Lord shall lead thee." The Jews during their dispersion, having been a people worn down with perpetual terrors. But they were terrible to inimical nations from ancient date. The text may allude to either, or both of these characteristics.] As the land addressed is described as away over the mouths of the Nile; so various characteristics in the address are suggested from thoughts associated with that river, and the people on its banks; as the bulrush vessel just noted; and here the measuring line. The river Nile periodically overflowed its banks, and swept away the boundaries of every man's inheritance on its interval. Every man, then, had to depend on a noted line, to measure anew and find his land. So the Hebrews, having by their sins, and expulsion from Canaan, and from the covenant of Abraham, lost all the visible boundaries of their inheritance, have no ground of hope of regaining their standing either in Palestine, or in the covenant of grace, but the line of the mere and sovereign promise of God, for their restoration. The word is doubled, line, line; a mere Hebraism, to form a superlative. As peace, peace, means perfect peace. -Isai. xxvi. 3; and as good, good, means the best; so line, line, means superlatively of line, or altogether dependent on the mere promise of God. That the allusion is to the event noted is evident from what follows: "Whose land the rivers have spoiled." Whose inheritance (in the holy Land) has been torn from them, and overrun by neighbouring hostile nations, often symbolized by rivers, even as the lands by the sides of the Nile often had their boundaries swept away by the overflowings of that river. Thus the Romans first, then the Persians, the Saracens, the Egyptians, and the Turks, have overflowed and possessed the Holy Land. But the line of divine promise will restore it to the Hebrews. [Much perplexity has rested on the passage, a nation of line, line, till the above solution occurred to mind. With this I am fully satisfied. It is natural, as the bulrush navigation. It agrees with facts, and is confirmed by the clause following; "whose land the rivers have spoiled." Here the long occupancy of their beloved Canaan by hostile invading nations, is noted by a figure, alluding to the overflowing of the Nile; -which confirms the idea that the phrase, "a nation of line, line," alludes to the same overflowing of the Nile, sweeping away boundaries and rendering the use of the line necessary to ascertain every man's bounds.]

Go thou protecting people; shadow with thy wings my ancient family, as though the Most High should say. For thus it is written; "Surely the isles shall wait for me, (or lands away over sea from Palestine,) and the ships of Tarshish first, (a people expert in navigation,) to bring my sons from far." A far distant land over sea shall be engaged in this work.

Verse 3. "All ye inhabitants of the world, and dwellers on the earth, see ye when he lifteth up the ensign on the mountains, and when he bloweth a trumpet, hear ye." After the land shadowing with wings is under way in fulfilment of the divine requirement; an apostrophe is made by the Most High to all nations, to stand and behold the banner of salvation now erected for his ancient people; and to hear the great gospel trumpet, the blessed Jubilee, now to be blown for their collection and their freedom.

The ancient silver trumpets in Israel collected their solemn assemblies.

And the same trumpets. with joyful and peculiar blasts, ushered in the Jubilee morn, and loosed every bond slave of the Hebrews. And the antitype of the event shall now be accomplished.

This standard of salvation at that period, is a notable event in the prophets. See Isai. xi. 12, where God sets his hand a second time to gather his Hebrew family from all nations and regions beyond sea; doubtless from America, as well as other nations; and it is promised, "He shall set up an ensign for the nations, and shall assemble the outcasts of Israel, and gather together the dispersed of Judah from the four corners of the earth." If from the four corners of the earth, then surely from America! In this passage are the descriptive situations from which the two great branches of the Hebrews are recovered; Judah from being dispersed among the nations; and Israel from being outcast from the nations; thrown out of sight of the social world; precisely as they have been in the wilds of America for more than two thousand years, provided our natives are of Israel.

Verse 4. "For so the Lord said unto me, I will take my rest, and I will consider my dwelling place like a clear heat upon herbs, and like a cloud of dew in the heat of harvest." The event and the figures in this passage are best explained by those found in synchronical passages, or prophecies alluding to the same event. And according to them, it is as though the Most High should say; I am now about to renew my ancient dwelling place. I will again have a fixed habitation in Canaan; as Zech. i. 16: "Thus saith the Lord, I am again returned to Jerusalem with mercies; my house shall be built in it;" and viii. 3; "Thus saith the Lord, I am returned unto Zion, and will dwell in the midst of Jerusalem." And the event shall be as "life from the dead" to the nations; Rom xi. 15. Therefore, ye Gentile lands, now behold. I will now be to my ancient heritage like the genial heat of the sun to promote vegetation after the death of winter; as Isai. xxvi. 19, "Thy dew is as the dew of herbs," which in the spring shall vegetate. "And I will be like the fertile cooling cloud in the sultry heat of harvest." The Hebrews shall now become "as the tender grass springing out of the earth, by the clear shining after rain; 2 Sam. xxiii. 4. Yes; "I will be as the dew unto Israel; he shall grow as the lily, and cast forth his roots as Lebanon. His branches shall spread, and his beauty shall be as the olive tree, and his smell as Lebanon; Hos. xiv. 5, 6. The nations shall behold this fulfilment of divine grace to Israel, and shall find instruments raised up adequate to the work.

But a tremendous scene to the anti-christian world shall be found intimately connected.

Verse 5. "For afore the harvest, when the bud is perfect, and the sour grape is ripening in the flower, he shall both cut off the sprigs with pruning hooks, and take away and cut down the branches." Or near the fulfilment of this event of the last days, a vast scene is to be accomplished. Prophetic notice is ever given relative to that period, that the salvation of the friends of Zion shall be ushered in with a proportionable destruction to her enemies. The harvest and vintage of divine wrath, called "the battle of that great day of God Almighty," must be accomplished; and at the time of the restoration of the Hebrews, that tremendous event shall be at the doors. As in the natural vineyard, when the blossom is succeeded by the swelled pulp, which soon reaches the size of the full grape, indicating that the vintage is near; so at the time of the service here divinely demanded, wickedness shall have blossomed; pride shall have budded in anti-christian realms. The sour grapes of their tyranny, violence, and licentiousness, will be found to be arriving at their growth; indicating that the time for the casting of the vine of the earth into the wine press of the wrath of God, is just at hand.

Verse 6. "They shall be left together unto the fowls of the mountains, and the beasts of the earth; and the fowls shall summer upon them, and the beasts of the earth shall winter upon them." Soon the most prominent branches of the anti-christian vine of the earth, shall be collected and trodden upon the mountains of Israel, in the noted scene of Armageddon; Rev. xvi. 16. The passage noted in Ezek. xxxix. 17-20, (at the time of the slaughter of Gog and his bands, and which is given as an illustration of the text,) shall then be accomplished. "And thou son of man, thus saith the Lord God, speak unto every feathered fowl, and to every beast of the field, Assemble yourselves, and come; gather yourselves on every side to my sacrifice that I do sacrifice for you, even a great sacrifice upon the mountains of Israel, that ye may eat flesh, and drink blood. Ye shall eat the flesh of the mighty, and drink the blood of the princes of the earth; of rams, of lambs, and of goats, of bullocks, all of them fatlings of Bashan. And ye shall eat fat till ye be full, and drink blood till ye be drunken, of my sacrifice which I have sacrificed for you. Thus ye shall be filled at my table with horses and chariots, with mighty men, and with all men of war, saith the Lord God." Also the further illustration of the same, Rev. xix. 17, 18; "And I saw an angel standing in the sun; and he cried with a loud voice, saying to all the fowls that fly in the midst of heaven, Come and gather yourselves together unto the supper of the great God; That ye may eat the flesh of kings and the flesh of captains, and the flesh of mighty men, and the flesh of horses, and of them that sit on them, and the flesh of all men, both free and bond, both small and great."

Verse 7. "At that time shall the present be brought unto the Lord of hosts of a people scattered and peeled, and from a people terrible from the beginning hitherto; a nation meted out and trodden under foot, whose land the rivers have spoiled, to the place of the name of the Lord of hosts, the Mount Zion." Just at that period of the world, the present which I claim of you shall be brought to the Lord of hosts, of that scattered and outcast people; of that people so terrible in ancient times to their enemies by the presence and power of their God with them; that people of "line, line," or depending solely on the measuring line of promise, or the entail of the covenant, found in the sacred oracles, for their restoration to their ancient inheritance in the church of God, and in the promised land; inasmuch as the boundaries of their inheritance in both these respects have long since been swept away. A present of this people must be brought by you, sequestered land shadowing with wings, unto the place of the name of the Lord of hosts, the Mount Zion.

Ye friends of God in the land addressed; can you read this prophetic direction of the ancient prophet Isaiah, without having your hearts burn within you? Surely you cannot, if you can view it as an address of the Most High to you. God here exalts you, in the last days, the age of terror and blood, as high as the standard to be raised for the collection of the seed of Abraham; "on the mountains." Nor is this the only passage, in which this your exaltation is recognized. See the same honour alluded to, in Zeph. iii. 10. -There, nearly connected with the battle of the great day of God, in which he there asserts he "will gather the nations, and assemble the kingdoms, to pour upon them his indignation, even all his fierce anger, and all the earth shall be devoured with the fire of his jealousy;" and that he will then "turn to the people a pure language, that they may all call upon the name of the Lord, and serve him with one consent;" he informs, as in the address in Isaiah; "From beyond the rivers of Ethiopia, my suppliants (or a people who are my worshippers,) shall bring mine offering, even the daughter of my dispersed," (as the verse should be read). Here is the same people, away in the same direction, over the mouths of the Nile, who are called God's suppliants, and who, in those days of vengeance, are to bring their offering to God, consisting of the descendants of his ancient people.If these views be correct, Christians in our land may well bless God that it is their happy lot to live in this land shadowing with wings; this protecting realm, an asylum of liberty and religion; a land so distant from the seat of anti-christ and of the judgments to be thundered down on old corrupt establishments in the last days. And their devout gratitude to Heaven ought to rise, for the blessing of having their existence so near the period alluded to in this sublime prediction, when this land of liberty is beginning to feel her distinguishing immunities compared with the establishments of tyranny and corruption in the old continent. We may rejoice to have our earthly lot with a people of whom such honourable mention is made by the prophetic spirit of old; and to whom so noble a work is assigned. Our children coming upon the stage may live to see the meaning and fulfilment of this prophetic chapter, which is most rich in sentiment, and which will not fail of accomplishment.

The great argument found in this sacred address, to induce to a compliance with the duty demanded, is the terrors of the days of vengeance on eastern corrupt nations; which seems to imply some good degree of exemption in our wn case, and our happy leisure for the business assigned. Heaven will show despotic nations, and old corrupt empires, the difference between them, and a land "shadowing with wings;" a happy asylum of liberty and religion in the west.

Can a motive be wanting to induce us to maintain the character implied in this address, and to obey the injunction of Heaven here urged upon us?

Should any say, what can be done? Let this be the reply; be devoutly disposed and prepared to obey; and Heaven will, in due time, make the duty plain. By prayer, contributions, and your influence, be prepared to aid every attempt for the conversion of the Jews and Israel; and God will be his own interpreter, and will make the duty plain.

A leading step has already been taken in a Jerusalem mission. This may prove, in relation to a fulfilment of our text, a cloud like a man's hand, which shall afford a sound of great rain; and shall water the hills of ancient Zion. How great effects spring from little causes! A purling stream from the threshold of the sanctuary, soon rises to the ankles, to the knees, to the loins, and to an unfordable river, which heals the Dead sea; Ezek. xlvii. Already has the bulrush vessel slipped from the "land shadowing with wings," across the mighty waters, over which the prophetic eye glanced; over the Atlantic and the Mediterranean, by the mouths of the "rivers of Ethiopia," and has landed her "ambassadors," for a Jerusalem mission! Bless the Lord, O children of Abraham, for this ray of light from the land of the going down of the sun. This may shed an incipient lustre on the noted passage in our evangelical prophet. It may prove to the children of Abraham, in these days of signal phenomena, a morning rising in the west to break their long and dreadful night! Let us, dear countrymen, second this attempt with our intercessions, our contributions, and our influence. May all societies formed in behalf of the Jews, and all solicitations in their favour, meet our most fervent patronage. And God will not fail of fulfiling by us his gracious designs. The blessed business will be brought within our reach, and will be accomplished.

The ten tribes, as well as the Jews, belong to the "nation scattered and peeled, and terrible from the beginning." Yes, the stick of Ephraim is to become one in the hand of the prophet, with the stick of the Jews; Ezek. xxxvii. 15. -If it is a fact, that the aborigines of this "land shadowing with wings," are the tribes of Israel; we perceive at once what can be done to fulfil the noted demand of God, as it relates to them. -And all who fear God will leap for joy, that as the Jerusalem mission is already under way; so missions to these tribes of Israel are already under way!

　　Should we find ample conviction that our natives are of the lost tribes of the house of Israel, and that the address noted is directed to us; we may in the light of this address, and of evangelical considerations connected with it, imagine ourselves as though seated in the audience of the prophet Isaiah; - may imagine him sighing at the long and dreadful exilement of his brethren of Israel; - and uttering the following sentiments of the holy prophetic spirit; "Ho thou nation of the last days, shadowing with thy wings of liberty and peace; pity, instruct, and save my ancient people and brethren; especially that outcast branch of them, who were the natives of your soil. Pity that degraded remnant of a nation so terrible in ancient times, but who have been now so long wretched. Bring a present of them, ye worshippers of Jehovah, to the God of Abraham. Give not sleep to your eyes, till a house be builded to your God, from those ancient and venerable materials. -Were not your fathers sent into that far distant world, not only to be (in their posterity) built up a great protecting nation; but also to be the instruments of gathering, or recovering the miserable remnant of my outcasts there, in the last days? [The duty of christianizing the natives of our land, even be they from whatever origin, is enforced from every evangelical consideration. Rev. Mayhew accordingly remarks; "as the conversion of the heathen (in this land) was from the first one professed aim of our forefathers in settling New England; so almost all the royal charters, grants, letters patent, and acts of government in England relative to this country, have made mention of, and encouraged, yea enjoined upon settlers, the prosecution of this pious design." The same author notes in the new charter granted by William and Mary to Massachusetts, as express recognition of this object, viz "to win the Indians to the knowledge and obedience of the only God and Saviour of men." The same is expressly recognized in the charter granted by king Charled II to William Penn of Pennsylvania. How sadly has the object been neglected and forgotten! If our natives be indeed from the tribes of Israel, American Christians may well feel, that one great object of their inheritance here, is, that they may have a primary agency in restoring those "lost sheep of the house of Israel." Those Hebrews first occupied the blessing of the covenant under the old and dark dispensation. Then the Christian Gentiles came into possession of the blessings of this covenant, under its last, the Christian dispensation. Noah, more than four thousand years ago, in prophetic rhapsody, uttered the following prediction. Gen. ix 27; "God shall enlarge Japeth; (i.e. the Gentiles) and he shall dwell in the tents of Shem," (or of the Hebrews.) But this event is only until the fulness of the Gentiles be come in; Rom. xi 25. Then shall the Hebrews again take their place, as God's first born. (Jer. xxxi 20, 21; Zech. i 16; Isai lx.) Let us be active in restoring their long lost blessing.]

Rejoice, then, ye distinguished people in your birth-right, and engage in the work by Heaven assigned. Let not those tribes of my ancient people, whom I have borne as on eagles" wings for so many ages; let them not become extinct before your eyes; let them no longer roam in savage barbarism and death! My bowels yearn for Ephraim, my first born." "For since I spake against him, I do earnestly remember him still." "I have seen his ways, and will heal him. I will restore peace to him, and to his mourners; peace in the renewal of my covenant. I will again bear him on eagles" wings, and bring him to myself. For you, (my suppliants in the west,) this honour is reserved;" Zeph. iii. 10. The wings of your continent have long borne him in his banishment. Let now the wings of your liberty, compassion, and blessed retreat, bear him from his dreary wilds to the temple of God.

Look at the origin of those degraded natives of your continent, and fly to their relief. -Send them the heralds of salvation. Send them the word, the bread of life. You received that book from the seed of Abraham. All your volume of salvation was written by the sons of Jacob. And by them it was transferred from Jerusalem to the lost heathen world, and to you; otherwise you had now been heathen, and eternally undone. Remember then your debt of gratitude to God's ancient people for the word of life.

Restore it to them, and thus double your own rich inheritance in its blessings. Learn them to read the book of grace. Learn them its history and their own. Teach them the story of their ancestors; the economy of Abraham, Isaac and Jacob. Sublimate their views above the savage pursuits of the forests. Elevate them above the wilds of barbarism and death, by showing them what has been done for their nation; and what is yet to be done by the God of their fathers, in the line of his promise. Teach them their ancient history; their former blessings; their being cast away; the occasion of it, and the promises of their return. Tell them the time draws near, and they must now return to the God of their salvation. Tell them their return is to be as life from the dead to the Gentile nations. Tell them what their ancient fathers the prophets were inspired to predict in their behalf; and the charge here given for their restoration. Assure them this talk of an ancient prophet, is for them, and they must listen to it and obey it. That the Great Spirit above the clouds now calls them by you to come and receive his grace by Christ the true star from Jacob, the Shiloh who has come, and to whom the people must be gathered. Inform them that by embracing this true seed of Abraham, you and multitudes of other Gentiles, have become the children of that ancient patriarch; and now they must come back as your brothers in the Lord. Unfold to them their superlative line of the entail of the covenant; that "as touching this election, 'they are beloved for the fathers" sakes;" that they were for their sins excluded for this long period, until the fulness of the Gentiles be come in, and so all Israel shall be saved.

Go, thou nation highly distinguished in the last days; save the remnant of my people. -Bring me a present of them "to the place of the name of the Lord of hosts, the Mount Zion."

Note: -Since publishing the first edition of the View of the Hebrews, the writer has for the first time obtained sight of an exposition upon this chapter of Isaiah by Dr. McDonald, and feels himself strengthened in a persuasion of the correctness of applying this address of the prophet to America. As the two expositions are before the public, the writer forbears to make any remarks, except upon one idea. Dr. McDonald, upon the bulrush navigation of the nation addressed, conceives that it may have, perhaps, considerable reference to the boat and canoe navigation of internal streams. And observing that "the central and eastern regions of Asia are generally supposed to be the present seats of Israel's dispersion; what nation then of Christendom can convey with so much ease and expedition, as the Americans, their messengers to the shores of that vast and unexplored country? What nation is better qualified to search and to discover them in their unknown retreats? Sheltered in the capacious bosom of mountains, that reach the clouds, occupying the extensive sides of rivers rapid and broad, whose waves never felt the keel, and on whose banks a highway has never been stretched; to European missionaries their retreat would be inaccessible, without great expense of time and labour. But these obstacles oppose difficulties easily surmounted by the nation of the canoe. Bred with the paddle in their hand, and taught to construct vessels lighter than the bulrush, they can ascend every stream, wind round the foot of every mountain, and as circumstances require, they can carry their canoe, or be carried by it." Had this author been led to believe that the natives in the vast wilds of America are the ten tribes of Israel; and that it comes within the prescribed duty of the people addressed by the prophet, to recover these outcast tribes; he would have perceived the application he makes, to come with still greater force to the sons of America, in relation to their searching out the wild tenants of the forests in the west, and through the wilds of America. It is a fact, the bulrush navigation, or light boats and birch canoes, have been a powerful auxiliary to travellers among the Indians, in ascending and descending their streams, in coming at their villages, and winding round the feet of mountains, carrying their canoes, or being carried by them in turn, to learn the existence and the customs of the natives. And the same means must be pursued, (and have already in a measure been pursued,) in carrying to them the word of life, and blessings of civilization. While the writer of these sheets still believes the leading object in the allusion to the ancient bulrush navigation of the Nile, when addressing our land, is to fix our characteristic of expertness in the navigation of seas and oceans - "who sendeth messengers by the sea even in vessels of bulrushes" -yet he feels no difficulty in admitting that it also comprehends our great facilities in inland navigation; especially considering our astonishing recent improvements in canal navigation. The eye of the prophetic spirit might partially rest on this circumstance, in fixing this characteristic of the nation in the west, who was the subject of the message.

In relation to the American people having a favourable agency in meliorating the condition of the Jews, as well as the tribes of Israel, it appears the thought has struck the minds of some on the eastern continent, as well as the western. Consult the following:

Extract of a letter from Erasmus Hermanus Simon of Stockholm, to the Secretary of the American Meliorating Society, dated April 26, 1823.

"I am constrained to congratulate you, western Christians, on the glorious prospects which are before you. It has become evident to me, that the Lord reserves for the Christians of America the scriptural means of effectually benefitting the lost stock of Israel. Nothing can be conceived worse than the present state of religion over the continent (of Europe) in general.

And nothing so subversive of that little serious impression, which a month or two of superficial teaching may have made, than their being left to the danger which abounds on every hand in what are denominated places of Christian worship. The reception which proselytes with the best desires and characters meet with, is truly deplorable. The Society of Frankfort, had it not been for the American Meliorating Society, would have degenerated into a mere tract society, having constantly heard of the miseries which beset those proselytes whom they sent seeking for employment among Christians."

In another letter from the same place, the writer says; "I unite my voice of thanksgiving and praise to the Supreme Disposer of hearts, who has in this time of Israel's extremity, turned so many in America to undertake their neglected cause. Our souls are refreshed by the prospect which is held out, of a lodge in the wilderness for the wayfaring men of Israel, where they may hasten to escape from the storm and tempest. Happy country, which affords a refuge for Abraham's believing sons!"

The following is ascertained from ample authority; that in many of the old establishments of Europe, the convicted anxious Jew can obtain little or no evangelical instruction. Such an one applying to a professed minister of the reformed church, was informed, "that it was not necessary to his salvation to believe in the Divinity of Christ. It would be sufficient should he persevere in the duty of being a good member of society."

"To a minister in Wurtemburg, (one of the most religious parts of Germany) a young Israelite came for instruction. He said he found no consolation in the present state of Judaism, as an immortal being, guilty before God. And that he wished candidly to inquire into Christianity. The instructor said to him, (clapping him on the shoulder,) are you an honest man? and do you disturb nobody? If so; you need not give yourself any trouble about being saved; you are sure enough of that!" Must not these things operate as a thousand arguments on the people of our Christian land, and of our superior advantages, to aid the children of Abraham, from whom we have received the blessings of salvation, and who in their turn are in a perishing state, and are stretching out their hands, and directing their wishful eyes across the Atlantic to us, for a return of that same word of eternal life? May they here find a present asylum; and here be led to the "Balm of Gilead, the Physician there."

Conclusion

1. It becomes us to be deeply affected with the excommunication of the ancient people of God. In the temporary rejection of those two branches of the Hebrew nation, the truth is solemnly enforced, that the God of Zion is a God of government; and that he will be known by the judgments that he executeth. The casting out of the ten tribes for their impious idolatries, is full of instruction. The wonders God had done for them, and all their privileges in the land of promise, could not save, when they rejected the stated place of his worship, and united in the abominations of the open enemies of God. They should be excommunicated from the covenant, hurled from the promised land, and abandoned to a state of savage wretchedness, for two and a half millenaries. Their sin in those dark ages of the old dispensation was no trifle. Its consequence is held up as an awful warning to the world. It impresses the following language; "Know thou and see that it is an evil thing and bitter that thou hast forsaken the Lord." To that event people under evangelical privileges ought to turn their eyes, and take the solemn warning. The God of Abraham is a God of judgment; while blessed are all they that put their trust in him.

The judgments of Heaven on the Jews were still more dreadful. The Lord of that vineyard did indeed come in a day when they looked not for him, and in an hour when they were not aware; and did cut them asunder. He came and miserably destroyed those husbandmen, and burned up their cities, as he foretold. Upon their turning him off with hypocrisy and will worship, and rejecting the Saviour, the denunciation, "Cut it down; why cumbereth it the ground?" was fulfilled with unprecedented decision. Let all rejectors of Christ, behold and tremble. The Jews were confident in a fancied security, to the last. But an impious confidence can never save. It is but a dead calm before a fatal catastrophe. Such presumptuous leaning upon the Lord, and saying, "Is not the Lord among us? no evil shall come upon us;" was so far from saving, that it was a sure precursor of perdition, and of the coming of wrath upon them to the uttermost. Let gospel rejectors beware. "Behold, ye despisers, and wonder, and perish." "Let him that thinketh he standeth, take heed lest he fall."

2. How evident and rich is the entail of the covenant which will recover the two branches of the house of Israel! Truly they are "a nation of line, line" (Isai. xviii. 2, in the Hebrew, and margin of the great Bible.)

Though they be infidels, and rejected, and as touching the gospel are enemies for our sakes; yet as touching the election, (the entail of the covenant,) they are beloved for the fathers' sakes; Rom. xi. 28. -This entail insures their ingrafting again into their own olive tree, which shall be as life from the dead to the nations. This is the infallible hold upon them, which shall finally recover them again to Palestine, and to the covenant of their God. It is upon this covenant hold upon them, that the God of Abraham promises to take away their stony heart out of their flesh, and give them a heart of flesh; to sprinkle them with clean water, and to make them clean; to put his spirit within them and cause them to walk in his statutes, and make them keep his judgments and do them; Ezek. xxxvi. 24-27. It is upon this entail, that God thus engages to bring them in under his new covenant, or the Christian dispensation; that their children shall be as aforetimes, and their congregations established before him; and "that all who see them shall acknowledge they are the seed which the Lord hath blessed;" "that they are the seed of the blessed of the Lord, and their offspring with them." It will then be understood, that though blindness in part had happened to Israel, it was that the gentiles might take their place, and only till the fulness of the gentiles be come in; and then all Israel shall be saved. The Jewish church will thence be a kind of capital and model of the Christian world; see Isai. lx. and many other promises of the same tenor.

The entail of the covenant may be expected thenceforth to have its proper and perfect effect in the fulfilment of such promises as the following, which relate to that period; "I will pour my Spirit upon thy seed, and my blessing upon thine offspring; and they shall spring up as among the grass, as willows by the water courses;" Isai. xliv. 3, 4. "As for me, this is my covenant with them, saith the Lord. My spirit that is upon thee, and my words which I have put in thy mouth, shall not depart out of thy mouth, nor out of the mouth of thy seed, nor out of the mouth of thy seed's seed, saith the Lord, from henceforth and forever;" Isai. lix. 21. This will indeed bring a season of salvation to man.

3. On reading the prophetic scriptures relative to the restoration of the Hebrews, and the calls of Heaven to aid in the event; the question becomes interesting. What is first to be done

relative to this restoration? The first object, no doubt, must be, to christianize them, and wait the leadings of Providence relative to any further event. God will in due time, be (to all who are willing to wait on him) his own interpreter; and to such he will make the path of duty plain. In his own time and way, after his ancient people shall be duly instructed, and taught the Christian religion, God will open the door for the fulfilment of his designs relative to any local restoration; and will bring that part of them, whom he designs, to their ancient home. All the Jews did not return to Palestine from their seventy years captivity. Many chose to continue where they were planted in the east. Something of the same may be realized in the final restoration of Judah and Israel. A remnant only of the ten tribes is to return. This is clearly taught. Isai. x. 20-22: "And it shall come to pass in that day that the remnant of Israel, and such as are escaped of the house of Jacob, shall no more again stay upon him that smote them; but shall stay upon the Lord, the Holy One of Israel, in truth. The remnant shall return, even the remnant of Jacob, unto the Mighty God. For though the people of Israel be as the sand of the sea; yet a remnant of them shall return." Here the number restored is comparatively small; as Jer. iii. 14, upon the same event; "Turn, O backsliding children, saith the Lord; for I am married unto you; and I will take you one of a city (village) and two of a family, (tribe) and will bring you to Zion." One from an Indian village, and two from a tribe, would indeed be a small remnant. This proportion may here be proverbial; but certainly indicates that but a small number compared with the whole will return. A proportion of that nation will in due time be offered, to return to the land of their fathers, where they may form a kind of centre or capital to the cause of Christ on earth. Relative to many particulars of the event, the holy oracles are not express. They have strongly marked the outlines or leading facts of the restoration; and the unrevealed particulars, the events of Providence must unfold. That great numbers will return, there seems not room to doubt. But the actual proposition to return, will doubtless be a free-will offering of those whose hearts God shall incline. The first duty must be to recover them to the visible kingdom of Christ. To this our prayers, alms, and all due exertions must devoutly tend.

4. Viewing the aborigines of America as the outcast tribes of Israel; an interesting view is given of some prophetic passages, which appear nearly connected with their restoration.

In Isai. xl. 3, relative to this restoration of the ancient people of God, we read; "The voice of him that crieth in the wilderness; Prepare ye the way of the Lord; make straight in the desert a highway for our God." This received a primary and typical fulfilment in the ministry of John the Baptist, in the wilderness of Judea, to introduce Christ. Hence the passage was applied to him. But it was to receive its ultimate and most interesting fulfilment at a period connected with the commencement of the Millennium, when "the glory of the Lord shall be revealed, and all flesh shall see it together;" as the subsequent text decides. It is intimately connected with the restoration of the Hebrews; as appears in its context.

"Comfort ye, comfort ye, my people, saith your God. Speak ye comfortably to Jerusalem, (a name here put for all the Hebrew family, as it was their capital in the days of David and Solomon,) and cry unto her that her warfare is accomplished, that her iniquity is pardoned; for she hath received of the Lord's hand double for all her sins." Here is the final Hebrew restoration, after the time of their doubly long corrective rejection for their sins shall have expired. The voice in the wilderness then follows, as the great means of this restoration.

A wilderness has justly been considered as a symbol of a region of moral darkness and spiritual death. It has been considered as a symbol of the heathen world; and it is a striking emblem of it. And the emblem receives strength from the consideration, that it is in a sense literally true. The voice, which restores Israel, is heard in the vast wilderness of America, a literal wilderness of thousands of miles, where the dry bones of the outcasts of Israel have for thousands of years been scattered. The voice crying in the wilderness has a special appropriation to these Hebrews. As it had a kind of literal fulfilment in the preaching of the forerunner John, for a short time in the wilderness of Judea; so it is to have a kind of literal fulfilment, upon a much greater scale, in the missions, which shall recover the ten tribes from the vast wilderness of America.

Of the same period and event, the same evangelical prophet says, Isai. xxxv. 1. "The wilderness and the solitary place shall be glad for them; and the desert shall rejoice and blossom as the rose; it shall blossom abundantly and rejoice even with joy and singing. The glory of Lebanon shall be given unto it, and the excellency of Carmel and Sharon; they shall see the glory of the Lord and the excellency of our God." In such passages, while the perdiction [sic] is to have its mystical and full accomplishment in the conversion of the heathen world to God, the prophetic eye evidently rested with signal pleasure, on a literal restoration of his long lost brethren, as involved in the event, and as furnishing the ground of the figure. They will be literally, and the fulness of the Gentiles mystically, restored and brought to Zion. Is it not an uncommon thing for prophetic passages to receive a kind of literal fulfilment; while yet the passage most clearly looks in its ultimate and most important sense to mystical fulfilment. Take the following instances for illustration. In Isai. xxxv. 5 -predicting the blessed effects of the mission of Christ on earth- the prophet says; "Then the eyes of the blind shall be opened, and the ears of the deaf shall be unstopped, then shall the lame man leap as an hart, and the tongue of the dumb shall sing." This had a literal fulfilment in the miracles wrought by our Lord on earth. And yet its mystical import upon the souls of men is infinitely more interesting, and will be extensively fulfilled in the introduction of the Millennium. This stands connected with the wilderness and the solitary place being glad; and the desert rejoicing and blossoming as the rose; and is followed by the clause; "For in the wilderness shall waters break out, and streams in the desert." And as the one was prefaced by a literal fulfilment; the other may be accompanied with a kind of literal fulfilment.

Again; Zech. ix. 9; "Rejoice greatly, O daughter of Zion; shout, O daughter of Jerusalem; behold thy king cometh unto thee; he is just, and having salvation; lowly, and riding upon an ass, and upon a colt the foal of an ass." This stands connected with the time, "when (verse 1) the eyes of men, as all the tribes of Israel, shall be toward the Lord; and when (verse 10) the battle bow shall be cut off; and he shall speak peace unto the heathen; and his dominion shall be from sea even to sea, and from the river even to the ends of the earth." It stands connected with the battle of the great day, and the introduction of the Millennium; and is a striking emblem of the means used by Christ, (in the estimation of the scoffing infidel world,) to introduce his kingdom "by the foolishness of preaching" "not by might, nor by power; but by my spirit, saith the Lord of hosts." Yet even this must be preluded by a literal fulfilment, in the riding of Christ into Jerusalem. See Matt. xxi. 1; Zech. xi. 1. "Open thy doors, O Lebanon, that the fire may devour thy cedars." This is to have its ultimate accomplishment in the battle of the great day of God Almighty," of which the destruction of the temple and of Jerusalem was but a type. But this too must be prefaced with a literal accomplishment. Josephus, assuring us of the miraculous portents of the destruction of Jerusalem, says; "About the sixth hour of the night, the eastern gate of the temple was found to open without human assistance."

"It was secured (he adds) by iron bolts and bars that were let down into a large threshold consisting of one entire stone." The Jews considered this as a manifestation that their divine protection was fled." M. Johanan, directing his speech to the temple, said; I know thy destruction is at hand according to the prophecy of Zechariah, "Open thy doors, O Lebanon" (Scott.)

Thus mystical texts often have a kind of literal fulfilment. And accordingly the predictions of the restoration of Israel, in the last days, while they deliver them from a mystical wilderness of spiritual wretchedness, of ignorance and moral death; may at the same time redeem them from a vast literal wilderness! And the prediction of the former may be phrased from this very circumstance.

As the wilderness of Judea in a small degree rejoiced and blossomed as the rose, when John the Baptist performed his ministry in it; so the wilderness and solitary place of our vast continent, containing the lost tribes of the house of Israel, will, on a most enlarged scale, rejoice and blossom as the rose, when the long lost tribes shall be found there, and shall be gathered to Zion. The event in relation to these ancient heirs of the covenant, stated in the last verse of this chapter, will then receive a signal fulfilment; "And the redeemed of the Lord shall return and come to Zion with songs and everlasting joy upon their heads; they shall obtain joy and gladness, and sorrow and sighing shall flee away." Upon this final restoration of his brethren, this prophet exults in lofty strains. Several of the many of these strains shall be here inserted. Isai. xlix. "Listen, O isles, unto me; (or ye lands away over the sea) harken ye people from afar. I will make all my mountains a way; and my highway shall be exalted.

Behold, these shall come from far; and lo, these from the north, and from the west; and these from the land of Sinim. Sing. O heavens; and be joyful, O earth; and break forth into singing, O mountains; for the Lord hath comforted his people, and will have mercy upon his afflicted." Such texts have a special allusion to the lost tribes of the house of Israel. And their being called over mountains, and over seas, from the west, and from afar, receives an emphasis from the consideration of their being gathered from the vast wilds of America.

With the prophet Hosea, the rejection and recovery of the ten tribes are a great object. In, chapter 2d, their rejection, and the cause of it, are stated, and also a promise of their return.

God threatens to strip them naked, and "make them as a wilderness." "And I will visit upon her the days of Baalim, wherein she burned incense to them;" i.e. to Baalim, her false gods. This visiting upon her her idolatries was to be done in her subsequent outcast state, in which God there says; "she is not my wife, neither am I her husband." But he says, v. 14, "Therefore, behold, I will allure her, and bring her into the wilderness, and speak comfortably unto her. - And I will give her her vineyards from thence, and the valley of Achor for a door of hope; and she shall sing there as in the days of her youth, and as in the day when she came up out of the land of Egypt." Here is Israel's restoration; and it is from the wilderness, where long they had been planted during the period of their outcast state. In this wilderness God eventually speaks comfortably to them, and restores them, as he restored from Egypt. Here God gives them "they valley of Achor for a door of hope." The first encampment of the Hebrews in the valley of Achor, was to them a pledge in their eventual possession of the promised land, after the Lord had there turned from the fierceness of his wrath; Josh. vii. 26.

Upon the same event God says; Isai. xlii. 19, 20; "Behold, I will do a new thing; now it shall spring forth; shall ye not know it? I will even make a way in the wilderness and rivers in the desert. The beasts of the field shall honour me; the dragons and the owls; because I give water in the wilderness, and rivers in the desert, to give drink to my people, to my chosen." If such texts have a glorious, general, mystical fulfilment in the conversion of pagan lands; yet this does not preclude, but rather implies the fact, that the people whose restoration is in them particularly foretold, shall be recovered from a vast wilderness; and their conversion shall be almost like the conversion of dragons and owls of the desert. Rivers of knowledge and grace shall in such wilds be open for God's chosen.

It will then truly be fulfilled that God in comforting Zion, will "make her wilderness like Eden, and her desert like the garden of the Lord;" Isai. li. 3. Such passages will have a degree of both literal and mystical fulfilment.

A signal beauty will then be discovered in such passages as the following; Isai. xli. 14. "Fear not, thou worm Jacob, and ye men of Israel; I will help thee, saith the Lord God, thy Redeemer, the Holy One of Israel. I will open rivers in the high places, and fountains in the midst of vallies: I will make the wilderness a pool of water, and the dry land springs of water. I will plant in the wilderness the cedar, the shittah tree, and the myrtle, and the oil tree; and I will set in the desert the fir tree, the pine, and the box tree together, that they may see and know and understand together, that the hand of the Lord hath done this, and the Holy One of Israel hath created it." The view given of the place of the long banishment of the ten tribes, gives a lustre to such predictions of their restoration. -These will have a striking fulfilment in the vast wilds of our continent, when the glad tidings of salvation shall be carried to the natives of these extensive dreary forests and those regions of wretchedness and death shall become vocal with the high praises of God, sung by his ancient Israel.

In Micah vii. is a prediction relative to Israel's restoration. Micah, as well as Isaiah, lived in the days of Israel's dispersion. He began his ministry about eighteen years before this event; and continued it about twenty-five years after the event. Though he was of Judah, Scott says, "He addressed his messages both to Judah and Israel." Of the passage, verse 11-13, Bp. Lowth says, "The general restoration of the Jews shall not be brought to pass till after their land hath lain desolate for many ages."

Bp. Newcomb says, of verses 14-17; "They may likewise have a reference to the times of the future restitution." Scott says of the verses following, "They evidently related to Christ, and the success of the gospel to the end of time; and the future restoration of Israel." In verse 12 the application for this restoration is made to them "from sea to sea; and from mountain to mountain." The prophet then prays for them, verse 14; that God would feed his people, "the flock of his heritage, which dwell solitarily in the wood;" that he would feed them in the midst of Carmel, Bashan and Gilead, as in the days of old. Where are this people to be found "from sea to sea; from mountain to mountain; and in the wood?" This answers to nothing of ancient date. But to the situation of Israel of modern date, (if they be in the wilds of America) it well accords. Here they must indeed be sought "from sea to sea; from mountain to mountain;" and "in the wood." And this event is to be, verse 13, "after that their land hath been desolate;" as Scott renders it from the original. And this is to be in fulfilment of "the truth to Jacob, and the mercy to Abraham, which God had sworn from the days of old;" verse 20. God then, as in verses 18, 19, pardons the transgression of the remnant of his heritage, retains not his anger forever, but turns again and has compassion on them, and casts all their sins into the depth of the sea. All these expressions seem to apply perfectly to the final restoration of Israel; but not to any thing antecedent to that event. This branch of Israel are to be found then, "dwelling solitarily in the wood;" and are to be sought "from sea to sea; and from mountain to mountain."

5. If it be a fact that the native Americans are the tribes of Israel, new evidence is hence furnished of the divinity of our holy scriptures. A new field of evidence is here opened from a race of men, "outcast" from all civil society for a long course of centuries. Impressed on these wild tenants of the forest, (these children of nature, without books or letters, or any thing but savage tradition,) striking characters are found of the truth of ancient revelation.

The intelligent vindicator of the word of God has never feared to meet the infidel on fair ground. His triumph has not been less certain than that of David against Goliath. But in the view taken of the natives of our continent, the believer will find additional arguments, in which to triumph. He will find more than "five smooth stones taken out of the brook," (1 Sam. xvi. 40.) each one of which is sufficient to sink into the head of an impious Goliath, challenging the God of Israel.

Let the unbeliever in revelations undertake to answer the following questions.

Whence have the greater part of the American natives been taught the being of one and only one God; when all other heathen nations have lost all such knowledge, and believe in many false gods?

Whence have the Indians, or most of them, been kept from gross idolatry, which has covered the rest of the heathen world? and to which all men have been so prone?

Whence have many of them been taught that the name of the one God, the Great Spirit above, is Yohewah, Ale, Yah, (Hebrew names of God,) who made all things, and to whom alone worship is due?

Who taught any of them that God, at first, made one man from earth; formed him well; and breathed him into life? and that God made good and bad spirits; the latter of whom have a prince over them?

Whence came the idea among the untutored savages, that Yohewah was once the covenant God of their nation; and the rest of the world were out of covenant with him, -the accursed people? God was the God of Israel, and of no other nation during their commonwealth. "I entered into covenant with thee, and thou becamest mine."

Whence their ideas that their ancestors once had the book of God; and then were happy; but that they lost it; and then became miserable; but that they will have this book again at some time?

Whence their notion that their fathers once had the spirit of God to work miracles, and to foretel future events? Whence the general Indian tradition of offering their first ripe fruits. See Exod. xxii. 29; and xxiii. 19. Lev. ii. 14; and xxiii. 10, 11.

Who taught the untutored savages to have a temple of Yohewah; a holy of holies in it, into which no common people may enter, or look?

Who taught him a succession of high priests? that this priest must be inducted into office by purifications, and anointing? that he must appear in an appropriate habiliment, the form of which descended from their fathers of remote antiquity?

Whence their custom of this priest's making a yearly atonement, in or near the holy apartment of their temple? Lev. xxiii. 27, and vi. 30.

Whence their three annual feasts, which well accord to the three great feasts in Israel? Exod. xxiii. 14 and on.

Whence came their peculiar feast, in which a bone of the sacrifice may not be broken; and all that is prepared must be eaten; or burned before the next morning sun? and eaten with bitter vegetables. Exod. xii. 8, 10, 46.

Whence a custom of their males appearing three times annually before God at the temple? Exod. xxiii. 17, Deut. xvi. 16.

Who taught wild savages of the desert to maintain places of refuge from the avenger of blood; "old, beloved, white towns?" Joshua chap. xx.

Who taught them to keep and venerate a sacred ark, containing their most sacred things; to be borne against their enemies by one purified by strict rites? -That no one but the sanctified keeper might look into this ark; and the enemy feeling the same reverence for it, as the friends? Exod. xxv. 10, and on. 1 Sam. vi. 19. 2 Sam. xi. 11.

Whence came the deep and extensive impression among these savage tribes that the hollow of the thigh of no animal may be eaten? Gen. xxxii. 32.

Let the infidel inform how these savages (so long excluded from all intercourse with the religious or civilized world) came by the right of circumcision? and some of them an idea of a Jubilee?

Whence their idea of an old divine speech; that they must imitate their virtuous ancestors, enforced by "flourishing upon a land flowing with milk and honey?"

Whence their notion of the ancient flood? and of the longevity of the ancients? also of the confusion of the language of man at building a high place? evidently meaning the scene at Babel.

How came these wild human herds of the desert by various Hebrew words and phrases; and such phrases as accord with no other language on earth? See the table furnished, page 90.

Who taught them to sing, Halleluyah, Yohewah, Yah, Shilu Yohewah; and to make the sacred use they do of the syllables, which compose the names of God? singing them in their religious dances, and in their customs; thus ascribing all the praise to Yohewah? I ask not, who taught them the spirit or holiness of such religious forms? For probably they have little or no intelligent meaning. But whence have they brought down these traditional forms?

How came their reckoning of time so well to accord with that of ancient Israel?

Whence their tradition of twelve men, in preparing for a feast similar to the ancient feast of tabernacles; taking twelve poles, forming their booths; and their altar of twelve stones, on which no tool may pass; and here offering their twelve sacrifices? and some tribes proceeding by the number ten instead of twelve? indicating their tradition of the twelve tribes; and their subsequent ten, after the revolt.

Whence came their tradition of purifying themselves with bitter vegetables? also fasting, and purifying themselves when going to war, as did Israel.

Who taught them that at death their beloved people sleep, and go to their fathers?

Whence their custom of washing and anointing their dead; and some of them of hiring mourners to bewail them; and of singing round the corpse (before they bury it) the syllables of Yah, Yohewah?

How came they by their tradition answering to the ancient Jewish separations of women? Lev. xii. 1-6, also a tradition of taking their shoes from their feet, on solemn occasions? Exod. iii 5. Deut. xxv. 9.

Whence were some of them taught in deep mourning to lay their hand on their mouth, and their mouth in the dust?

And whence came their tradition of their ancient father with his twelve sons, ruling over others? and the mal-conduct of these twelve sons; till they lost their pre-eminence?

Let it be remembered, it is not pretended that all the savages are in the practice of all these traditions. They are not. But it is contended that the whole of these things have been found among their different tribes in our continent, within a hundred years. A fragment of these Hebrew traditions has been found among one tribe; and another fragment among another; and some of the most striking of these traditions have been found among various and very distant tribes; as has appeared in the recital from various authors, traders and travellers.

Let the unbeliever in revelation set himself to account for these events.

No account can be given of them, but that they were derived from ancient revelation in Israel. And hence in the outcast state of the ten tribes of Israel, (in their huge valley of dry bones, in this vast new world,) we find presented a volume of new evidence of the divinity of the Old Testament, and hence of the New; for the latter rests on the former, as a building rests on its foundation. If the one is divine, the other is divine; for both form a perfect whole.

We are assured by the chief apostle to the Gentiles, that the restoration of the ancient people of God in the last days, when "all Israel shall be saved," shall be to the nations "as life from the dead;" Rom. xi. 15. Its new and demonstrative evidence of the glorious truth of revelation, will confound infidelity itself; and fill the world with light and glory. These Indian traditions may be viewed as beginning to exhibit to the world their quota of this new evidence.

In our subject, we find a powerful evidence of the truth of revelation, extending through a wild continent, in savage traditions; which traditions must have been brought down from 725 years before the Christian era.

The preservation of the Jews, as a distinct people, for eighteen centuries, has been justly viewed as a kind of standing miracle in support of the truth of revelation. But the arguments furnished from the preservation and traditions of the ten tribes, in the wilds of America from a much longer period, must be viewed as furnishing, if possible, a more commanding testimony. And it is precisely such evidence as must have been expected in the long outcast tribes of Israel, whenever they should come to light;

and just such evidence as must rationally be expected to bring them to the knowledge of the civilized world.

6. The people addressed by the prophet Isaiah, (be they America, or Britain, or who they may,) are highly honoured of God. They are a "land shadowing with wings." God is abundantly represented as shadowing his people with his wings. "Hide me under the shadow of thy wings." "The children of men put their trust under the shadow of thy wings." To Israel as brought from Egypt, God said; "I bare you on eagles" wings, and brought you unto myself." Wings, and especially eagles" wings, are much used in the holy oracles, to denote special aid, and that of the most dignified kind. Of the children of God it is said; "They that wait on the Lord shall renew their strength; they shall mount up with wings as eagles; they shall run and not be weary; they shall walk and not faint."

And if the ancient tribes of the Lord are to be recovered at last by an agency well denoted by a "land shadowing with wings;" this rich prophetic imagery is certainly very honourable to the nation addressed; as the business assigned them is also very honourable. And probably no other nation on earth can, from its national character, the excellency of its government, and its local situation, lay so good a claim to this inspired characteristic. The American Eagle is a term well known in the civilized world. And no other nation has so good a right to this honour.

7. May the people addressed by the prophet Isaiah, awake to a diligent performance of the duty assigned them. Here is a rich opportunity of being workers together with God in a business, which will excite the attention of heaven and earth. "All the inhabitants of the earth, see ye when he lifteth up the ensign on the mountains; and when he bloweth the trumpet, hear ye." The ancient restorations of Israel were remarkable. Nations that stood in their way sank, as under a deluge; -as Egypt. Babylon, Amalek, and many others could testify. The Ammonites and Moabites were branded with infamy, "because they met not Israel with bread and water when they came forth out of Egypt."

And the final restoration of Israel is to exceed all antecedent restorations. "It shall no more be said, The Lord liveth who brought up Israel from Egypt; but, The Lord liveth who brought them from all the countries whither I have driven them." Divine judgments then, may be proportionably greater against all who withstand the final restoration. "I will undo all that afflict thee." Wo will be to them, who shall have the unbelief or temerity to place themselves before the wheels of divine providence when Christ shall ride forth in the chariot of salvation to bring the dispersed Jews, and outcast Israel to himself. God will arise, and his enemies will be scattered. As smoke is driven away; and as the wax melteth before the fire; so God will drive away and melt the enemies of his ancient people. He will ride in the heavens by the name Jah. And while his friends rejoice, his enemies shall tremble at his presence. God will go before his people, and march through the wilderness. The earth, it is said, shall shake; and the heavens shall drop at his presence. Though his long banished people have lain among the pots; yet now shall they be as the wings of a dove covered with silver, and her feathers with yellow gold. The mountains and hills shall leap at the presence of the Lord, at the presence of the God of Jacob. And God will wound the head of his enemies, and the hairy scalp of them that oppose his march, when he shall again bring from Bashan, and recover his banished again from the depth of the sea. Their foot shall be dipped in the blood of their enemies; and men shall again see the stately march of the God of Zion; and shall bless the Lord, even the Lord from the fountains of Israel. Little Benjamin, and his ruler (or chief) shall be there, with the princes of Judah and their counsel. God will command his strength. He will rebuke the armies of the spearmen, with the bulls and calves of their mighty coalition. He will scatter those who delight in war, till every one shall submit himself with pieces of silver.May the suppliants of God in the west, in the land shadowing with wings, be hid in that day of the Lord's anger. May they be found in the chambers of his protection, until the indignation be overpast; faithfully obeying the direction to bring his present of the people scattered and peeled, to the place of the name of the Lord of hosts, the Mount Zion.

Appendix

Some objections to the scheme in the preceding pages have been noted. The writer is desirous that due attention should be paid to every objection; hence the following things are appended.

The Afghans in Persia have by some been conjectured to be of the ten tribes of Israel. Mr. Vansittart of England has given notice of them. While he was in the east, he met with a Persian abridgement of a book styled, Ararul Afghainah; or secrets of the Afghans. This he translated, and sent to Sir W. Jones, who then presided over the Asiatic Society. He observes that it opens with a very wild description of the origin of that tribe of people, and conveys a narrative, which is by no means to be offered upon the whole as a serious and probable history. This book unfolds some notions of their having descended from Melic Talut, supposed to be king Saul. And a number of things they mention, which seem to have arisen from the ancient history of Israel. But not a rite or ceremony is noted of them, which seems to bear any resemblance to the ceremonial system of ancient Israel. Afghan, a noted ancient leader, (they inform) "made frequent excursions to the mountains, where his posterity after his death established themselves, lived in a state of independence, built forts, and exterminated the infidels." When Mohammedism was propagated in the east, the Afghans embraced it with avidity, and have remained under that delusion to this day. Surely this favours not their being of Israel.

This people have latterly divided themselves into four classes. The first class consists of those who are purely Afghan. The second, of those whose fathers were Afghan, and their mothers of another nation. The third of those, whose mothers were Afghan and their fathers of another people. The fourth of those whose connexion was still more remote.

A question arises, whether this history of their apparent descent from Israel might not have been furnished to this class of people from the grand imposter, Mohammed? They were a brave warlike race. They at once embraced his system; upon which they boast that he said to them, "Come, O moluc, or kings;" -that Mohammed gave them his ensign; and said "that the faith would be strengthened by them." He knowing that Israel were once planted in that region, might think further to please them by furnishing them with a legend of their having descended from that people. This he might have done by the Jewish apostate who assisted him in forming his system of delusion. But it is said that their account of the time of their departure from Palestine does not at all agree with the Old Testament account of the same. Mr. Faber upon the circumstance says; "It must be confessed, that this Afghan tradition bears a strong resemblance to many of those Mohammedan legends, which are founded upon scripture accounts, (i.e. allude to them, to strengthen the imposition) whence it is certainly not impossible that a tribe of Mussulmans might be in possession of it, without being descended from the house of Israel."

But should the Afghans prove to be of Israel, they may be from a tribe, or scattering people of ancient Israel, who tarried behind when most of that people set off for this continent. The Indian tradition says, "that they once lived in another country, where the people were very wicked; and nine tenths of their people took counsel, and left that wicked people, and were led into this land. The posterity of that one remaining tribe may possibly now be found somewhere in the east. But the Afghans, according to their own account, have much mixed with other people. We are led to believe from prophecy that God would keep the tribes of Israel (as he designs they shall finally be known and recovered as such) free from any considerable degree of mixture. -And it would appear that Israel, as such, must be ascertained by evidence less liable to imposition than the aforenoted book of the secrets of the Afghans.

Doctor Buchanan gives an account of white and black Jews at Cochin, East Indies. The Most High speaks of gathering his ancient people from the east, and from the west. If nine tenths of Israel migrated to this continent; the residue of them might migrate to the East Indies. Doctor Buchanan informs that the white Jews there emigrated from Europe in later times. The black Jews have a tradition that they arrived to the Indies not long after the Babylonish captivity. And Doctor Buchanan adds; "What seems to countenance this tradition is, that they have copies of those books of the Old Testament, which were written before the captivity; but none of those whose dates are subsequent to that event." It seems most probable then, that these black Jews are descendants of those Jews, who turned their course to that region of the east, when they were liberated from Babylon, instead of returning to Jerusalem. Some of the Jews manifestly did thus part from their brethren, and migrate to the east. These were the Jews who abounded in eastern as well as western provinces of Ahasuerus, in the days of Haman, Esther and Mordecai; when the impious decree was obtained against them by Haman. Ahasuerus then "reigned over one hundred and twenty-seven provinces, even from India to Ethiopia." Esther i. 1. And Jews appear, at that time, to have scattered in all these provinces. Thence these black Jews became planted in India; and they had their bible as far as was written before the captivity. Their being blacker than modern Jews in Europe, may be accounted for upon the same principles, of different climates and habits of living, which have given to the American natives a darker skin than to the Jews of Europe; or than their ancestors possessed.

But two arguments testify against those black Jews of Asia having descended from the ten tribes.

1. They call themselves Jews. The Jews have ever been strict to retain the knowledge. of their descent. And the deep rooted prejudices mutually maintained between the Jews and Israel, forbid that the latter should ever relinquish their name for that of the former.

2. The tribes of Israel were threatened with the famine of the word, which has been already noted; Amos viii. 11, 12. Here the ten tribes in their long banishment, should wander from "north to east, and from sea to sea;" running to and fro, to find communication from Heaven; but should remain destitute of the word of life, till about the time of their restoration.

But the black Jews in Asia, as well as the white Jews there, have had their word of the Lord to this day, all the sacred writings, which were given before the Babylonish captivity. These reasons render it probable if not certain that these black Jews are not of the ten tribes of Israel.

Since preparing the above the writer has seen in communications from the London Jews Society, for May 1824, an extract of a letter from Thomas Jàrratt, Esq. at Madras, East Indies, giving account of Mr. Largon's mission in the east in search of the ten tribes. It is happy that such a mission has been undertaken, to ascertain whether any traces can be found of Israel in the east. Mr. Largon gives the following account of some people discovered by him in Hindostan.

1. These people in dress and manners resemble the natives, so as not to be distinguished from them, but by attentive observation and inquiry.

2. They have some Hebrew names with local terminations.

3. Some of them read Hebrew. And they have a faint tradition of the cause of their original exodus from Egypt.

4. Their common language is Hindoo.

5. They keep idols, and worship them; and use idolatrous ceremonies intermixed with Hebrew.

6. They circumcise their children.

7. They observe the Kippoor, or great expiation day of the Hebrews.

8. They call themselves Gorah Jehudi, or white Jews; and they term the black Jews, Callah Jehudi.

9. They speak of the Arabic Jews as their brethren; but do not acknowledge European Jews as such, because they are of fairer complexion than themselves.

10. They use a Jewish prayer; Hear, O Israel; the Lord thy God is one Lord; Deut. vi. 4.

11. They have no priest, Levite, or nasi among them; though they have elders and a chief in each community.

12. They expect the Messiah; and that when he comes, he will go to Jerusalem, whither they shall return, to be dispersed no more."

For these reasons Mr. Jarratt seems inclined to view this people as of the ten tribes. Should they prove to be thus, they may be descendants of the small part of Israel who stayed behind, according to the Indian tradition, when nine tenths of their nation journeyed to this country. But relative to their origin, let the following things be considered.

1. They are found in the country of both the white and the black Jews; and seem to have no essential distinction from them. They may then be of the tribe of Judah. Any circumstantial difference between them and the other Jews may be accounted for at least as easily, as we can account for the different complexions of the white and black Jews; or for the different complexions among the different tribes of our natives, or among any other different tribes of men, when all sprang from Noah. They appear from their name to be not so black as the black Jews. And they appear not to be so white as the European Jews from their aversion to them on account of their whiter complexion. From some circumstance they have a shade half way between the white and black Jews. But this forms no greater objection against their being of the Jews, than against their being of the ten tribes.

2. They call themselves Jews. Why then shall we not credit them, and believe they are Jews? The ten tribes after the separation, were never called Jews. And such was their inveterate enmity against the Jews, that they would never be likely to assume their name in a rejection of their own, as has been noted. It is predicted in Isai. xi. 13, as one peculiarity of these two branches of Israel, after their final restoration, that they shall envy each other no more. Neither this prediction, nor the nature of the case, admits that Israel, -long ages before the restoration,- should be so in love with Judah, as to adopt his name instead of their own. This new clan of Jews, half way between the white and black Jews, say the Arabian Jews are their brethren. Grant this to be a fact, and they no doubt are of the descendants of Judah.

3. The two ancient branches of the house of Israel were to be long lost from each other; as has appeared. This seems to warrant the belief that they were to be planted in different regions of the earth. But this does not accord with the idea of their having been found in a measure intermixed, or in the same vicinity. The ten tribes were to wander northeast, and from sea to sea; from one extreme ocean to another, in a famine of the word; Amos viii. 11, 12. While the American natives appear fully to answer to this description; the same cannot be said of that people in Hindostan.

4. We are led to believe (as has been noted,) that God would furnish a place of retreat and safe-keeping for his outcast tribes of Israel for 2500 years; that they might be kept, and not be lost among the nations. Would Israel then be led into the heart of the populous Hindostan? -or into any of the crowded empires of the east? It is inadmissible. The Jews were to be dispersed through the cities and nations, and were to be kept and known as Jews. But this cannot be said of the ten tribes. Fact forbids it; and facts are stubborn things. The Jews have been known as such, over the nations, in all ages since their dispersion. The ten tribes have never been known; but have been lost from the world. Some have objected to the distinction recognized in this book between dispersed and outcast. I wish every part of this subject to be thoroughly examined; but I wish it to be examined with candour, and with an acknowledgment of plain facts. This distinction is plainly made in the word of God. Of the final restoration it is predicted Isai. xi. 12; "And he shall set up an ensign for the nations, and assemble the outcasts of Israel, and gather together the dispersed of Judah from the four

corners of the earth." This is one of a number of texts recognizing this distinction. Had not providence illustrated and fulfilled this distinction, we might with better grace say, it is a mere accidental expression, or a mere expletive. But when we find the thing exactly fulfilled for so many centuries; that the Jews are dispersed, and known as Jews for 1800 years; and the ten tribes have been outcast and unknown both to the Jews and the civil world for between two and three thousands of years; we are warranted to say (all groundless doubts of it notwithstanding) that there is a manifest meaning in this inspired and repeated distinction. As well might any other manifest facts be denied as this! But this fact does highly favour the belief, that the ten tribes would have been, and doubtless were, planted in regions very different from the populous regions of the East Indies.

5. Compare the evidences which have been adduced in favour of the hypothesis, that the natives of our continent are the tribes of Israel, with the above evidence in favour of the Hindoo Jews being the ten tribes; and what will be the result? The question is cheerfully submitted to every impartial reader. And it is cheerfully submitted whether more than ten times as much evidence has not appeared in favour of the former, as has ever yet appeared in favour of any other people on earth.

Some have objected to the following effect against the theory in the preceding pages: Who knows but such traditions and religious customs, as are said to be found among the natives of America, may not be found among all or most of heathen nations? Let such be asked in their turn; Who knows but much of the rites of the christian religion may not be found among all or most of the heathen nations? Who knows that these rites are from heaven, and are not of heathen origin? This is a more glaring case; but is perhaps upon the same scale of reasoning. The objection must be too loose and general, if not uncandid. If such rites and religious traditions as are found among the Indians of America, can be found among any other heathen nations; let the fact be adduced, and something is accomplished. But idly to say, who knows -is an easy way of answering not only human writings, but the word of God itself. And it is an objection unworthy of a serious answer.

That some traditionary notions of the flood, of the ark, of the confusion of tongues, and of sacrifices, have been handed down in heathen mythologies, is so far from being denied, that Christians glory in the fact, as adding an incontestible argument to the divinity of revelation.

And that some nations living in the twilight of ancient revelation, caught some rays of the light shining from heaven, and blended various shreds of bible sentiment and bible morality with those of the heathen, is admitted as a manifest fact. Says a first character of our nation; "Neither Plato nor Aristotle would have taught even their purblind ethics, had not the light of divine revelation shone. They moved in the twilight made by the tradiations from the church. Philosophy was not born in Greece, till after the Jews were dispersed among the heathen by Nebuchadnezzar. Pythagoras, the earliest of the Grecian philosophers, and the cotemporary of Thales, the founder of the first school, began to flourish half a century after that event. He spent twenty years in Egypt, where much of the Jewish religion had long before been known. He visited Phoenicia and Chaldea. He conversed with the Persian Zoroaster, and also with the Jewish prophets. Thales travelled in pursuit of knowledge to Egypt, where the Hebrews had lived hundreds of years, and in the neighbourhood of which they had lived nine centuries." These correct remarks of Doctor Griffin suggest the aid derived by ancient heathen philosophers from their contiguity to a people blessed with the true light from heaven. This principle may account for all the excellencies found in the morals of Seneca, and other heathen moralists. They caught some of the rays which shot off from the true Light of Israel. The golden age of Virgil was no doubt borrowed from the Kingdom of the Messiah in the prophet Isaiah. But while we admire various of the sayings of Seneca, Cicero, and some other heathen writers; we are not in the least staggered at the divine assertion that "the world by wisdom knew not God." But we are led to admire the word of prophecy shining in ancient Israel; the distant twilight of whose rays could light up in unsanctified heathen minds ideas so correct and so sublime. These things are cheerfully admitted.

And it is also admitted that various heathen nations in the contiguity of the light of Israel, having their superior and subordinate divinities of heathenism, might borrow the name of the God of Israel, and attach it to their superior false divinity. Yes, the Romans had their Jove, the Moors their Juba, and the Greeks their Iou. And other contiguous heathen nations might symbolize with them in some similar facts.

But I ask the objector; can these ancient facts afford him a satisfactory account how the American natives (granting them to be of Tartar extraction) came to possess so many traditions of the Mosaic ceremonial law? Behold these natives, filling this western world, far separated from the old continent, living at a period of between two and three thousand years later than the ancient heathen round about Israel, destitute of letters, children of nature, roaming for more than two millenaries in wild forests; and yet possessing many manifest traces (what ancient heathen even in the vicinity of Israel never possessed) of the ceremonial laws of Moses! Too often did the sons of Jacob adopt the idolatrous customs of the heathen neighbours.

But when did their heathen neighbours return the compliment? Who of them ever adopted the ceremonial religion of the God of Israel? The Mosaic ceremonies were the distinguishing peculiarities of the chosen tribes. By these they were insulated from all other people of the earth, who were in gross idolatry. "You only have I known of all the families of the earth."

"He suffered all other nations to walk in their own way." While some traditionary notions of the flood, the ark, of Babel, and of sacrifices, taught long before, were floating in heathen mythologies; the peculiarities of the Mosaic ceremonial code were never adopted by heathen nations.

Let the objector then, (who cannot but be haunted with the thought, Who knows but a lively imagination can find just such things as these among all heathen nations?) be so kind as to inform us; how the ancient Scythians of the north, (barbarous, and far remote from all intercourse with the people of Israel,) should be supposed to be so intimately acquainted and delighted with the distinguished ceremonial religion of Israel, as not only to have adopted it themselves; but to have so deeply imprinted it in the minds of their posterity as that they should transmit it to their far distant sons through the wilds of America, for thousands of years? Men, seriously to adopt this alternative, must be far more wild, and fond of miracles, than ought to be admitted at this day of light and improvement!

And it must be extraordinary, to hear men of letters, and of Christian improvements, when so many distinct Indian traditions, manifestly from the ceremonial law of Israel, have been ascertained from a great variety of unimpeached witnesses, indulging in the vague objection, Who knows but such things exist among all heathen nations? Let it be asked also; Who knows that the Mosaic rituals descended from Heaven? Who knows but they were derived from heathen mythologies?

Let the fact be ascertained, that the Indians of our wilds have brought down ,from their ancestors a variety of the ceremonial laws of ancient Israel; and let who will object, or disbelieve, -I shall rest satisfied that a very considerable if not a sufficiency of that very kind of evidence is here found, which about this period of the world is to bring to light the long lost tribes of the house of Israel.

The writer has seen a review of his first edition in the United States Literary Gazette, in which objections are made which merit some reply. The Reviewer it seems does not believe in a literal restoration of the Jews and Israel to Palestine. He argues, that as "the prophecies relative to the advent of the Lord were misunderstood by the Jewish church," existing when Christ appeared; -as they were understood to speak of the restoration of Israel; but the dispersion of the two remaining tribes followed;" So "the existing Christian church believes that when the Millennium arrives the children of Israel will be restored to their promised land." But they may be under an equal mistake. The Reviewer seems cautious in being understood as adopting this as his own sentiment. But it appears manifest that it is his sentiment, and a ground of his reasoning. As far as the Reviewer makes reliance on this argument, I would briefly say, it does not follow, that because the Jews, when Christ appeared, had become extremely corrupt, perverted their own scriptures, were prepared to reject and crucify the Lord of Glory, and were just ready for destruction; that accordingly "the existing Christian church" may now be as grossly ignorant relative to the true sense of Israel's promised restoration. It is to be hoped the present church of Christ has more correct evangelical sentiment, and more grace, than had those Jews. They certainly have had more opportunity to investigate the true sense of the prophecies than had those Jews. And it is to be hoped many of them are far less corrupt.

The Reviewer informs us, that the words "Judah, Israel, Jerusalem, &c. used in the prophecies, which relate to this subject, are nearly synonimous with the word church." And he proceeds to inform that "those prophecies which had a primary reference to the consummation and devastation of the Jewish dispensation existing at the time they were revealed, were necessarily fulfilled in relation to those who were literally denominated Israel and Judah. But those which, speaking of Israel and Judah, relate in fact to the establishment, the condition and progress of another church, cannot be expected to have their fulfilment with any peculiar reference to that nation, because it has ceased to be Israel, in the prophetic sense of the term." With whatever extreme caution this sentence is phrased, its sentiment appears from all the use made of it, to be this; the Old Testament prophecies relative to the names of Judah and Israel, but which relate to periods subsequent to the destruction of Jerusalem have no further allusion to those particular people; but to another community under the same name, -the Christian church. If this is not the sense of the Reviewer I am unable to comprehend his meaning, or arguments. I understand it as being on this ground that he now believes that the many prophecies which seem to predict the literal restoration of Israel and Judah to Palestine, yet mean no such event. The Reviewer finds in Rom. xi. that the literal Jews are to be converted to Christ; but not to be restored to Palestine, as he conceives. But the ground he has assumed as much forbids their being brought to Christ as Jews, as their being as such restored to Palestine. If his premises contain his consequences; it can be only on the ground that no Old Testament prophecy relative to the literal Jews and Israel under the Christian dispensation, has any distinct appropriation to literal Jews and Israel; but to a Christian church under their name. And according to the same argument, their being brought to the land of their fathers can mean only their being brought into the kingdom of Christ.

But if this be correct, how strangely have "the existing church," and the most profound and pious commentators, been deceived in supposing that they have seen held up before the world, a tremendous fulfilment of Old Testament denunciations of signal judgments on the literal Jews now for about 1800 years. Those predictions foretold they should be removed into all kingdoms, for their hurt, their reproach; and they should be a proverb, and a taunt, and a curse in all places; Jer. xxiv, 9., Ezek. v. 15. Are we now to learn that such things were never to befall the Jews, as such under the Christian system? Should the present church decline this sentiment, and still adhere to their belief, that Old Testament predictions of evil are now fulfilling on the Jews as such; they may be likely still to infer that the connected predictions of the recovery of the same Jews, and their restoration to their own land, may likewise be expected to have a literal accomplishment. And if so, they may in like manner deem it a truth that the collateral predictions of the restoration of Israel with the Jews, will have a literal fulfilment.

Does the Reviewer mean to have it understood that the ten tribes, when expelled from Canaan, 725 years before Christ, amalgamated with the heathen world, and were lost? The writer was informed, before he saw the review, that this was the sentiment of the Reviewer. And I see not but the review carries this sentiment. But the existing Christian church will want more evidence than has yet been discovered, to adopt this belief. The names of Israel and the Jews, it is acknowledged, are in some sacred passages used in a mystical sense. But to take an occasion from this to annihilate all further use of these terms in the prophecies, as relating to that particular people, would indeed be extraordinary!

The reasoning of Paul, Rom. xi. to show that the temporal casting away of the Jews was consistent with the entail of the covenant of grace with Abraham, involved (among other things) the fact, that they as Jews should be recovered. And the same argument must hold equally true with the ten tribes.

Had the Jews disappeared from the world when expelled from Canaan, and never more been heard of as Jews; whatever difficulty might have attended to reconciling of this with the divine promises and predictions; the Reviewer would have had greater plausibility of reasoning on his side. But as the Jews do still as Jews exist; and are receiving the manifest fulfilment of ancient denunciations upon them as Jews; it must be a task indeed to show that the predictions of their restoration to the land of Canaan (where they shall in numbers, and in prosperity, far exceed all their ancient fathers,) are to receive no literal fulfilment. But if they are to be literally fulfilled, then the predictions which are blended with those of the event, that Israel shall in like manner be recovered to the same land, that the two sticks in the prophet's hand shall become one, Ezek. xxxvii. and all this over and above God's giving them a new heart and a new spirit; must likewise be literally fulfilled.

Had the general theory of the Reviewer been correct, probably nothing more would have been heard of the Jews, after the destruction of Jerusalem, than has long been heard of Israel. But the Jews have been wonderfully kept a distinct nation, for many centuries. And one of the brightest ornaments of the republic of science, (and one too who did not deem it beneath his dignity to study the prophecies) could say; "Whenever I see a Jew, I seem to see a standing miracle in favour of the truth of divine Revelation!"

Relative to the proofs adduced in the View of the Hebrews in favour of our Indians having descended from Israel; the Reviewer says; "Various degrees of credit are due to the authorities on which Mr. S. relies." Reply. I never heard these authorities impeached, unless this insinuation is designed to impeach them. It was designed that nothing dubious should be admitted. And the testimonies of authors are given in their own words, that nothing should appear coloured.

The Reviewer expresses his difficulty with the scheme, from a dissimilarity of the Indian features and countenance with those of the Jews. This objection has in the preceding pages received an answer, which will not here be repeated.

But granting all the facts stated in the View of the Hebrews, the Reviewer discovers nothing conclusive in all this. For he says; "We have no evidence that the customs and institutions of the Hebrews, which were sanctioned by divine authority, were all peculiar to that people, nor that they originated with them." It is admitted that various sacrifices were offered among other nations. And circumcision was practised among the descendants of Abraham in Arabia. But the chief reliance of the writer was on those rites, which he ever deemed peculiar to Israel. Have we then "no evidence" that the passover, the ark of the covenant, the special feasts in Israel, the separation of females, the annual atonement, cities of refuge, and the other ceremonial observances adduced; -have we no evidence that these originated in Israel? Have we now to learn that the ceremonial laws in Israel were only "sanctioned by divine authority there;" -but that they were not "peculiar to that people;" nor did they originate with them?" Let evidence of this be exhibited, and it shall have its weight. But till this is done, I shall stand firm in the old belief, that God did originate the ceremonial law in Israel. As soon should I believe that the rites of the Christian religion did not originate from God in his church, but originated among the heathen; and were only "sanctioned by God" in his church; as to believe the same relative to the rites of the ceremonial law, which have been noted.

The Reviewer adds; "Neither does it appear that the Jewish scriptures were the first that God gave to man. On the contrary; there is strong proof that parts of the first books were compiled from earlier scriptures. And the ancestors of the Indians might have had a book, without being Hebrew."

That communications were made from God to man, before the days of Moses, perhaps there is no room to doubt. And possibly the knowledge of some things which Moses was inspired to incorporate into his history, might have been correctly handed down by tradition. But if there is "strong proof" that eastern nations had possessed sacred writings before the writings of Moses, from which antecedent writings our natives may have brought down the tradition that their ancestors had a book of God, with no allusion to the writings of Moses; so that such a tradition is no evidence that those Indians descended from Israel; (which is the argument of the Reviewer;) how strange it must be that none beside the Indians of America, and the Reviewer, have any knowledge of such a book of God? Why have not the literary world been blessed with the knowledge of it? Why could not our literary Reviewer himself have laid his hand upon it, and presented it to us; or at least some of the "strong evidence" in its favour? The human family in the days of Abraham were going off to gross idolatry. God selected and covenanted with Abraham, in order that the true knowledge of himself might be maintained on earth. "He suffered all other nations to walk in their own way." And he said to Israel, "You only have I known of all the families of the earth." Moses, in this family, was inspired to write the book of God. And it is noted as the special privilege of the circumcised Israel, that "to them were committed the oracles of God." Now was there during all this time, in the other nations of the east, the knowledge of another book of God, so well known among the nations, and the sacred impressions of it so deep and universal, that the descendants of the northern barbarous nations might bring down many deep and correct impressions of it for three or four thousand years, in so distant and extensive a region of the world as this continent? So that all the rites of our natives, and their notions of an ancient book of God, afford no evidence of their being of Israel? Why has nothing of this kind ever been known in the learned world, till our literary Reviewer has brought it to light? Can he make it appear indeed, that although the natives of our continent claim the one Great Spirit as the God of their fathers, who they say were exclusively in covenant with him; who had his prophets to work miracles, and foretell future events; who had the ark of the covenant; places of refuge; high priests; yearly atonements; and many other exclusive Mosaic rites; yet all this amounts to no distinctive evidence that they descended from Israel? because they may have derived all these things from ancient heathen nations. One of two things, from the Reviewer's view of the subject, appears true; either the church of God have been under a great mistake relative to the origin of the Mosaic religion; or, deep literature does not always constitute a man a sound divine!

The Reviewer seems to be disturbed, that the writer should make the attempt he has done in this little book, to give an explanation to some prophecies relative to Israel. He informs that "the true mode of interpreting the prophecies is certainly little understood at this day."

He proceeds to allude to a dissertation on the prophecies of the writer published some time since; which he says received a quietus in the death of Buonaparte." The Reviewer certainly expresses these things with a sufficient degree of disrespect! One would imagine he was indeed much disturbed at any attempt to explain prophecy. But his assertion relative to the general ignorance "of the true mode of interpreting the prophecies," surely must be understood as indicating that he himself has been so happy as to arrive at a superior knowledge upon this subject. Now, whether he has reached this high attainment by close application, or instinctively, he surely should not object to others taking what they may judge the most proper methods to obtain a small degree of that knowledge, of which he is so happy as to have much! The information given by the Reviewer, relative to what the scriptures do or do not mean concerning the restoration of the Jews, certainly would seem to indicate, that he himself has made great proficiency in this knowledge. For one must possess considerable knowledge on this deep subject, before he can with modesty and propriety publish what shall sweep away at a stroke the long received rules and writings of such men as Mede, Lawman, Bishop Newton, Sir Isaac Newton, and other most profound and celebrated expounders of the prophetic scriptures! The Reviewer then should be willing, (if he has been so successful) that others should make their humbler attempts, even though they should arrive at some different conclusions from himself. If this seems foreign from the first professed object of the Reviewer; the blame will not be attached to the reviewed, when it is considered he is following only where he is led, in self-defence.

Relative to the duty of studying the prophetic scriptures, let the following divine testimonies be considered. To the Jews Christ said, when light was far inferior to what it now is, "How is it that ye do not understand the signs of the times?" The signs of the times were the fulfilments of prophecies then taking place. "Whoso readeth, let him understand." "Blessed is he that readeth, and they that hear the words of this prophecy, and keep those things that are written therein; for the time is at hand." Numerous were such testimonies many centuries ago. Light has been rising on the subject. And now it must be viewed as involved in inexplicable darkness! When then can so great a part of our holy revelation ever be understood? Or was it given in vain? Why has God commanded men to search and understand this part of his blessed word?

Every event for time and eternity, now future, is known only by prophecy.

And yet "the true mode of interpreting prophecies is certainly little known at this day." Does this hold true in relation to the judgment, and eternity? to the resurrection, to heaven, and to hell? Where shall we draw the lines? Are no opinions to be formed of the Millennium? -of the battle of that great day of God? Why then are ministers commanded to "blow the trumpet in Zion, to sound an alarm in God's holy mountain, that all may tremble for the day of the Lord, which is nigh at hand?" And if these vast events must be studied and known, why not other great events connected with them, and revealed with equal clearness?

But if the Reviewer may have mistaken as much in relation to the prophecies, as he has in stating that the writer's former Dissertation received a quietus in the death of Buonaparte; possibly his knowledge of this subject will not prove to be of great practical importance; and possibly his remarks may receive a "quietus" in a statement of facts.

1. The writer did about fourteen years ago publish a Dissertation on the Prophecies. He did it at the request of many, and with the special recommendation of more than half a dozen of the first literary characters in New England.

In this work Buonaparte was noted only as one signal leader of the last head of the secular Roman beast rising from the bottomless pit. But he was never identified with this beast; but was ever distinguished from it.

Hence let his death have taken place ever so soon, after the beast was exhibited in his characteristic marks, it would in no sense have given a quietus to Mr. S's. scheme. For as the first part of the ancient imperial head of this beast depended on no one emperor; but was accommodated with many in succession; so notice was given that it might be with the last imperial reign of the same head, recovered to life in these last days. See the following quotations from the first edition of the Dissertation. "And the king shall do according to his will, and he shall exalt himself and magnify himself above every god, and shall speak marvellous things against the God of gods."

"By a king in the language of prophecy, is generally to be understood a kingdom, or civil power, and not an individual person. In this sense we are to understand the king in this text.

In the passage we are presented with a great atheistical power, who in his commencement is to be anarchical. -His licentiousness is first noted; he "shall do according to his will;" breaking every restraint. His anarchy follows; "and he shall exalt himself above every God," i.e. above every king or legitimate ruler.

War with kings, was to be among his first characteristics. His atheism follows; "and shall speak marvellous things against the God of gods." He shall blaspheme and deny the God of heaven. "But in his estate shall he honour the god of forces." After this power shall gain national importance, he shall honour military munitions, or pay his first attention to the arts of war.

"And a god whom his fathers knew not, shall he honour with gold and silver, and precious stones, and pleasant things." Although his father's god, and all gods (kings) have been rejected; yet a god, or ruler of foreign descent shall by and by come to be acknowledged by this power, and honoured with the greatest magnificence. "Thus shall he do in the most strong hold with a strange God whom he shall acknowledge and increase with glory; and he shall cause them to rule over many, and shall divide the land for gain. This infidel power shall overrun strong holds, and powerful nations, with this foreigner at their head, who shall be received as their supreme ruler, and honoured with the highest dignity. And he shall lead them to subdue states and nations; and shall distribute their governments among his favourites. "And at the time of the end the king of the south shall push at him; and the king of the north shall come against him like a whirlwind." The Ottoman empire may provoke the infidel power to its own ruin. "Whether this will be the case; or whether some other two powers, one on the south, and the other on the north of the infidel power, will be found to unite, with a view to crack their common enemy; time will decide."

This power is ever treated of in this dissertation as an empire, and not as any emperor, or succession of emperors.

This beast in his last head, (in the scheme of the seven vials given in the Dissertation, which scheme has never been disproved, but has met with general, if not universal approbation) was to continue through the three last and greatest vials, the fifth, sixth and seventh. The periods of these vials was to be distinguished from each other by various reverses experienced by this power. Says the writer in his first edition, "Floods of delusion, of wicked agents, of falsehoods and abuse, if not of national rage, armies and bloody violence, will be excited, as though belched out of the mouth of the old serpent, like an overwhelming torrent; in so much; that nothing can save the cause of Christ from destruction, but signal interpositions of Providence in counteracting those violent measures, and confounding the enemy, like the earth opening her mouth and swallowing up floods of water."

2. Great reverses in the state of this power of the last days were thus implied in the first edition of this work.

And it occurred to the writer, while preparing his second edition, (soon after) that these reverses were clearly held up in various collateral prophecies, as being far greater than he had expressly stated; while yet the power (not any individual leaders of it) would continue its mystical existence, till it should sink in perdition at the close of the seventh vial, subsequently to the restoration of the Jews. It was to be "part of iron, and part of clay; partly strong and partly broken." Of this the writer gave ample notice in his second edition in the following sentences, and many similar ones; "To how great a degree these reverses may proceed, God only knows. Should the brokenness of this last part of the Roman power be now made in some degree as conspicuous as his antecedent strength, (as the text "the kingdom shall be partly strong, and partly broken," seems to warrant us to expect) that wicked power would indeed be prostrated. But should this be the case, should all the horns of the anti-christian beast be torn off, and the wretch lie bleeding and fainting; yet it appears evident that all his work is not yet done. He does not go into final perdition, till the battle of that great day of God, which is subsequent to the restoration of the Jews."

3. "The enormous power or influence, symbolized by the beast from the bottomless pit, (says the writer) depends on no one man; though it has been accommodated hitherto with a leader truly prepared for the work of judgment. In the first reign of the imperial head of the Roman beast, emperors were set up and deposed, and numbers slain, in thick succession.

And it repeatedly seemed as though destruction had fallen upon the empire; still that imperial head continued, (i.e. till the days of Constantine.)

That genius of the people continued, which would not be governed by any thing short of a military despotism. And this (it may be expected) will be the case on the Roman earth henceforth, till the battle of the great day.

Should revolution succeed revolution, it would not alter the case. The nature of the beast from the bottomless pit is not changed. It rests on the broad basis of a general systematic corruption, which will never be purged, but by the exterminating fire of the great and notable day of the Lord."

Much of this kind of notice was given in this publication, which fully accords with the subsequent death of Buonaparte, and the prostration of his particular schemes of ambition, which was so terrible under the fifth vial. It was anticipated in the following words on the king of the north coming against him like a whirlwind, &c. "The phraseology seems to intimate great success against the infidel power. For a mighty whirlwind usually prostrates every thing in its way."

"Between the present time and the battle of the great day, (the writer adds) as great intervals of light may be experienced as might be expected to form a transition from the events of one great vial of wrath to another."

The scheme of the vials, in this Dissertation, makes the events of the French revolution the fulfilment of the fifth vial, poured on the throne of the Papal beast, and filling his kingdom with darkness. The sixth is to be fulfilled in the subversion of the Turks. And the seventh in the utter destruction of the great secular Roman beast, which arose in his last head. He is clearly to continue in some kind of existence, till the battle of the great day; though with the reverses which have been hinted.

In relation to the general scheme of this Dissertation, the writer of it has never found occasion to alter his mind. He as much believes, as when he wrote, that his scheme of the last head of the Roman beast, and of the seven vials, is essentially correct; and has to the present day been more and more confirmed in the opinion, by the events of the times. He anticipated and published his opinion, that between one vial and its successor, there might be intervals of peace. He believes the fifth vial closed at the battle of Waterloo. He often from that time stated to his friends his apprehension that the sixth vial, to subvert the Turkish government, might next be expected.

This was the scheme of his Dissertation. And events thus far appear fully to accord with the hypothesis.

The Reviewer then, on re-examining the subject, may possibly be convinced that his attack on the Dissertation was not only unprovoked and gratis, but wholy incorrect.

His following assertion is no less incorrect. He says; "But he (Mr. S.) maintains boldly that the prophecies respecting the restoration of the Jews, and the Millennium, must be fulfilled about this time." The writer's time for the commencement of the Millennium, (and his reasons for it) he gave to the public in his second edition, published ten years ago; which is stated to be about the year 2000. And never since that time has a word been by him uttered or written in opposition to this opinion.

In the first edition of his Dissertation, he stated the scheme of a noted author, and several things that might render it probable; which scheme introduces the Millennium before the close of the present century. But attending further to the subject, in his second edition, the writer became of opinion that the Millennium will not commence before the year A.D. 2000.

4. Such representations then cannot be for the benefit of the public, or of the author reviewed; and hence cannot be for the honour of the Reviewer!

Some other things in the Review might be noticed, but shall pass. If the Reviewer's conscience is satisfied with them, they may rest in silence. The writer of the preceding pages is not insensible that such an attempt as he has made, is not only a task; but one that will excite obloquy from a certain class of men. He solicits information on the subject of his book from all who may find it convenient to communicate it. And every objection to his scheme, stated with candor, shall be gratefully received. But he shall never feel grateful for any communications to the public calculated to bring attention to the prophetic scriptures into disrepute; or to prevent a candid attention of the public to any evidences adduced relative to the state and recovery of the long lost tribes of Israel.